The Alpine 4000m Peaks
by the Classic Routes

On the shoulder of the Matterhorn's Hörnli Ridge

The view north from the summit slopes of
Mont Blanc. Mont Blanc du Tacul is on
the left. The five 4000m pinnacles of the
Aiguilles du Diable dominate the ridge
leading down to the Grand Capucin and
the Glacier du Geant. Mont Maudit's
Frontier Ridge, its halfway gendarme
Pointe de l'Androsace prominent,
parallels the Diable Ridge in the middle
distance.

THE ALPINE
4000m PEAKS
by the Classic Routes

by Richard Goedeke

Bâton Wicks · London
Menasha Ridge Press · Birmingham, Alabama

This second edition of *The Alpine 4000m Peaks* is adapted from the German *4000er Die Normalweg*. The author and UK/US publishers wish to thank the following photographers who have contributed new images for this edition: **John Allen** 52, 64, 83, 84, 167, 184, 189, 208/209, 228; **Willi Burkhardt** 40 (lower); **Leo Dickinson** 224; **Colin Foord** 109, 128, 159; **Wil Hurford** 89; **Jim Teesdale** 74/75, 141, 162, 212, 216; **Martin Welch** 201; **Dave Wynne Jones** 9, 31, 42, 43, 147, 148, 150. In addition **Bill O'Connor**, **Martin Moran**, **John Wilkinson** and **Simon Richardson** gave valuable additional topographical information and advice. The english text is adapted from an original translation by the late **Jill Neate** with additional work by **Gill Round**.

For editorial advice credit should also be given to Heinrich Bauregger, Gotlind Blechschmidt, Hartmut Eberlein, Klaus-Jürgen Gran, Andreas Hartmann, Susanne Hornburg, Joachim Linde, Helmut Krämer, Axel Naujoles, Wolfgang Rauschel, Barbara Spies, Hans Steinbichier and Thomas Stephan.

Maps and topos were prepared by **Eckehard Radehose**. Apart from a few minor changes they are left unaltered with German/French/Italian hut and feature names. *Frühstuckplatz* and *Salle a Manger* might be found convenient places to pause for an early morning bite. In the text *bergschrunds* will be just as problematic in German regions as the *rimayes* girdling French-named peaks. Illogically abseils rather than rappels are required to descend French peaks.

A warning: Great care has been taken in the compilation of this guidebook to ensure that accurate topographical, grading and timing advice is given. Using this advice the climber will make the judgement (according to weather conditions, ability and fitness) on how best to tackle the mountains. This is an alpine region and thus subject to steady change, a factor increased by global warming. Thus mountains can alter and errors and discrepancies cannot be ruled out. Therefore no guarantee can be given for the accuracy of every piece of information and climbers should, as always in dangerous terrain, rely on their own judgement and caution for route-finding and weather and time assessment. Anyone embarking on an alpine expedition is taking part in a hazardous pursuit and no legal liability is accepted by author or publisher for any accidents or damages sustained.

Copyright by © J.Berg, an imprint of Verlagsgruppe, Bruckmann, Munich, 1998 English translation © by Bâton Wicks, London, 2006.

Published simultaneously in the UK and the USA in 2003 by Bâton Wicks, London and Menasha Ridge Press, Birmingham, Alabama.

This revised edition was reprinted in 2010 in Singapore by MRM / PWGS.

Trade enquiries in the UK and Commonwealth to: Cordee, 3a De Montfort Street, Leicester LE1 7HD. Trade enquiries in the USA and Canada to: The Globe Pequot Press, P.O. Box 480, Guilford, CT 06437, U.S.A. Tel. (800) 243-0495

British Library Cataloguing in Publication Data:
A catalogue record for this book exists at the British Library   ISBN 1-898573-56-5

Library of Congress Cataloguing in Publication Data:
A catalog record of this book exists at the Library of Congress   ISBN 0-89732-559-1

Contents

Pennine Alps, Frontier Crest: Monte Rosa Group

Pennine Alps, Central Frontier Crest

Pennine Alps West

Mont Blanc Massif East

Mont Blanc Massif

Preface

The Alpine 4000ers are quite beautifully big, quite beautifully cold and quite beautifully wild. Though modest in height when matched against peaks of other continents, they rise further above the snow-line than many summits in the Himalaya and the Andes. They are also more convenient to reach – served by roads, railways and airports – and once there valley resorts with cableways, mountain railways and high mountain huts ensure rapid access to many mountains. Though many alpine valleys no longer convey the rustic charm of the old Alps they make up for it by the sheer speed and convenience of access. Thus alpinists need not make excessive demands on their professional and family lives in order to partake in a still wild and challenging pursuit. Small wonder that many people collect 4000ers.

Many of the Normal Routes on these peaks involve climbs of some challenge. They usually take the lines of least resistance working through savage glaciers and alongside fierce rock and ice faces. For this reason they are invariably spectacular and as they are often the first ascent routes, they also give us a link with alpine history. Despite traffic they renew themselves constantly with fresh snow, indeed weather changes lend them the unpredictability that is part of the fascination of big mountains, making these Normal Routes, anything but 'normal'.

In this new edition I have incorporated the 1994 UIAA peak changes. Previously 62 summits had formed the generally accepted list, but some prominent heights had been relegated, ignored or overlooked. These are now part of a new official total of 21 new 'summits' (with just the Balmenhorn demoted to a 'top') making a UIAA total of 82. Using the new col-depth tenets I believe that 9 more peaks should be added to make a total of 91 'summits' and 89 minor 'tops' (see pp.232–235).

Such pedantry may be scorned, but a glance at the new additions shows that most are perfectly logical. The extra summits on Liskamm, Breithorn, Grand Combin and the Grandes Jorasses lend these mountains added interest and dimension. The four Aiguilles du Diable of Mt. Blanc du Tacul introduce one of the great alpine rock excursions. Pic Luigi

Amedeo and Grand Pilier d'Angle prompt ascents of two great Mont Blanc ridges. I have identified a number of rock spires as prominent as the Diable four. Of these the Weisshorn's Grand Gendarme will involve an ascent of the classic North Ridge or the fine Younggrat rock spur, and the Pilier du Diable adds a new expedition of real challenge above the Glacier du Geant.

In aspiring to the 4000ers the crucial importance of good alpine skills and judgement cannot be overstressed. This is not an alpine instruction book. However, I urge new 4000m peak collectors to prepare themselves properly for these great ascents.

All the key route information they need will be found here so that, apart from the appropriate detailed maps, no further references are necessary. This English-language adaptation introduces 35 additional photographs. The route descriptions too, have benefited from the extra advice of British alpinists.

If there are changes on the mountain that require route variations, I will be grateful to learn of them to improve further editions. In the meantime, I wish you much joy and a safe return.

RICHARD GOEDEKE
Braunschweig 2006

Technical Guidance

Each chapter has a section called **Difficulties** with overall difficulty given first, then technical grade, length, rock quality, altitude and seriousness. The French grades customary in the Western Alps are:

F	*facile*	easy	D	*difficile*	hard
PD	*peu difficile*	not very hard	TD	*très difficile*	very hard
AD	*assez difficile*	fairly hard	ED	*extrêmement diff.*	extremely hard

After that, technical difficulties on dry rock are given UIAA grades (e.g. III+) and for ice and snow the maximum steepness in degrees (e.g. 50°) are given. Remember that the difficulty of rock-climbs can change considerably under snow and ice; likewise, bear in mind that it makes an enormous difference on snow or ice whether there is an established track or line of steps.

Under **Dangers**, only objective dangers are mentioned. Naturally, anyone can lose their life very quickly on objectively

At the summit of Dent d'Herens looking east to the nearby Matterhorn and the Mont Rosa group in the distance. On the Matterhorn the Italian Ridge is on the right and the Zmutt Ridge on the left.

safe terrain, if they misjudge the weather, their own ability, or make errors with equipment or technique. It is also wise to be circumspect when climbing below another group of climbers keeping alert for stonefall or ice chips, or worse, falling climbers (there have been several catastrophic accidents of this type).

The UIAA rock climbing grading scale converts as follows:

I	Moderate	5.1–5.2	IV	Severe	5.5–5.6
II	Difficult	5.2–5.3	V	Very Severe	5.6–5.7
III	Very Difficult	5.4	VI	HVS	5.8–5.9

In considering this one should note that classic rock pitches routes on high alpine peaks are usually tackled when heavily accoutred in boots (sometimes in crampons), anoraks and with heavy sacs. Pitches are sometimes wet, iced, snow-covered or loose and may have to be climbed in dawn light, during inclement weather, or later in the day when the early freeze has long since ceased to weld loose sections. The climber's abilities may also be reduced by fatigue or altitude weakness.

To prepare for this it is well to spend a few days of simulated alpine climbing before setting out for the Alps. At your alpine destination a further session of glacier training is always valuable (even for experienced teams) allowing cramponing, ice-axe technique (particularly braking involuntary slips), belaying, crevasse rescue and alpine rope technique to be practised. A training climb will then allow these skills to be polished, reveal the fitness of each climber and tune up the habits of speedy movement. Then select a climb to match the abilities of the party – alpine climbing soon exposes overambition, demoralisation or excessive fatigue being the usual result.

In the route descriptions 'right' and 'left' are used for the principal direction of travel. Abbreviations used are:

B	bed spaces (including Matratzen lager)
LKS	Landeskarte der Schweiz (Swiss maps)
IGN	Institut Geographique National (French maps)
m	metre
mH	height gain in metres
orogr.	orographically seen in direction of flow
SAC/CAF/CAI	Swiss/French/Italian Alpine Clubs

The guide gives only general route-finding advice and not finite instructions. Alpine peaks are constantly changing: rocks fall, glaciers recede or advance, snowfields develop, melt or turn to ice, cornices appear, avalanche conditions lurk, séracs collapse and storms arrive. To judge the best tactics remains the task for all who climb and this includes knowing when to turn back. If, despite all care, we get into difficulties the following information is important:

Alpine Distress Signals
If help is required make a visible or audible signal *six times in a minute* then a minute's pause before repeating the sequence. The reply, showing that the distress call has been understood, is a signal given *three times per minute* with minute's pause before a repeat.

Helicopter Rescue Signals and Advice
A signal with <u>*both arms held up at 45° above the head*</u> means '**Help! Please land**'. Conversely a signal with <u>*one arm high and the other low*</u> means '**Do not land, we do not require anything**'.
1. For the landing site, a horizontal place (no hollows!) of 30m x 30m is required with no obstacles in a 100m radius.
2. Remove objects which can be whirled into the air by the suction of the approaching helicopter.
3. The approaching helicopter is directed, back to the wind, by a person taking up the 'Yes' position (both arms stretched high).
4. Only approach the helicopter frontally on a signal from the pilot.

Helicopter Rescue Alarm REGA Tel. 01-383-11-11 and when phoning from outside Switzerland 0041 333 333 333
When reporting an accident important details are: name, location, telephone number, when and what happened, type of injury/illness; exact location, weather and obstacles (e.g. cables) in accident area. Patrons of the Swiss Air Rescue Service receive free rescue service inside Switzerland. (Swiss Air Rescue Service, Mainaustrasse 21, CH-8008 Zurich, Tel. 01-385-85-85; annual subscription currently about 20 Euros. Rescue/Hospital Expense Insurance is important – your national mountaineering organisation will be able to advise.

The following technique books are useful:

Handbook of Climbing by Allen Fyffe and Iain Peter. Pelham Bks (London)
Glacier Travel and Crevasse Rescue by Andy Selters. Mountaineers (Seattle)
Avalanche Safety for Skiers and Climbers by Tony Daffern. Rocky
    Mountain Books (Calgary) and Bâton Wicks (London)
Alpinism by Peter Cliff. Published privately (Distributed by Cordee)

The Big Isolated Peaks

Apart from the three highest mountain chains, which contain most of the four-thousand metre peaks, there are three lower ranges in which, in each case, only the highest summit achieves the requisite height. Nevertheless, these are quite independent massifs and the mountains of all three underline, by their originality and form, how foolish it is to be focussed solely on height. But in this book we are concerned solely with the 4000m peaks:

Piz Bernina 4049m

Along the strikingly straight valley furrow of the Engadine, the Bernina Alps rise above the magic height with the icily brilliant Piz Bernina. Whether this "Ballroom of the Alps", as Walter Flaig called them, is the most easterly group of the Western Alps or the most westerly of the Eastern Alps, belongs to the arcane discussions of the categorizers. The main point is that this splendid mountain massif, in the elegance of its lines and impact of its bulk, is one of the most architecturally appealing in the Alps; a refreshing change from the greater ranges to the west.

The first ascent was made in 1850 by the Swiss surveyor Johann Coaz and the brothers Jon and Lorenz Ragut Tscharner taking a route up the Morteratsch Glacier to the Fuorcla Crast'Agüzza and thence up the South Ridge (Spallagrat) which is today's Normal Route. The celebrated Biancograt (in Romansh, Crast'Alva) leads to the summit from the north and was first climbed in 1876 (to Pt. Alva) by Henri Cordier and Thomas Middlemore with their guides Johann Juan and Kaspar Maurer. The final stretch to the summit was added in 1878 by Paul Güssfeldt guided by Hans Grass and Johann Cross.

A view along the Spallagrat to the summit of Piz Bernina

Difficulties: PD. Predominantly a glacier route with long and complicated approaches to the hut below the final summit ridge (pitches of II and I) which are made easier (but not beautified) by fixed ropes.

Effort: The climb to the Marco e Rosa Hut from the Diavolezza Hut is 1050mH (5–6 hrs). Summit climb (by the Spallagrat): 500mH (2 hrs). Other routes: From Morteratsch via the Boval Hut 600mH + 1100mH (2–3 + 4–6 hrs), from Franscia via the Marinelli Hut 1250mH + 1000mH (4 + 3–4 hrs).

Dangers: On all glacier ascents to the Fuorcla Crast'Agüzza, especially from the north, there are many crevasses and occasionally also possibility of avalanches. The least dangerous approach is from the Diavolezza. On the narrow summit ridge beware of cornices. In a crowd, discipline and circumspection while passing or overtaking is important, especially on the the Biancograt. In poor visibility, particularly if the track is lost, there are considerable route-finding problems on the Morteratsch Glacier. In bad weather the descent from the Marco e Rosa Hut can be arduous. This is true both of the wire ropes (severe danger from lightning in thunder storm) on the Italian side, and of the glaciers on the north side when the risks of crevasse falls in new snow are increased.

Pleasure: The highest summit of the Eastern Alps with splendid views of the adjacent Bernina peaks.

Maps: LKS 1277 *Piz Bernina* 1:25,000; LKS 44 *Maloja* 1:100,000.

Travel: By rail via Zürich-Chur-St Moritz or by car through the valley of the Engadine to Pontresina (1805m, summer/winter tourist resort plus a youth hostel, Tel. 082-67223) and Bernina railway to Hotel Morteratsch (1896m, 6km from Pontresina); valley station of the Diavolezza cableway at Bernina-Suot (2093m, 10km from Pontresina). On the Italian side, by rail to Sondrio in the Val Tellina 23km and by car through the Val Malenco to Franscia (1565m, mountain village), possibly as far as the lower reservoir Lago di Gera (1996m).

Hut climb from the Diavolezza Hut: (2973m, private, 170B, Tel. 082-66205. Managed from June–September and December–April). Descend path south-westwards to cross (in the same direction) the Vadret Pers Glacier. On its west bank work up south to pass under the rocks of the Chamuotsch Hut, following the usually (in good weather) broad track, and then move up steeper snow slopes to the broad ridge of the Fortezzagrat.

Continue along the narrowing ridge (pitches of II and I) and a steeper step, which can be turned on the west side, to reach a snow slope. Climb this to the Bellavista Terraces. Before reaching the notch of the Fuorcla Bellavista, turn right and traverse west and south-west on the snow terraces, staying at about the same height, as far as north of the most westerly Bellavista summit (at the 'Eck' [corner], in sight of the prominent spire of the Crast' Agüzza). Descend steeply (big crevasses) into the uppermost snow trough of the Morteratsch Glacier. Before reaching the ice-falls, descend further to about 3600m and then traverse west to the flat saddle of the Fuorcla Crast'Agüzza. In the same direction and at the same height, traverse another 300m to the rocky shoulder with the two Marco e Rosa De Marchi Huts (3597m / 3609m, CAI, 45 B, often crowded, managed July to mid-September, Tel. 0342-515370).

The view west over the Bellavista Terraces to Piz Bernina with the Spallagrat on the left and the Biancograt the right skyline.

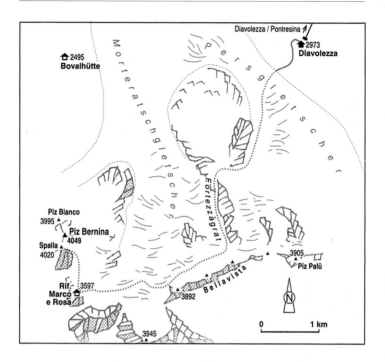

Hut climb from Morteratsch: A path takes the western moraine of the Morteratsch Glacier to reach (2 hrs) the Boval Hut (2495m, SAC, 100 B, managed from June to October as well as Easter/Whitsun, Tel. 081-842 6403). From here, first of all cross the Morteratsch Glacier eastwards to the foot of the rocky Fortezzagrat. Go along the foot of the rocks as far as the height of the rock island P.3087 on the glacier. Cross over to the right (west) towards this rock island, to the Schnapsbödeli – a small plateau. From here between the Fortezzagrat (left) and another ridge with séracs (right), climb straight up southwards to the Bellavista terraces, where the Diavolezza route is joined.

One can also climb up to the Fortezzagrat from further below on the left and ascend this (time-consuming but avoiding the glacier) to reach the Bellavista Terraces. Two other (heavily crevassed) routes lead further west through the ice-falls of the 'Buuch' and the 'Labyrinth' respectively, directly up to the Forcella Crast'Agüzza.

The approach from the Italian side, from Franscia (1556m) heads north-west (marked path) to the Scerscen Hut (1813m) and continues north, crossing the valley to the Alpe Campascio (1844m). Climb north-east through the wood to the Alpe Musella (2021m). Continue north-east over the increasingly sparse ground to the Bocchetta delle Forbici to the Carate Hut (2636m, CAI). Go round the North-West Spur of the Cime di Musella to a lake under the little Vedretta di Caspoggio Glacier and continue, with a right-left bend, to the Marinelli Hut sited on a rock ridge (2813m, c.50B, managed in summer). From there, head north-eastwards near the rock ridge, over debris and snow to the Passo Marinelli occidentale (3087m) which lies above the ridge. Pass northwards under the rocky spur of Piz Argient to the upper Vedretta di Scerscen Glacier. Cross this and move under the rocks of Crast'Agüzza passing the ice/snow couloir descending from the Fuorcla Crast'Agüzza (crevasses) to the northern boundary spur of the couloir. Cross the bergschrund and climb the spur (wire ropes) or gully to gain the Marco e Rosa Hut.

Summit climb by the Spallagrat: From the hut head north over the steepening snow slope to the rocks of the south-eastwards orientated ridge. Follow this (II, fixed rope), up to the fore-summit (Spalla) from whence a narrow snow ridge with one rock section (II) leads to the summit of Piz Bernina.

View: To the south-west are Piz Bernina's two impressive neighbouring peaks Piz Scerscen and Piz Roseg, to the north Piz Morteratsch, to the east Piz Palü and to the south-east Piz Zupo. In addition there are also magnificent views north-westwards down to the Tschierva Glacier and north-eastwards down to the Morteratsch Glacier.

Adjacent peaks: The Spalla (La Spedla) 4020m, the southern top, is prominent but not very independent. The northern summit, Piz Bianco (Piz Alb / Piz Alv, 3995m), marks the end of the Biancograt, from where the main summit can only be reached via the airy and not easy connecting ridge (III in places).

Other worthwhile routes: *The Biancograt* (AD) is so famous that the crowds often remove the pleasure of an otherwise magnificent excursion (pitches of III, mixed, snow or ice up to 50°). From the Tschierva Hut 1450mH (7–8 hrs) of which 600mH (4 hrs) from the Forcella Prievlusa is the ridge itself.

Guidebook: *Bernina and Bregalia* (Alpine Club 2002)

Looking down to the Eselsrücken. The Emanuele approach comes up the left slope to join the Chabod route that gains the shoulder more directly.

Gran Paradiso 4061m

This is the highest summit of the Graian Alps which lie between Mont Blanc to the north and Dauphiné range to the south. It is not prominent from the closer valleys, being hidden behind its surrounding mountains. Only from distant summits is its impact obvious. The name arouses concepts of a tremendous unscathed world – easily imagined in this area with its dreamy cirque lakes and lonely screes and snows, with occasional views of the prehistoric-like herds of ibex. However, although this quality can be discovered around the peak it is singularly absent in the valleys and on the mountain's Normal Route – a popularity ensured by the 'National Park' publicity tag. What one finds on the peak is a busy, well-trodden track up one of the 'easy' 4000ers. This reputation guarantees its ascent by climbers with a wider age range than is usual on mountains of this height.

Despite the popularity its ascent is far from effortless. It demands over 2000m of height-gain from the car-park at Pont to the summit, and all of this must be made on foot. The first ascent was made by John Jermayn Cowell and W. Dundas with the guides Michel Payot and Jean Tairraz in 1860. They did not have the advantage of the hut, named in honour of Vittorio Emanuele II to commemorate his founding of the national park.

Difficulties: F+. Up to summit ridge this is a rather monotonous rubble/snow plod, mostly on a deeply worn track, with a slope of 35°, which can be icy in late season. The final metres to the summit call for some exposed rock work (II and I).

Effort: Hut climb 700mH (2–3 hrs), summit climb 1350mH (4–5 hrs). Crossing the rubble slope of big blocks immediately behind the hut in the dark is really troublesome. The climb can also be unpleasant on account of the crowds at the hut, during the ascent, and on the summit.

Dangers: Small crevasses occasionally appear on the glacier but otherwise there is little objective danger. However, in bad visibility or storms, because of the scale and height of the mountain, very rapid and dramatic developments are possible.

Pleasures: In contrast to those peaks which have been made docile and palatable to consumers by means of cableways or mountain railways, the Gran Paradiso gives the satisfaction of a high peak gained solely by personal effort. Especially impressive is the view which, after a rather monotonous ascent, suddenly develops on the final approach to the summit, with fine aspects on all sides.

Map: IGC 1:50,000 No.62003 *Gran Paradiso.*

Travel: By rail through the Aosta valley to Sarre, 6km west of Aosta. By bus up the little road branching off the main road at Villeneuve, 11km west of Aosta, 25km southerly through the Val Savaranche to Pont (1945m, hotel / camping / big car-park).

Hut climb from Pont: A broad path heads up the valley and soon drops down to a stream descending in waterfalls on the left (east). Then ascend the valley slope in wide bends through the wood. Continue over sparse pastures and moraines to the barrel-shaped Vittorio Emanuele II Hut (2775m; CAI, 143 B, winter room with 43 B, mostly overcrowded, managed from the end of April to 25 September, Tel. 0165-95920). Alternatively, from 2km below Pont (camping/car park) take a path to Rifugio Chabod (2750m. CAI, 100B, Tel. 0165 905798).

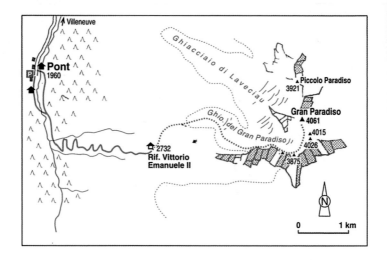

Summit climb by the West Face: From the hut, head north-wards over the 'block field' (very tiresome in the dark) to the moraines leading up to the Gran Paradiso Glacier. Follow these and then a small valley climb over snow keeping below the now receded glacier snout. Instead of going up this (old way) follow cairns to the left of it and then up steep and unpleasant rock and scree to the lower part of the ridge. Go up this to where it narrows (Eselsrücken) and leads along the edge of the glacier to the saddle in front of the pinnacle Becco del Moncorvé towering up on the right at the edge of the south cliff. **From the Chabod Hut** go along the northern edge of the Ghiacciaio di Laveciau until the glacier can be gained. A south-easterly line is taken to join the Emanuele route at the Eselsrücken. Now ascend north-wards over the steeper slopes, below the rock ridge of the 'Roc' to the rimaye. Cross this (usually without problems) and go up a short rocky ridge, with a final surprisingly exposed section (I) to gain the fore-summit (Madonna). The highest point, which lies behind at the north-west end of the summit ridge, may be reached by more rock climbing (II and I) in about 15 minutes.

View: To the north-west the Mont Blanc massif can be seen, to the north-east the Pennine Alp frontier crest, to the south-west the Dauphiné with the Barre des Écrins and to the south Monte Viso. There is a fine view down the East Face.

Looking south from Gran Paradiso's Madonna summit to Il Roc (4026m).

Adjacent peaks: The Madonna summit (c.4058m) is only a little lower than the highest point. The Central Summit (c.4015m), also crowned with several rock pinnacles, is quickly and easily climbed from the Normal Route (II and I). The same goes for the somewhat more difficult (II) East Summit (Il Roc 4026m) rising on the connecting ridge. The Piccolo Paradiso (3923m) rises on the ridge running northwards from the main summit.

Other worthwhile routes: *East Face* (AD, II, mixed and 50°; 900mH from the Pol Bivouac).

North-West Face (D, ice or snow 50°, 600mH from the rimaye).

North Ridge intégral (D, IV and III, 1700mH, 15 hrs from the Leonessa Bivouac).

Guidebook: *Graians East* (West Col, 1969).

Barre des Écrins 4101m

In the Haut Dauphiné, far to the south-west, the Alps reach up into more rarefied air, in a row of impressive mountains. Unfortunately some of the most beautiful lie just under 4000m and the Barre des Écrins alone towers above this level. But the satellites of the majestic Barre are the essential parts of this splendid ensemble of pinnacle ridges and gloomy ice walls high above the glaciers. Those who scorn the peaks that fall below the critical height, are missing the whole point of alpinism and some very fine climbs.

Almost the entire high mountain region of the massif is a national park and thus permanently(?) protected from the building of téléphériques. As a result this untouched scenery can be experienced only by those prepared to climb from the valley under their own steam. It is nevertheless threatened permanently, as are many other areas of Europe, by accidents in the atomic reactors installed in the Rhône valley just west of Grenoble.

The first ascent of the Barre in 1864 fell to Adolphus Warburton Moore and Edward Whymper, led by Michel Croz from Chamonix and the Swiss guide Christian Almer. They busied themselves in delicate step cutting up the North Face and the upper part of the East Ridge and, on descent, cleaned up the then very unstable West Ridge, over which today's Normal Route leads. Whymper's account of it in *Scrambles Amongst the Alps* still makes fascinating reading. The rugged South Face was climbed in 1880 by Henri Duhamel and the local guide Pierre Gaspard and his son. The ascent of the overwhelming line of the South Pillar, towering above the Glacier Noir the summit, fell to the extreme climbers Jean and Jeanne Franco in 1944.

> **Difficulties:** PD. On the summit ridge, exposed climbing on good, stabilized rock, with pitches of II, mostly I. The rest is glacier climbing with snow up to 40°. The bergschrund at the Brèche Lory can be troublesome.
>
> **Effort:** Hut climb 1350mH from the Cézanne Hut (5 hrs), summit climb 1000mH (4 hrs).
>
> **Dangers:** On some parts of the lower glacier, there is a mild danger from falling ice and some of the crevasses in the upper section should be treated with respect. Otherwise, an objectively safe ascent. Nevertheless, one should not get caught by storm high on the mountain.
>
> **Pleasures:** The ascent from the bottoms of the valleys through the unspoiled scenery of the Écrins Nature Park 'creates, in its consistency and gradually impinging impressions, the pre-conditions for an especially profound and fascinating mountain experience'.

Maps: IGN 241 *Massif des Écrins, Meije, Pelvoux* 1:25,000, also IGN itinéraires pedestres et à ski 6, *Écrins et Haut Dauphiné* 1:50,000.

Travel: By rail from the south via Gap through the valley of the Durance to l'Argentière-la-Bessée (16km south of Briançon) or from Italy via Turin and Susa to Oulx and then by bus via Col de Montgenèvre to Briançon and l'Argentière-la-Bessé. This can also be reached from the west by bus from Grenoble railway station via Col du Lautaret and Briançon. By car, by the motorways from Paris and Switzerland to Grenoble, then highway N91 over the Col du Lautaret or, from the Po plain, motorway to Turin and then highway E13 via Susa-Oulx-Col du Montgenèvre to Briançon and south to l'Argentière-la-Bessé (979m). From there, by bus 18km to Ailefroide (1503m, mountain village over-run with hotels; camping Tel. 49223-3200).

Hut climb from Ailefroide: Near the valley bottom, take a path for 5km, first on the road then, cutting off its bends This leads to the Cézanne Hut (1874m, hotel, car-parks, often crowded).

Cross over the fields of debris to the bridge over the outflow from the Glacier Noir. After that, take the grassy slope on the right in bends, over a rock-studded spur and traverse to the tongue of the Glacier Blanc. Move up over polished rocks on the right (east) of the glacier (on an ugly steel staircase with railings), past the ruins of the old Tuckett Hut, and northwards to the Glacier Blanc Hut (2550m, 2–3 hrs from the Cézanne Hut; CAF, c.100B, managed, often less crowded than the Écrins Hut). Continue 2km up along the edge of the glacier to a rock spur (P.3016). Beyond this climb right in an arc to the already visible Écrins Hut, high above the glacier (3170m, CAF, 100B, May–September, Tel. 049223 4646 – usually full in good weather.

Summit climb – North Face and West Ridge: From the Écrins Hut go down to the glacier to join the route ascending from the Glacier Blanc Hut. Continue up the northern edge of the glacier, to the proximity of the Col des Écrins, sunk between the Roche Faurio (north) and the Barre des Écrins (south). Before reaching the rock towers of the Clochetons de Bonne Pierre, climb (with despatch) obliquely left up the steep, avalanche-scarred slope which is threatened by the séracs above. Then follow a (usually distinct) track in the direction of P.3791 on the East Ridge of the Barre, and when close under the rimaye, traverse to the right along a slightly inclined terrace to the Brèche Lory (3974m). If the rimaye is too wide traverse further right and climb steep snow slopes (often icy) to the summit of Dôme de Neige.

From Brèche Lory cross the rimaye and at first ascend the steep, mixed face to gain the exposed, narrow ridge (II, unpleasant when icy) which leads up to Pic Lory. After crossing a notch on the narrowing and more exposed ridge head up to the easternmost and highest point of the mountain.

View: To the east and north far below is the impressive Glacier Blanc, and to the south the Glacier Noir. Behind that are the Pelvoux and the Ailefroide, and to the south-west Les Bans, to the north the Roche Faurio and beyond that La Meije.

Adjacent peaks: The very obvious Pic Lory (4086m) was

Barre des Écrins from the north-east from the Refuge des Écrins.

Crossing Pic Lory, the narrowest part of the West Ridge of Barre des Écrins. The main summit is on the lower left.

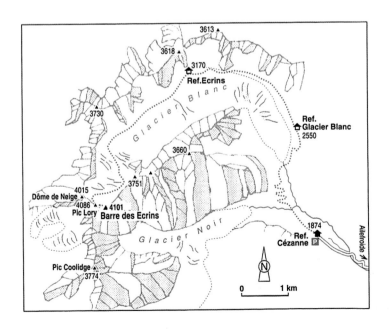

crossed during the ascent. This is the connecting point between the West Ridge from the the Brèche Lory and the steep ridge running south-west to the Col des Avalanches. The Dôme de Neige (4015m) can be easily climbed from the Brèche Lory.

Other worthwhile routes: *East Ridge* (AD, III and II, mixed, snow to 50º, 450mH and 2 hrs from the Brèche des Écrins).

South Face (AD, rock with longer passages of III and II, mixed, snow to 55º, from the Temple Hut 1700mH and 6–8 hrs, of that 630mH and 3–4 hrs from the Col des Avalanches).

South Pillar (TD, IV+, with passages of V+, is a splendid classic Alpine route, serious because of the lack of escape possibilities, 1100mH and 6–9 hrs from foot of face).

Guidebook: *Écrins Massif* (Alpine Club, 2002).

Dôme de Neige 4015m

The caravan summit of the Écrins is now considered independent according to the UIAA list – one of the less exciting additions in that it is easily attained during an ascent of the Barre, but taken strictly as a project on its own it offers considerable interest. There are also interesting routes on other faces including a clutch of intriguing TD rock climbs above the Glacier Bonne Pierre.

> **Grade:** F– Usually a peaceful glacier route.
> **Effort:** summit ascent from the Refuge Écrins 900m (3 hrs).
> **Dangers:** Advisable to take a rope on the glacier because of crevasses.
> **Highlights:** impressive glacial terrain.

Summit route: As for the Barre des Écrins to the Brèche Lory, then without problems to the summit along the snow ridge.

View: Very restricted by the Barre to the south, though it is interesting to watch, at close quarters, parties traversing that fine historic peak.

Other worthwhile routes: From the Barre's Normal Route up the North Face, *La Calotte* (AD) moves right at half height (passing below a sérac barrier) and takes a direct line to the Dôme up the exposed snow/ice face (J. Girand and client, 1944).

Bernese Alps

The Bernese Alps is not the highest range of the Alps but, situated on its northwestern edge, with tremendous, steep flanks facing out over the foothills, it attracts especially heavy precipitation that feeds enormous glaciers. Both of the longest glaciers in the Alps are thus to be found here. To the north a high altitude railway offers a comfortable spring-board to some of the most prominent summits. But apart from that, the approaches to the peaks are long and arduous.

Aletschhorn 4195m

The mighty pyramid of the second highest summit in the Bernese Alps dominates, with the hanging glaciers of its North Face, the snow basin of the Grosser Aletsch Glacier, the largest ice stream in the Alps. Here it is still possible to view a relic of the Ice Age when such ice masses pushed themselves through all the big Alpine valleys to the fringes of the foothills. Even the arid and rockier southern flanks of the mountains are still framed by glaciers littered with the tell-tale debris of the varying rock bands scoured by this great glacier and its feeder streams.

The Normal Routes on this mountain, offer a choice of difficulties, either on glacier and snow or on the rock. There is the North-East Ridge reached from the Mittelaletsch Glacier that was taken during the first ascent in 1859 by Francis Fox Tuckett, J.J. Bennen, Pete Bohren and Victor Tairraz. This is also the customary route for ski ascents. The rockier South-West Face approach was pioneered in 1879 by L. Lichti, A. Kummer and a porter, but may have been climbed five years earlier by Thomas Middlemore and party. Taken together they provide a large-scale traverse. A harder, but still more splendid traverse is offered by the ascent of the stylish Hasler Rib on the left side of the North Face to gain the North-East Ridge. This was climbed to the summit by Gustav Hasler and party in 1902 but the rib itself was probably first done in 1888 by C. Lüscher and party.

Difficulties: *North-East Ridge* PD. On the erratically disrupted Mittelaletsch Glacier with its ever changing conditions, then by a snow ridge and slopes up to 40°, with short sections of easy rock climbing on the summit ridge. *South-West Face* AD– with longer passages of rock climbing (II). In snowy conditions, when used for descent, it can be quite difficult to find.

Effort: *By the North-East Ridge*: 800mH ascent to the Mittelaletsch Bivouac Hut (5–7 hrs), with a summit climb of 1200mH (5 hrs). *By the South-West Ridge*: 700mH, 8km (4 hrs) to the Oberaletsch Hut, summit climb of 1700mH (7–8 hrs).

Dangers: On account of its situation amidst large glaciers and its isolated, wind-exposed position, the Aletschhorn is an unusually cold mountain, on which warm and wind-proof clothing is especially important. There is stonefall risk on the summit block of the South-West Face. On the glaciers there are the usual crevasse dangers. Otherwise both are objectively very safe climbs.

Pleasures: A magnificent, untouched mountain in a wild, isolated position.

The chief thing to bear in mind is that because of its size and the diversity of its demands, the ascent of the Aletschhorn remains a comprehensive alpine undertaking.

Maps: LKS 1269 *Aletsch Glacier* and LKS 5004 *Berner Oberland*.

Travel: Along the Rhône valley by rail or car as far as Betten (830m; 5km south-west of Fiesch, 10km north-east of Brig, 3km from Morel). This is the valley station of the cableway to the Bettmeralp (1950m) a tourist resort on the shoulder of the ridge between the valley of the Grosser Aletsch Glacier and the Rhône valley and the starting point for the North-East Ridge/ Mittelaletsch approach. For the South-West Face leave the Rhône valley at Brig (684m), and thence 9km by bus or car to the tourist village of Blatten (1322m).

Hut climb to the North-East Ridge: Start from Bettmeralp and descend to the Bettmersee and take a path to P.2292 on the ridge which runs south-west from the Eggishorn. A track leads in the direction of the Marjelensee on the West Face of the Bettmerhorn to almost below the Eggishorn. At P.2348.6 descend on the left to the Gross Aletsch Glacier and cross this (often laboriously) to the junction with the Mittelaletsch Glacier. On this, first climb over moraine debris, then move onto the ice in the middle of the glacier. Above 2700m, avoid a badly disrupted area by a path on

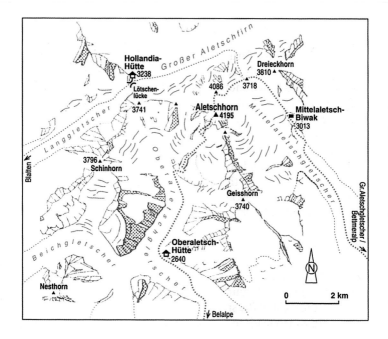

the eastern (right) bank leading to the Mittelaletsch Bivouac Hut at 3013m (SAC, 13 B, blankets, no kitchen, no wood).

Hut climb to the South-West Face: Go from Blatten by cableway, or by car, to Taatsche 1750m, then 1 hr on foot on a zig-zag path, or by a little road, to the cableway station on the Belalp (2094m). Head north-eastwards on broad path to Hotel Belalp (2130m). Behind it, descend a broad zig-zag track and then cross grassy slopes towards the head of the valley. Further on, climb to the moraines of the Oberaletsch Glacier descending from the left. At about 2200m, the moraines are traversed. After that, ascend the dry glacier for about 3km to beyond and behind the spur on which the hut stands (easily seen, high above the polished rock). When beyond the confluence of the various glacier arms quit the glacier on a newly built path (red markings at start; pegs, wire ropes and chains) going up over the steep slabs 150mH to the very picturesque (but impractically placed for the Aletschorn ascent) Oberaletsch Hut (2640m; SAC Chassertal, 60 B, managed in summer, Tel. 027-9271767).

Summit climb / North-East Ridge: From the Mittelaletsch Bivouac Hut, head north-west up over the crevassed slopes to the Aletschjoch (3629m). Turn to the west and follow the narrow corniced ridge of P.3718 (also reached from the north by the impressive Hasler Rib) to a broad snow slope. Climb this to the snow hump P.4086.3 which is crossed or turned on the south to gain the snow shoulder beyond. Finally climb a short steep slope, cross a bergschrund, finish up a snow and rock ridge to gain the summit.

Summit climb / South-East Face: From the Oberaletsch Hut, descend the path back to the glacier and ascend it to about 2700m. After that, cross the marginal crevasse at a suitable place and, on a series of ledges and terraces (tracks; difficult to find in the dark) head obliquely right up to grass slopes. Climb the hollow between a rock rib (on the left) and a moraine (on the right) then go up a gully on the left to the crest granite spur with large blocks, and climb it to P.3382 at the upper end.

From here, take a right-left curve up the glacier (crevasses) to the foot of the rock spur descending from the summit. At first climb on the right of the spur, then move to the left to use a small snow-field which leads to the steeper gneiss rocks of the summit

The North Face of the Aletschorn with the Hasler Rib on the left linking up with the North-East Ridge.

block. Keep right of the edge, taking a steep gully and straight on to a less steep snow-field which leads to the summit.

View: The summit provides a magnificent panorama. To the west is the Bietschhorn, and to the north and east the other Oberland peaks. To the south, somewhat further away, are the Pennine Alps.

Adjacent peaks: On the North-East Ridge is the modest snow top of P.4086, on the W.N.W. Ridge the scarcely more significant P.4071 and, further west, the Kleines Aletschhorn (3755m). On the South-East Ridge is the prominent tower of P.3947.

Other worthwhile routes: *North Rib* of P.3718 (Hasler Rib) and *North-East Ridge* (AD+, pitch of III, mostly II and I, mixed, and snow to 50°, objectively safe; 700mH from the Grosser Aletschfirn to the ridge, then a further 500mH to the summit, 5–7 hrs from the Hollandia Hut.

South-East Ridge (AD–, II, mixed, 1600mH from the Oberaletsch Hut 8 hrs).

West-North-West Ridge (AD+, III and II, 6–8 hrs from the Oberaletsch Hut), most interesting as part of the large-scale *Sattelhorn/Aletschhorn/Dreieckhorn Ridge* traverse (AD+, up to III; 11–15 hrs from Hollandia Hut to Konkordia Hut).

North Face (D/TD, thoroughbred ice climb, up to 50°, but lower part menaced by falling ice, 1100mH, 5–8 hrs).

Guidebook: *Bernese Oberland* (Alpine Club, 2003).

Jungfrau 4158m

The name of this peak lends wings to the imagination, either as poetry or trivial jokes. For anyone who wants to read something original about the peak I recommend Alphonse Daudet's delicious Alpine satire, *Tartarin on the Alps*, which has lost nothing of its freshness in over a century since it was written. This third highest summit in the Bernese Alps is especially striking seen from the north. There the faces and snow slopes fall, a breathtaking 3000 metres, to the Lauterbrunnen valley. This magnificent mountain wall, together with its neighbours Mönch and Eiger, may be seen on clear days from the equally impressively frontages of the Swiss federal capital Berne. From the south the Jungfrau appears, by comparison, less magnificent, although even from there it still rises a good 1000 metres above the snow basin of the Grosser Aletsch Glacier.

The first ascent was made in 1811 by Johann Rudolf Meyer and Hieronymus Meyer with the chamois hunters Alois Volker and Joseph Bortis in a four-day expedition from the Lötschental. The rack-railway, built in 1912, tunnels up through the Eiger and Mönch to Jungfraujoch. The outbreak of the First World War luckily prevented the planned continuation to the summit of the Jungfrau. The shortest approach to the Normal Route, previously a major expedition in itself behind the Eiger and over the Unter and Obermönchjocher is thus reduced to a fraction of its previous length by using the tunnel railway. Ascending this peak from the valley bottom entirely on foot remains a major undertaking.

Difficulties: PD+, climbing to II (mostly mixed) and snow or ice up to 40° and in part 50°. Late in the year, the bergschrund below the Rottalsattel can give problems.

Effort: The ascent from Jungfraujoch involves 850mH, and 150mH on the return (4 hrs from the Mönchsjoch Hut). From south from Fiesch:1100mH of ascent (3–4 hrs, avoidable by cableway) plus 750mH over 10km to the Konkordia Hut. Summit climb of 1350mH over a further 7km stretch (5 hrs).

Dangers: A peak with a high accident rate, surely increased by the proximity to the railway, which encourages less well prepared (and unacclimatized!) people to rash deeds? After fresh snow, the traverse to the Rottalsattel itself is often avalanche prone; also the cornices on the Rottalhorn can give trouble. More frequently the traverse from the Rottalsattel to the rocks is under-estimated. If everybody used in-situ iron posts for belaying it would cut down the calls on the mountain rescue. On the glaciers there is constant crevasse danger. Due to the dangerous snow conditions in the second half of the day it is strongly advised to make an early start from the hut rather than a later one using the first morning train.

Pleasures: Magnificent views but in good weather the descent is often spoiled by the crowds using the rail approach. An early start from the Mönchsjoch Hut enables one to avoid the worst of the congestion.

Maps: LKS 5004 *Berner Oberland* and LKS 264 *Jungfrau*.
Travel: By train from Berne via Interlaken to Grindelwald (1034m; from there take the train to Jungfraujoch). By car to

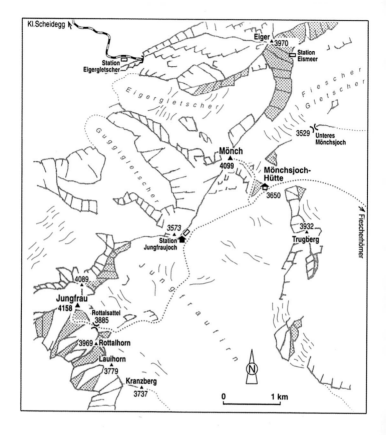

Grindelwald where there are the usual parking problems.

Hut climb: From the Jungfraujoch station (3475m) go through the Sphinxstollen tunnel and traverse under the South Face of the Mönch on a slightly ascending track to the Ober Mönchsjoch (1 hr) and then up east to the Mönchsjoch Hut (3660m, private, 125 B, managed in spring and summer, Tel. 033-9713472). For approach to the Konkordia Hut, see Gross Grünhorn (p.45).

Summit climb: From the Mönchsjoch Hut, return to the Sphinxstollen and go south across the highest part of the Jungfraufirn to skirt round the base of the Kranzbergegg (the Rottalhorn's East Ridge), turning west and north to gain the ridge crest above P.3411.1.

Climb the broad scree-covered ridge (rain gauge) to a steep step which is passed by a 20-metre crack leading to a narrow ledge under a high wall (abseil point for descent). Move left (south) and ascend slabby rocks and snow straight up to the ridge. Continue on snow ridge to about 3800m. Then make a rising rightwards traverse across the face of the Rottalhorn, over the bergschrund, to gain the Rottalsattel (3885m). The original way directly up the snow/ice couloir to the Rottalsattel is often difficult on account of large bergschrunds and steep ice.

The Rottalhorn and the Jungfrau from the Mönch.

Mönch (right) and Eiger (left) seen from the Jungfrau to the south-west. Mönch's Normal Route takes the rock-flanked right ridge.
Jungfraujoch is the lowest point on the bottom right of the photo.

From the Rottalsattel, make a tricky rising traverse left (north-westwards) on the steep slope to the rocks. It is worth belaying here – an accident blackspot. Continue up (numerous iron posts for belays) with technically easy climbing and then take the 35° snow slope leading to the summit rocks and highest point. The direct ascent from the Rottalsattel up over the 45° snow ridge is only advised in excellent conditions and even then it is more difficult than the described route.

View: Virtually all the great Oberland peaks and glaciers are laid out in sumptuous panoramic view.

Adjacent peaks: The Wengener Jungfrau (4089m), the apex of the North Face, will attract 4000-metre purists (allow an extra 70 minutes). South of the Rottalsattel, the Rottalhorn (3969m) and beyond it the Lauihorn (3779m), are worthy secondary goals.

Other worthwhile routes: *S.W. Ridge* (*Innerer Rottalgrat*) (AD, III/II, 1750mH+1400mH, 6 hrs from Rottal Hut).

N.W. Ridge (*Rotbrettgrat*) (D, if using fixed rope III, 1660mH+1500mH, 9 hrs from Silberhorn Hut).

Guggi Route (D+, A North Face traverse up hanging glaciers, serious, 480mH+1400mH, 8–10 hrs from the Guggi Hut).

N.E. Ridge (D+, V/IV, 700mH, 8–9 hrs from Jungfraujoch).

Guidebook: *Bernese Oberland* (Alpine Club, 2003).

Mönch 4099m

The Mönch lies so close to the Jungfraujoch that the ascent by the Normal Route, just like that of the Breithorn and Allalinhorn, has received undue emphasis; for in doing so one gets to know merely the uppermost few hundred metres of the mountain. Yet that should not be taken lightly, especially if one is unfit. Under-estimating the task can lead to over-straining and failure as the technical difficulties of the climb are far from negligible and when icy are often increased. The first ascent was made in August 1857 by the well-known Grindelwald guide Christian Almer and Ulrich and Christian Kaufmann with the Viennese

Siegmund Porges. The daring coup of the first ascent of the popular Nollen on the north-west flank was first climbed in 1866 by the Berne climber Edmund von Fellenberg with the guides Christian Michel and Peter Egger. Done years before adequate ice equipment was introduced, the climb was a truly hair-raising undertaking (a 10-metre ladder taken as an aid proving useless).

Difficulties: PD. Rock climbing to II, mixed, and snow or ice to 45°.
Effort: To summit from Mönchsjoch Hut 500mH (2–3 hrs).
Dangers: Under-estimating the demands of the mountain and trying to 'bag' it without adequate acclimatization, practice and experience. On bare ice, belaying with ice screws is recommended. Look out for cornices on the very narrow summit ridge! Even without cornices it is very precarious. It is best to keep just below the crest on the south side.
Pleasures: A short, elegant climb that can be opportunely 'snatched'.

Maps / Travel / Hut climb: See Jungfrau.

Summit climb: From the Ober Mönchsjoch, traverse south-westwards for 400m to the foot of the South Spur P.3651 (also gained by a north-easterly trek from the railway terminus). On the spur, climb debris then slabs, at first on limestone then further up more steeply on reddish gneiss, past the rain-gauge to P.3887. Here the South Spur joins the East-South-East Ridge.

Continue along an almost horizontal snow or rock ridge (beware of cornices) to a steeper, rocky piece of ridge. Climb its edge, awkward when icy, to a further snow ridge. Climb this, partly broken by rock steps, to a steeper ice passage. This leads to the junction (fore-summit, 4065m) with the branch of the ridge ascending from the north-east. The sharp, easy-angled, snow/ice ridge (sometimes corniced) leading to the summit plateau needs the utmost care in both ascent and descent.

View: The view is dominated by the contrast between the steep drop and the grassy foothills to the north, and the extensive glaciers and icy summits to the south. To right of the Eiger (north-east) is the Schreckhorn (east) and, to the south-east the Fiescherhornen, the Finsteraarhorn and Gross Grünhorn. In the western quarter the Aletschhorn and Jungfrau dominate.

Other worthwhile routes: *South-West Ridge* (AD–, direct from the Jungfraujoch, III and II, 650mH, 3–4 hrs).

North-East Face (D, snow or ice to 57°, mostly 45°, 250mH, 3 hrs from starting climb).
North-West Spur or *Nollen* (D, ice to 65°, from the Guggi Hut 480+ 1300mH, 7 hrs).
North Face Rib (*Lauper/Liniger Route*) (D+/TD, rock to V– and ice to 60°; 1300mH, 10–12 hrs from the Guggi Hut).
Specialist guidebook: *Bernese Oberland* (Alpine Club, 2003).

Gross Fiescherhorn 4049m

Seen from Grindelwald, where its impact vies with that of the Eiger, the Gross Fiescherhorn, and its eastern summit the Ochs, displays a wild and menacing ice wall that offers some of the most difficult ice and mixed routes of the Alps. Viewed from the Ewigschneefeld the massif is more enticing, flaunting an attractive snowy ridge crest. The peak was first climbed in 1862 by Adolphus Warburton Moore and Hereford Brooke George with their local guides Christian Almer and Ulrich Kaufmann.

Difficulties: PD. By a choice of three glacier routes with climbing to II and I.
Effort: From the Mönchsjoch Hut the summit climb involves 750mH, with a reascent of 350mH when returning. From the Konkordia Hut it is 1350mH; from Finsteraarhorn Hut 1000mH.
Dangers: Guarded by crevassed glaciers. Falling ice can threaten in places on the Konkordia and Finsteraarhorn approaches. On the final slope to the Fieschersattel, there is stone-fall danger when following other parties.
Pleasures: A wonderful vantage point in the centre of the wildest part of the Oberland. In Spring it is justifiably popular with ski mountaineers.

Maps / Travel / Hut climb: See Jungfrau, Grünhorn and Finsteraarhorn.
Summit climb: *From the Mönchsjoch Hut* head east and then south-east down across the Ewigschneefeld to 3300m. (This part is also reached from Konkordia via the Ewigschneefeld ice-fall taking a line to the south of the main fall. This is less crevassed but more menaced by falling ice than the Mönchsjoch Hut

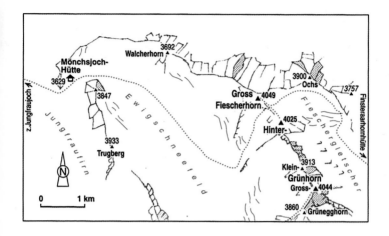

approach.) Now ascend on the left (north) of the rock rib leading to P.3981 of Hinter-Fiescherhorn. At P.3415 continue, keeping left, up under the West Face of the Hinter-Fiescherhorn. On the final section the best line is to the left of the saddle fall line, over the often big bergschrund and then, keeping right, over the steep and usually icy slope to brittle slate rocks to gain the Fiescher-sattel (3923m, 3–4 hrs from the Mönchsjoch Hut). The final bit can be avoided by traversing to P.3711 on the rock rib left of the crevassed slopes and following this to the summit.

From the Finsteraarhorn Hut, ascend the upper Fiescher Glacier as far as west of point P.3443.8. Beyond this, head up the ice-fall, keeping right, for about 120mH. This is a steep slope riddled with hungry crevasses and dangers of falling ice. Then work round to the left, towards Ochs, on the flatter, upper slopes of the glacier to about 3700m, and thence west up to the Fiescher-sattel (4–5 hrs from Finsteraarhorn Hut; see Grünhorn and Lauteraarhorn sketches, p.44 and p.49).

From the Fiechersattel (junction with Mönchsjoch route), continue on the South-East Ridge to a slabby rock tower. Climb this (III–) or turn it on the right on steep snow or ice. Continue up a

Top left: Gross Fiescherhorn's North-West Ridge from the summit.

Left: The Fiescherhorn group and Gross Grünhorn (centre right) from the Eiger with the Ewigschneefeld on the right.

The view south-east from the summit of Gross Fiescherhorn to Hinter-Fiescherhorn and, beyond, the Gross-Grünhorn.

firm gneiss ridge to the summit (from Mönchsjoch Hut, 4–5 hrs; Finsteraarhorn Hut, 5–6 hrs; Konkordia, 6–7 hrs).

View: The Hinter-Fiescherhorn and the Gross-Grünhorn (see above), to the east the Finsteraarhorn, to the north-east the Schreckhorn and the Lauteraarhorn, to the west and north-west the Mönch and Eiger and to the north the view down the imposing Fiescherwand.

Adjacent peaks: The Hinter-Fiescherhorn but with an ascent of over 100m from the intervening col this might add (ascent and descent) an extra 2 hours to the itinerary. The Ochs (Klein-Fiescherhorn) 3900m, to the east-north-east, reached along a narrow, corniced ridge, is a feasible addition if based at the Finsteraarhorn Hut.

Other routes: *North-West Ridge* (AD, III, mixed, and ice to 50°, a 4km ridge from the Unteren Mönchsjoch, often luxuriantly corniced, 4–5 hrs from the Mönchsjoch Hut. *North Rib to P.3804* (TD+, IV and III, mixed and serious with a broken glacier approach and then an ascent of 1000mH, 10 hrs).

North Face Direct (ED, IV mixed, ice to 65°, 1300mH, one of the hardest ice faces in the Alps).

Guidebook: *Bernese Oberland* (Alpine Club, 2003).

Gross Fiescherhorn from Hinter Fiescherhorn.

Hinter-Fiescherhorn 4025m

The southern neighbour of the Gross Fiescherhorn is climbed (PD) from the Fiechersattel in about an hour. The ridge is usually corniced so it is best to keep on the eastern slopes, and only on the final part go directly on the snow ridge. From the Ewigschneefeld approach one can also climb the inclined rock rib south of the Gross Fiescherhorn route (traverse the big rock tower on the left, II) to the prominent rocky South Ridge Summit P.3981 and from there traverse the summit (PD). For further information, see Gross Fiescherhorn.

Gross-Grünhorn 4044m

A beautifully formed peak with stylish rock ridges high above
wild glaciers. The summit block consists of firm amphibolite.
Its situation, far from mountain railways and motor passes, still
guarantees the ascent a really alpine character.

At the Konkordia Hut, the glacier shrinkage of the last 140
years is especially noticeable. At the time of the glacier high
point in 1850, the rock shoulders, where the huts were built, were
just above the level of the Grosser Aletsch Glacier. Yet today,
even after a decline in height of some 100m, the thickness of
the ice at the Konkordiaplatz, by seismic measurements, still
amounts to about 900 metres.

Edmund von Fellenberg with Peter Egger, Peter Michel and
Peter Inäbnit made the first ascent in 1885 from the west.

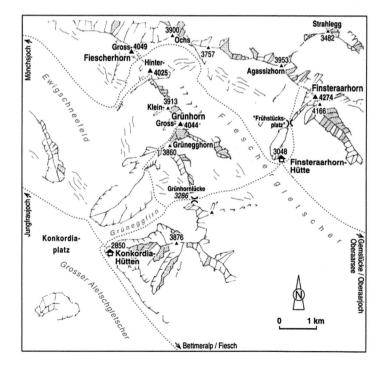

Gross-Grünhorn (left) and Grünegghorn seen from its fore-summit (3787m) on the S.W. Ridge.

Difficulties: AD–. On approach to the Grünegghorn, snow to 40° and easy climbing (pitches of I). On the summit ridge there are exposed sections of III– and II, which can be quite difficult when icy.

Effort: The hut climb from the cableway station above Fiesch is 750mH and 12km, 5 hrs. If the cableway is shunned, there is an additional 1100mH and 4km, 3–4 hrs. Alternatively, approach from the Jungfraujoch to the Konkordiaplatz (2–3 hrs). From the hut, the summit climb is 1400mH.

Dangers: There are some crevasses on the Grünegfirn otherwise, in good conditions, this is an objectively safe climb.

Pleasures: The peak offers everything that an alpinist treasures – remoteness, history, excellent views, good climbing.

Maps: LKS 1249 *Finsteraarhorn*, for approach from south LKS 1269 *Grosser. Aletsch Gletscher* or LKS 5004 *Berner Oberland*.

Travel: By rail or car through the Rhône valley to Fiesch (1049m; not too large a tourist resort with attractive old houses in the town centre, cableway to Eggishorn). For approach from Jungfraujoch, see Jungfrau.

Hut climb – Aletsch Glacier approach: From the middle

station of the Eggishorn cableway (Chuebodenstafel, 2221m), go north-east on a broad track along the slope. Then climb around a ridge (P.2386, view of Fiescher Glacier) and descend west across the Marjelenalpe to the picturesque Marjelensee, which is dammed in by the ice of the Grosser Aletsch Glacier. Move onto the dry (in summer) glacier, first amidst crevasse zones, then on clearer terrain. Head north on the eastern side of this impressive ice stream, then north-north-west. In mist, the debris ramparts of the central moraines assist route-finding. After several kilometres, regain the eastern glacier bank (often transverse crevasses full of snow), pass under the huts and then, from the west, reach the iron ladders/stairs screwed to the steep polished rock. Ascend 100mH to the Konkordia Hut (2850m; SAC Grindelwald; 130B, managed in spring and summer, Tel. 033-8551394).

Hut climb – from Jungfraujoch: From the Jungfraujoch station, go through the Sphinxstollen to the Jungfraufirn. Descend this keeping close to the eastern (left) edge under the slopes of the Trugberg and then below the ice-falls of the Ewigschneefeld

An early morning view across the Fiescher Glacier from the Finsteraarhorn Hut to Gross-Grünhorn and Hinter-Fiescherhorn.

coming in from the east, to the glacier morass of the Konkordia-platz to arrive at the iron ladders from the north.

Summit climb by the South-West Ridge: From the Konkordia Hut descend the ladders and ascend eastwards over the Grüneggfirn to about 3000m. Keeping to the northern edge of the glacier, ascend more steeply for about 400mH. Then turn left (west) over snow slopes and a short steep gully to the south-west snow slope of the Grünegghorn. Follow this to the fore-summit (3787m). Continue along an exposed rocky ridge with a final rise, keeping away from any cornices on the right, to reach the summit of the Grünegghorn (3860m, 3–4 hrs from the Konkordia Hut).

Descend the steep rock ridge to the saddle beyond (c.3800m) This point can be reached from the Ewigschneefeld by the serious, complicated glacier route of the first ascent. This can be time-consuming but less so in spring snow conditions.

From the saddle continue along the rocky South-West Ridge, sometimes using the slope to the left, to the summit of the Gross-Grünhorn.

View: To the west there is an impressive view of the source of the longest Alpine glacier with the icy Aletschhorn and the Jungfrau above it. The impressively towering Finsteraarhorn is to the east. The Fiescherhorn, Eiger and Mönch are to the north.

Adjacent peaks: The Grünegghorn (3860m), immediately to the south-west, is traversed on the Normal Route. The Klein-Grünhorn (3913m), a similar distance away to the north-west, is more easily climbed from the Ewigschneefeld over the Kleine Grünhornlücke and the North-North-West Ridge (II) (5 hrs from the Konkordia Hut).

Other worthwhile routes: *North-North-West Ridge* from the Klein-Grünhorn (D, IV and III, 3–4 hrs from summit to summit).

South-East Ridge and South-East Face (AD+, III, mixed, from the Finsteraarhorn Hut 1000mH, 4–6 hrs).

East Spur (TD–, V–, mixed; worthwhile rock-climbing, 650mH of rock, 7–9 hrs from foot of face).

Guidebook: *Bernese Oberland* (Alpine Club, 2003).

The Grosser Aletsch Glacier, the biggest ice stream in the Alps.

Eastern Bernese Oberland

These mountains between Grimsel and the Fiescher Glaciers and Eismeer are especially wild and remote with a particularly grand and dominant character.

Schreckhorn 4078m

The most rugged and hardest of the Bernese 4000s is largely a rock peak. Despite its considerable difficulty, it was first climbed as early as 1861 by way of the Schrecksattel and the East Ridge (when its snow cover may have been greater) by Leslie Stephen with the guides Christian and Peter Michel and Ulrich Kaufmann. Today's customary Normal Route was discovered in 1907 by the guideless trio of John Wicks, Edward Bradby and Dr. Claude Wilson. The enormous approaches from all quarters maintains the Schreckhorn as one of the most exacting peaks in the Alps. This climb is covered in a chapter 'Storm on the Peak of Terror' in Frank Smythe's *Climbs and Ski Runs* where the author describes an arduous retreat in a thunderstorm.

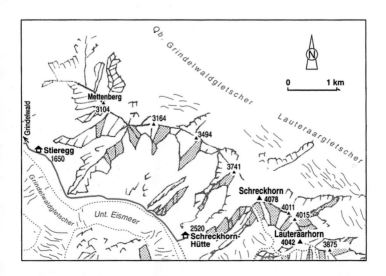

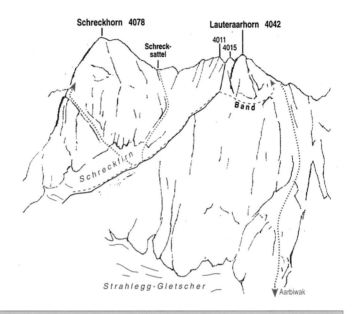

Schreckhorn 4078   Lauteraarhorn 4042

Schreck-sattel   4011   4015

B a n d

S c h r e c k f i r n

Strahlegg-Gletscher   Aarbiwak

Difficulties: AD+. Rock-climbing III and II, mixed. However, after new snow it dries off quickly at the critical places. Nevertheless, the traverse from the glacier to the rock can present problems. This climb is particularly tiring because of the sustained nature of the difficulties, both on the ascent and descent. Perhaps because of this it has recently been equipped with bolts, a highly controversial action regarded (by critics) as both an unreasonable visual pollution and the vulgarizing of a classic and challenging route climbed by amateurs nearly a century earlier without such 'aids'.

Effort: Hut climb 1570mH (5–6 hrs; with use of cableway 1160mH, 4–5 hrs), summit climb 1558mH (of which 600mH is on the summit tower (7–8 hrs).

Dangers: In contrast to the first ascent route (Schreckhorn Couloir/ Schrecksattel) today's customary ascent, the South-West Ridge, is objectively less dangerous. However, it should not be under-estimated; here too crevasses lie in wait on the glacier and the ramp is exposed to stone-fall and problematic (in descent) if overtaken by bad weather – afternoon storms being a feature of the northern Oberland peaks.
 Pleasures: Varied climbing on sound gneiss, in an impressive position.

Maps: LKS 1229 *Grindelwald*, also LKS 5004 *Berner Oberland*.
Travel: To Grindelwald, see Jungfrau notes on page 34.
Hut climb from Grindlewald: Take the Pfingstegg cableway to

1392m and then traverse south-west to join the hut path at P.1386 (or reach the same point on foot, starting at the Lutschinen Bridge and taking a marked track to Uf der Halten and thence south of the Toldislouwina, climbing the zig-zag path through the wood).

Continue southwards on a shelf above sections of steep rock to Begg and then a slight descent to Gasthaus Stieregg (1650m, accommodation, 2–3 hrs from Grindelwald). Now ascend east over grass and moraines and continue south to the spur of the Banisegg. After that, go east above the Unterey Eismeer Glacier to the steep rocks of Rots Gufer. Traverse across and climb these on constructed paths (ropes, pegs, aluminium ladders) and cross some streams. Then, just short of the remains of the old Schwarzegg Hut, work left (east) over a moraine to the new Schreckhorn Hut (2520m, SAC Basle, 90 B, managed in summer, Tel. 033-8551025).

Summit climb: From the hut, descend to the Obers Eismeer and continue along the old hut path to the remains of the Strahlegg Hut (destroyed by avalanches). Ascend north-east up the snow and debris-filled Gaagg valley to about 2950m, then move left to the notch above P.2844 on the brittle rock rib of the 'Gaagg'. Climb this, in part on unstable blocks, to reach a snow-field (3150m).

After a short ascent up a snow slope on to the left, traverse to the upper part of the Schreckfirn and across in an arc to the foot of the conspicious South Face Couloir bisecting the red rocks of the South Face (3 hrs). The objectively dangerous Lower Schreck Couloir (the 1861 line of ascent) leads directly to this point.

Cross the bergschrund on the left of the couloir (late in the year this is often exciting) and work up and then across left to the bottom left edge of a ramp which slants up to the left. Ascend the rocky edge of the big, mostly snow-filled, ramp (III in good conditions, but when iced it is more pleasant to climb the snow of the ramp) to a shoulder of the South-West Ridge (c.3800m). Climb the ridge keeping close to the steep and narrowing knife-edge (III) and continue until a steep step bars the way. Climb this direct (IV) or on the left side (III) and regain the ridge which is followed steeply, with fine climbing (III) to a snow ridge which leads (cornice possible) on to the summit.

View: Uniformly impressive. To the north lies Grindelwald dominated by the limestone summit of the Wetterhorn and to the

Schreckhorn from the Lauteraarhorn with the South-West Ridge (left) and the East Ridge (right) above the Schrecksattel.

east is the Lauteraar Glacier. To the south, beyond the nearby Lauteraarhorn is the majestic Finsteraarhorn, with the Fiescherhorner and the Grünhorn to its right. To the west, above the icefalls of the Eismeer, are the Mönch and Eiger and behind them the tip of the Jungfrau.

Descent: From the fore-summit on the South-West Ridge make three 40m abseils on the edge or climb down 20m on the west side and then use a ledge to get back to the edge, on which one can then climb down further to the shoulder at the beginning of the steep ramp (if the snow is rotten late in the day, then it is better to climb down the edge of the ramp).

Other worthwhile routes: *North-West Ridge* (Andersongrat) (D, III, mixed, 1750mH, 8 hrs from the Gleckstein Hut).
South Pillar (TD–, V– and IV, enjoyable climbing for experts, from foot of face 600mH, 5–6 hrs).

Guidebook: *Bernese Oberland* (Alpine Club, 2003).

Lauteraarhorn 4042m

This southern high peak of the 10km Schreckhorn crest is curiously upstaged by the surrounding peaks being unprepossessing in appearance and tucked away in the centre of the range, disguised by intervening ridges and spurs.

Up to 1976, an ascent still meant a voluntary bivouac had to be planned, but it should be remembered that in the days of the pioneers, this was the norm everywhere. The first to climb the peak in 1842, the geologist Arnold Escher from Linth and the glaciologists Eduard Desor and Christian Girard, made their bivouac in an uncomfortable situation by a gigantic block on the central moraine of the Unteraar Glacier.

From there they explored the glaciers in the vicinity, under the climbing leadership of the local men Melchior Bannholzer and Jakob Leuthold, and then climbed the Lauteraarhorn by mistake – the Schreckhorn having been their real goal.

Since the building of the Aar Bivouac Hut, the ascent can be aided by a comfortable night's sleep. This allows the most convenient final climb but with the long approach up the eastern

Oberland glaciers. If the brutal project of enlarging the Grimsel Reservoir (Super-Grimsel) should become a reality, despite all the protests, the initial part of this approach march will become considerably less convenient and enjoyable than today.

Difficulties: AD+. By the South Face Couloir with snow or ice to 40°, and thence by the South-East Ridge with rock-climbing of II, mixed. The couloir can be difficult to pinpoint in the dark.

Effort: The climb to bivouac hut involves 900mH and 19km of walking (7 hrs), the summit climb is 1300mH (5–6 hrs), of which 900mH is in the couloir and on the ridge. The summit ascent from the Schreckhorn Hut is 1550mH, 7–8 hrs, but with a slightly shorter approach.

Dangers: The South Face Couloir can be considerably threatened by ridge cornices. This is true even when one keeps to the flanking rocks. In the interests of safety, the timing must allow a descent of the couloir before the snow has softened. If the snow is soft in the morning, one should not start at all. The ascent 'Uber das Band' (Over the Ledge) is unstable and tricky at several points.

Pleasures: One of the most remote areas of the Alps.

Maps: LKS 1229 *Grindelwald*, LKS 1249 *Finsteraarhorn*, LKS 1250 *Ulrichen*, also LKS 5004 *Berner Oberland*.

Travel: By rail from the north via Berne and Interlaken to Meiringen, from the east via Chur and the Furka tunnel, from the south-west through the Rhône valley via Brig to Oberwald. From Meiringen and Oberwald, by bus to Grimsel Stausee [reservoir] and the Staumauer Grimselhospiz (1980m, beds for climbers).

Hut Climb: From the car-park terrace of the hospice, take the concrete steps into the basement and cross the dam wall to the north bank of the reservoir. There, climb steps and go through a tunnel, then under the artificial but very considerable waterfall of a supply tunnel. Continue along flagged paths past magnificent Arolla pines. These, together with the first pitches of the wonderful El Dorado slabs further up the valley, would be drowned if the Super-Grimsel was allowed. After the present (and hopefully the future) end of the reservoir, move over moraines to the Unteraar Glacier and follow the markings along a central moraine. Further on, the markings point to a big block on the northern bank, from whence a path on the side moraine leads to

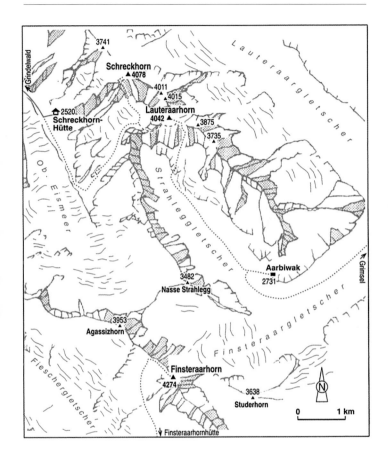

the Lauteraar Hut (2392m, SAC Zofingen, 50 B, managed in summer from time to time, Tel. 033-9731110; 4–5 hrs from Grimselhospiz; ladder path to the Unteraar Glacier).

After regaining the glacier, stay on the central moraine and subsequently go left to the Finsteraarhorn Glacier coming in from the south-west. Up this, along the central moraine, to the junction of the Strahlegg Glacier coming from the north-west. Now follow marker poles, staying on the level glacier, passing a crevasse zone on the east side, until as far as the fall line of the bivouac hut and only then (following coloured markings) cross to the Aar Bivouac Hut (2731m; SAC Pilatus, 17 B, blankets, no cooking equipment).

Summit climbs: South Face Couloir / South-East Ridge:
From the Aar Bivouac, climb up over the Strahlegg Glacier,
passing the ice of the steep tributary glacier embedded in the slope
on the right, until below the mouth of the prominent couloir. The
best line starts left of this, climbing blocks to a snow shoulder
(c.3250m). Continue up the ridge to the left (west) bordering rib
of the couloir. Climb this (I) to a small snow saddle somewhat
west of the prominent tower of P.3915. In good conditions this
can be reached more pleasantly but with more objective danger
by just climbing the couloir. From the snow saddle go directly
up the slabby gneiss ridge (II) enjoyably to the summit.

West-South-West Ridge / South-East Ridge: From the
Schreckhorn Hut take the Schreckhorn approach up to 3150m on
the snow-field above the Gaagg. Move right over snow, or the
rocks left of that (below P.3428) to gain the Strahlegg Pass
(3345m). From here continue up the somewhat brittle ridge to a
saddle. Then, keeping on the right, turn a steep rise (in part III–
and II) to gain a big shoulder (c.3750m) – serious in descent. From
here follow a snow ridge to the foot of the difficult summit wall.
To avoid this involves a long traverse across the South Face taking
a not very obvious ledge system (Über das Band), ascending and
descending (in parts delicate, pitches of II) crossing rock ribs and
gullies before finally using a friable chute/couloir to gain the
South-East Ridge and thence to the summit (6–7 hrs from the
Schreckhorn Hut).

View: Similar to that from the Schreckhorn, but with particularly
fine views of the Finsteraarhorn towering up to the south-west.

Adjacent peaks: P.4011 and P.4015 on the North-West Ridge,
can only to be reached by a long ridge climb (up to IV).

Other worthwhile routes: *North-West Ridge* from the Schreckhorn (D, pitches of IV, gives a classic long ridge climb that
incorporates P.4011. 5–6 hrs from summit to summit).

West-South-West Ridge Direct (TD, V and IV, splendid crack
climbing on the summit wall gives a direct finish to the above
described ridge route, 8–9 hrs from the Schreckhorn Hut).

East Rib of the North-West Ridge of P.4011 (D, IV, 1000mH from
the foot of the rib, 1600mH, 10–12 hrs from the Lauteraar Hut).

Guidebook: *Bernese Oberland* (Alpine Club, 2003).

Lauteraarhorn towers 4015m, 4011m

The prominent towers on the connecting ridge between the Schreckhorn and Lauteraarhorn fulfil the UIAA 'peak' criteria with the deepness of their adjoining cols and their singular character. They are accessible only by a long, rocky ridge climb. This was first done by two parties on 24 July 1902. It appears to have been the result of intense competition between two driven female climbers. This typifies the pre-war years at the turn of the century in which female ambitions in mountaineering, indeed in all spheres, were very evident. Starting from the Lauteraarhorn, Gertrude Bell and her guides Ulrich and Heinrich Führer traversed the ridge. They passed, *en route* (but 'not greeted with enthusiasm'), Fräulein H.Kuntze, and her guides P and R. Bernet who had approached via the Schrecksattel.

> **Grade:** D+ with long rock sections of IV, otherwise mostly III. There is often a really 'interesting' bergschrund in late season.
> **Effort:** The summit ascent to the Schreckhorn from the Schreckhorn Hut 1560mH (5–7 hrs), ridge traverse to the Lauteraarhorn 200mH, 1km, (4–5 hrs). Descent to the Scheckhorn Hut – long and laborious (4 hrs).
> **Dangers:** Indifferent rock, particularly on the descent, but the main risk is the remoteness and length of the itinerary which demands settled weather.

Summit route: Descend from the Schreckhorn by the South-East Ridge over the fore-summit and directly down the crest on good holds. Above the col turn a series of ridge towers down on the left flank (Elliotswängli) to gain the snow slopes leading down to the Schrecksattel (early in the season the sattel can be reached directly and quickly by the route from the Schreckfirn). Continue along the Lauteraarhorn's North-West Ridge over numerous small towers to the two big Lauteraarhorn towers. The most difficult place is a 5m gendarme halfway between the two towers which can be climbed using the left or the right side (III+). The South Face Couloir/Strahlegg Pass way (though quite serious) is preferable to 'Über das Band' which is very serious and unstable except when fully frozen.

Other worthwhile routes: *East Face Rib of P.4011* (IV, 1300mH, 10–12 hrs from the Lauteraar Hut; on solid slabby gneiss.

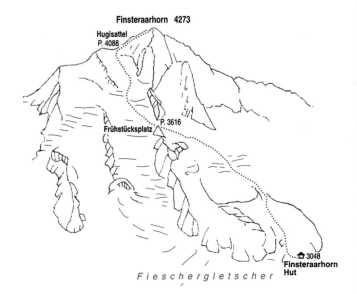

Finsteraarhorn 4273

Hugisattel
P. 4088

P. 3616

Frühstücksplatz

3048
Finsteraarhorn
Hut

F i e s c h e r g l e t s c h e r

Finsteraarhorn 4273m

The highest summit in the Bernese Alps, towering above all the surrounding peaks, provides a selection of elegant lines of ascent. Likewise, the glacier scenery of its surroundings is amongst the most imposing in the Alps. The Fiescher Glacier below, forced into a narrow valley, exceeds, in terms of length, even the great ice streams of Mont Blanc and Monte Rosa. Despite the length of its approaches this regal mountain is very popular. However, this happens mainly in the spring when skis allow a more rapid access. At this time the hut is frequently overcrowded during spells of good weather. In summer the endless trudging along the wide glacier basins deters all but the most dedicated alpinists.

The mountain appeared to have been climbed in 1812 by the South-East Ridge. Rudolf Meyer remained behind on a lower top while his three guides Alois Volker, Joseph Bortis and Arnold Abbühl continued. Their report of reaching the highest point was later disputed – it is now thought that they gained only the prominent high shoulder of the ridge. The agreed first ascent took place in 1829 – via today's Normal Route, the North-West

Ridge – by the guides Jakob Leuthold and Johann Wahren, while their employer, the glaciologist Franz Joseph Hugi, remained behind a little below the summit. A particularly impressive early ascent was that of the classy East-North-East-Spur in 1904 by the guide Fritz Amatter and his employer Gustav Hasler from Berne.

Difficulties: PD. To Hugisattel a glacier climb with snow to 35°. On the North-West Ridge of the summit block there is exposed climbing to II on firm gneiss (often icy, then distinctly harder).

Effort: Hut climb from Jungfraujoch via Konkordiaplatz, 1000mH descent, 500mH ascent, 13km (5 hrs); from Konkordia Hut 500mH ascent and 200mH of descent (3–4 hrs); plus from the cableway above Fiesch also 750mH and 123km; from Fiesch via the Fiescher Glacier 2100mH (8–10 hrs); from the Grimselsee via Oberaarjoch and Gemslücke, altogether 1500mH ascent, 7–9 hrs. Summ 1300mH (4–5 hrs).

Dangers: On the glacier there are occasionally awkward crevasses and cornices on the summit ridge. Otherwise, objectively, a very safe climb.

Pleasures: The climb is particularly fine on the summit block, as a comprehensive panorama gradually unfolds and broadens.

On the North-West Ridge of the Finsteraarhorn

The N.W. Ridge of the Finsteraarhorn from P.4088 above the Hugisattel.

Maps: LKS 1249 *Finsteraarhorn*, LKS 5004 *Berner Oberland*. See also Grünhorn and Lauteraarhorn sketches.

Travel: To Grindelwald (see Jungfrau chapter) or Fiesch (see Gross-Grünhorn chapter).

Hut climb from Konkordiaplatz: To the Konkordiaplatz, see Gross-Grünhorn (page 45). On the Grüneggfirn, ascend eastwards through the snow troughs to the Grünhornlücke and on the other side go down in the glacier trough (crevasses) to the Fiescher Glacier. After crossing it, there is a short ascent to the Finsteraarhorn Hut which lies below P.3231 on the east bank (3048m; 115 B, managed in spring and periodically in summer, Tel. 033-8552955).

Summit Climb: South-West Face / North-West Ridge:
From the hut follow a path to the north-east over the debris ridge (or on snow to the left) to the saddle by P.3231. Continue to the north over the glacier (crevasses), right of a rock spur up a trough to P.3616 on the S.W. Ridge ('Frühstücksplatz' – breakfast place).

Continue northwards on the glacier on the left of the South-West Ridge crossing bergschrunds higher to reach the Hugisattel (by P.4088, 4094 on Sheet 5004). Follow the North-West Ridge, first on the west side and then on the ridge proper (II) to the summit. If the Hugi Route is crowded, the South-West Ridge, direct from P.3616, is a slightly harder alternative, PD+.

View: To the north-east to the Lauteraarhorn and Schreckhorn, with their glaciers flowing towards the Grimsel Pass, to the east the Urner Alps, to the south-west, behind the crest of the Wannenhorn, the Pennine Alps, and to the west, the Gross-Grünhorn, with its rugged rocky East Face especially impressive.

Minor tops: P.4088 by the Hugisattel and P.4166 on the South-East Ridge are modest rising only 10m above their cols.

Other worthwhile routes: South-East Ridge (AD, III, mixed, and snow to 50°, a classic ridge, 2.5km long, 1100mH, 10–12 hrs from the Gemslücke to the summit starting from the Oberaarjoch Hut).

East-North-East Spur The 'Walker Spur' of the Oberland. (D+ to TD, long sections of IV+ on good gneiss, 850mH of rock, 8–10 hrs from start of climb. Some stonefall danger.)

Guidebook: *Bernese Oberland* (Alpine Club, 2003).

Pennine Alps (Valais or Wallis)

The Pennine Alps constitute the backbone of the Alps. This enormous massif includes more than half the 4000ers of this whole gigantic mountain system. From the frontier crest, along which most of the highest peaks are to be found, huge, deeply entrenched valleys run northwards to the Rhône valley which in the Ice Age was also fed by the glaciers of the Bernese Alps to the north. These valleys are, because of their situation to leeward of the high mountains, extra-ordinarily dry, so that traditional Alpine husbandry has, for many centuries, relied on artificial irrigation of the pastures. From the permanently flowing glacier streams, the water is led along the slopes to the meadows in laboriously con-structed trenches and canal systems and there distributed via branching ditches.

If the more recent tourist developments in the valley villages have robbed the Valais district of its traditional appearance, there are still, as witness to the old peasant culture, many groups of the typical wooden houses and granaries to be found, which to the visitors are as photogenic as the lofty, glittering snow mountain giants. One can really appreciate again the normal, mild world down below, when, worn-out and brutalised by exposure to the savage alps, one returns to the warm green of the valleys.

The description of the mountains starts with the mountain crests lying between the valleys, in each case from north to south, after that the frontier crest from east to west is described.

Eastern Pennine Alps Weissmies Group

This side crest has two different faces. The western Saastal is thoroughly developed with roads and cableways. The eastern side on the other hand is only accessible by car as far as Simplon. Otherwise access is by foot up long and tiring valleys which conspire to use up all reserves of energy, before the bases of the mountains are reached.

Lagginhorn 4010m

The most north-easterly and lowest 4000er of the Pennine Alps, at least as long as the plans to promote the northern neighbouring Fletschhorn from its 3993 metres (through building measures) to a 4000er are not realized. The Lagginhorn reaches the magic line without such assistance, only by ten metres it is true, but with elegance. The summit soars small and airy over deep abysses. Its first ascent was made in 1856 by the Saas pastor Johann Joseph Imseng and his servant Friedrich Joseph Andenmatten, as well as seven other companions. These included four Englishmen, their

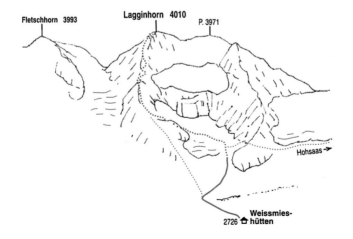

Looking north to the Lagginhorn from Weissmies. The Normal Route takes the ridge on the far left with Weissmies's North Ridge leading up to the near right from the Lagginjoch

presence a harbinger of the development of the tourist industry. The classic ascent route was then, as now, by the rocky West Ridge. Indeed the Lagginhorn is, in summer, mostly a very rocky mountain, with snow-fields and glaciers mere arabesques on the extensive gneiss faces.

Difficulties: PD. Easy rock-climbing with a section of II, otherwise I and scrambling on good gneiss.
Effort: 1280mH ascent, 4–5 hrs from the Weissmies Hut; 960mH, 3–4 hrs from the cableway station at Hohsaas.
Dangers: Objectively a very safe climb. The crevasses on the small Lagginhorn Glacier are avoidable by an ascent from the base of the West Ridge. In the upper part there may be stone-fall danger from climbing parties above.
Pleasures: Some entertaining rock-climbing in the middle part of the ridge. An open panorama from summit. In reliable weather a later departure is possible as the ascent can be made without using the snow slope.

Maps, Travel and Hut climbs: See Weissmies on page 69.
Summit route by the West Ridge: From the Weissmies Huts head north-east over grassy ridges and a broad ramp to the glacier stream. Ascend the path on the left (north) of this on moraine ridges (with steep, short bends near the top) to the beginning of the prominent ridge which divides the Hohlaub Glacier (south) from the Lagginhorn Glacier (north). Ascend on the left over moraine debris and snow, pass south of the tongue of the Lagginhorn Glacier and then go up over the glacier to its northern upper end. From there move left (west) to a big block terrace (2 hrs). To reach this point from the Hohsaas cableway station: head north-east, descending somewhat to the Hohlaub Glacier. Traverse under the tongue, following little cairns, over debris and slabs (delicate when icy!) to the other side of the glacier. There, ascend obliquely left over a slabby ramp (little cairns, pitches of II), then traverse and finally climb again to the ridge between Hohlaub Glacier and Lagginhorn Glacier. Move to the other side until almost level with the Lagginhorn Glacier and continue as previously described to the block terrace (1 hr).

From the block terrace head north-eastwards, following the picturesque cairns to the ridge (which can also be climbed direct,

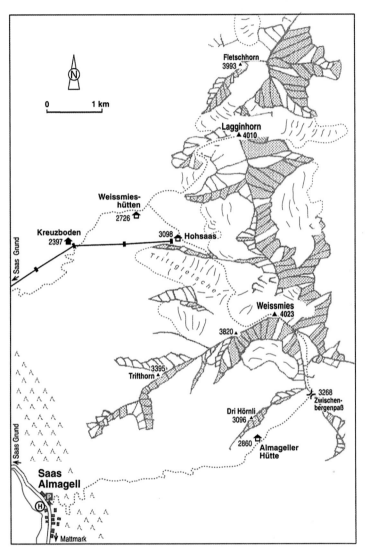

without reference to the glaciers). Follow the crampon scratches and path on the southern flank (various possibilities) moving steadily upwards in the direction of the mountain. Finally go directly along the crest, with a touch of exposure on the view down to the Fletschhorn Glacier. Continue (pitch of II on a slab) to the notch before the poorly defined upper part of the ridge. Climb debris and rock. Avoid the snow-field by traversing right as low as possible and thence go up to the summit block. Continue, keeping near the edge on the right to finally make a surprisingly airy finish to gain the highest point.

View: To the south the nearby Weissmies with its icy North-West Face dominates. On the far side of the Saas valley is the mighty crest from Monte Rosa to the Nadelgrat. To the north, behind the nearby Fletschhorn, are the Bernese Alps, and to the east the Simplon, the Engadine and, in the distance, the Bernina.

Adjacent peaks: South Summit (3971m) is a not very prominent elevation on the South Ridge.

Other worthwhile routes:

South Ridge (AD, III and II, mixed, brittle to start with), via the Lagginjoch, 5 hrs from Hohsaas.

North Ridge (AD, III and II, mixed, in part corniced), 2–3 hrs from the Fletschhorn, via the Fletschhornjoch.

East Spur (AD+, III, brittle, 1700mH, 6–7 hrs from the Laggin Bivouac Hut).

Guidebook: *Valais Alps East* (Alpine Club, 1999).

Weissmies 4023m

This is the highest mountain in the north-eastern Pennine Alps, east of the Saas valley, and is at the same time the most beautiful. Its ice-armoured North-West Face contrasts strongly with the steep, mostly bare gneiss face of the south side over which mighty summit ridge cornices project.

Correspondingly different are its Normal Routes. The older and easier (not assisted by the cableway) takes the South-East Ridge. This was the 1856 first ascent route taken by the guideless party of Peter Joseph Zurbriggen and Jakob Christian Häuser much to the irritation of the local guides. Today's customary ascent, by the North-West Face and the West Ridge, has more glacier work and an exposed upper slope. It is thus more serious but also more popular as it is reached by the Hohsaas cableway.

The north-western slopes of Weissmies bathed in crepuscular light in a view from Hohsaas Hut

An early departure from the hut offers the advantage of hard snow in the dawn hours, and better chance of distant visibility from the summit before the clouds obscure the view. Alternatively, those who wish to bag this mountain in a single day, can take the first cable car and climb fast before the snow deteriorates – a race which one always loses in fine weather.

> **Difficulties:** PD. Snow or ice, to 40°, with some exposure.
> **Effort:** From Hohsaas to the summit 1050mH in 3–4 hrs ascent. The worse part of the ascent to the hut can be avoided by using the cableway.
> **Dangers:** Occasional falling ice shortly after setting foot on the glacier and at the foot of the North-West Face. On the glacier there is some crevasse danger (mostly obvious), but there is almost always a worn track which makes things much easier, especially on the exposed summit ridge. Here there are big cornices all the way to the summit.
> **Pleasures:** Impressive glacier scenery and a fantastic panoramic view.

Maps: LKS 1329 *Saas*, LKS 5006 *Matterhorn-Mischabel*.

Travel: By rail up the Rhône valley to Visp and on to Stalden, from there 14km by bus. By car from Visp (Rhône valley) via Stalden and up the Saas valley 21km to Saas Grund (1559m) a tourist resort with campsites, tourist office, etc.

Hut climb: Take the cableway via Kreuzboden (2397m) to the Hohsaashaus (3098m) on the ridge above the Trift Glacier. There is a hut here (Saas Grund Community, 36 B, managed from the end of June to early October, Tel. 027-9571723). Alternatively, go to Kreuzboden (Chrizbode) and walk up to the Weissmies Huts (45mins) situated under big moraines (2726m, SAC, 124 B, managed from mid-July to late September, Tel. 027-9572554).

Those who spurn the cableway can ascend by a path from north of the town centre of Unter dem Berg, to Triftalp (2072m) and thence to Kreuzboden and the huts (1540mH, 5–6 hrs).

Summit route: From the Weissmies Huts take the path over the moraine above, heading south to the Hohsaashaus (45 mins). From there ascend east-south-east on the flat ridge to gain a crude ramp leading down the Trift Glacier. Climb this through a bare crevasse zone, to a flatter section, and then up over a steep

Weissmies from the Lagginhorn. The Normal Route takes the
shadowy glacier slopes on the right.

The north-western slopes of Weissmies.

snow slope. To avoid broad crevasses ahead, turn right and then continue up the face to the south-east. Before reaching the West Summit (P.3820) trend left to gain a saddle on the West Ridge. Keep left of the corniced ridge, on the face below the summit ridge (exposed, no rock belays) to eventually reach the summit.

View: To the south are the Portjengrat, the Stellihorn and Monte Rosa, to the west the whole long ridge crest from the Strahlhorn to the Nadelhorn. The nearby Lagginhorn dominates to the north with the distant Bernese Alps beyond. To the east are wild views down into the Zwischenbergen and Laggin valleys as well as, in the distance, the Engadine and Bernina ranges.

Adjacent peaks: The West Summit (3820m) can be reached with a short excursion from the saddle on the West Ridge.

Other worthwhile routes: *The South Face* and *South-East Ridge* (Original Route) from the Almageller Hut, 2860m, Tel. 027-9571179; (PD, climbing to I, little snow, 1180 mH to the hut plus 1140mH ascent, 7–8 hrs from the hut).

North Ridge (D, IV–/ III, finally snow, 6–10 hrs from Hohsaas).

Guidebook: *Valais Alps East* (Alpine Club, 1999).

The final section of the Weissmies route seen from the West Summit.

Nadelhorn with its satellites Stecknadelhorn and Hohberghorn in a view north from the slopes of the Lenzspitze.

North Pennine Alps

The magnificent single crest of the Mischabel group boasts seven principal 4000m peaks. Running north/south, it is defined and accessed by the the Saas valley on the east, and the Matter valley on the west. The northern part of this ridge bears the name 'Mischabel', which sounds exotic but means quite prosaically 'Mistgabel' (dung fork). In this part of the range there is only one minor cableway and climbing by one's own efforts is the name of the game – the mood at the huts and on the peaks correspondingly sportsmanlike.

Nadelgrat:
Dürrenhorn 4035m, Hohberghorn 4219m, Stecknadelhorn 4241m, Nadelhorn 4327m

The most northerly 4000er of the ridge crest is the Dürrenhorn. An ascent of this peak alone involves a route with very long approach. For that reason, it is better combined with a round of the northern Nadelgrat that includes the Hohberghorn and Stecknadelhorn and the dominating Nadelhorn (see map on p.79).

The first ascent of the complete Nadelgrat (from the Dom Hut over the Hohberghorn to the Lenzspitze and back to the Dom Hut) was made in 1892 by a group guided by Christian Klucker. The first traverse from the Lenzspitze to the Galenjoch was done in 1916 by Adrian Mazlam with Josef Knubel. The first ascents of each peak were as follows: the Dürrenhorn – Albert Frederick Mummery, William Penhall, Alexander Burgener and Ferdinand Imseng in 1879; the Hohberghorn – R.B. Heathcote, Franz Biner, Peter Perren and Peter Taugwalder in 1869; the Stecknadelhorn – Oscar Eckenstein and Matthias Zurbriggen in 1887.

It is worth considering carefully which is the best direction for the traverse. With a base at Mischabel Hut, if one begins at the Nadelhorn then its sharply cut North-East Ridge lies in the magic of the morning light and one can usually reach the summit before the clouds build up. The main drawback of this strategy is the anticlimax on the following summits and a tiring conclusion as

the return will be over the softened Ried Glacier. If the excursion is taken in the opposite direction (as described here), then the Ried Glacier should be in crisp condition, the Dürrenhorn ascent in the morning sun is thrilling, and the airy ridge to the Nadelhorn gives a fitting climax. The descent over the North-East Ridge may then be soft but has the advantage of being well-defined (helpful in poor visibility) and leaving no re-ascent at the end of the day. These alternatives offer an opportunity for

The Nadelgrat seen from the slopes of Balfrin. Peaks are (from the left) Ulrichshorn, Lenzspitze, Nadelhorn (with the Dom's summit peeping out behind) Stecknadelhorn and Hohberghorn.

debate during planning but on one point there should be no dispute – the need for reliable weather on such a long and remote expedition. A popular, shorter version of the ridge that avoids the Ried Glacier to traverse from the Nadelhorn to the Hohberghorn and then retrace one's steps but leaves the Dürrenhorn unclimbed.

Difficulties: AD. The principal difficulties of the route usually lie in the ascent up the steep couloir to the Hohbergjoch (especially in late summer when there is often big bergschrund; in bad snow or ice the steep couloir is avoidable on the crumbling rocks north of it). On the ridge between Dürrenhorn and Nadelhorn there is a pitch of II+, otherwise II– and I, mixed, partly also snow ridges. The Nadelhorn's N.E. Ridge is II– and I, mixed.

Effort: The hut climb involves a wretched 1550mH (4–5 hrs in the sun until midday) direct from Saas Fee or travel on the cableway to the Hannigalpe, 2349m. which still leaves 1000mH (3–4 hrs); the summit route to Dürrenhorn by the detour over Ulrichshorn and the Riedpass involves 1000mH (4–5 hrs) or by the more direct approach from the Windjoch to the Hohbergjoch Couloir 600mH, but this way can be crevassed. From the Hohbergjoch to Nadelhorn is a further 500mH ascent (3–4 hrs). Nadelhorn to the hut – 1000mH (2 hrs).

Dangers: Both the Hohbalm Glacier and the Ried Glacier are replete with unpleasant crevasses, but by using the detour over the Ulrichshorn and Riedpass the worst crevasse zones are bypassed. On the ascent to the Hohbergjoch there is stone-fall potential. Beware of cornices on the ridge itself.

Pleasures: An especially scenic and impressive ridge traverse.

Maps, travel, hut climb: (and on to Windjoch) see Nadelhorn. **Summit route with a finish over the Nadelhorn:** Climb to the Windjoch 3850m (1 hr from the Mischabel Huts). From here, in early season, with suitable snow cover, it may be feasible to head directly to Hohbergjoch Couloir by a traverse of the steep, upper Ried Glacier: climb for a short distance towards the Nadelhorn looking for a route working round above the prominent ice-fall to gain the foot of the couloir. It is more common to take the easier but circuitous route up the S.W. Ridge of the Ulrichshorn, 3925m, north-east to the Riedpass, and then west across the Ried Glacier to the foot of the Hohbergjoch Couloir. Cross the often awkward bergschrund and either climb the 45° snow or take the rocks on the right (now equipped with anchors for belaying or abseiling) to gain the Hohbergjoch (3916m; 4–5 hrs from the Mischabel huts). Either way is now likely to be hazardous in mid to late season because of lack of snow.

From the col ascend the Dürrenhorn (4035m) by its S.E. Ridge (brittle rocks of II and I) and return to Hohbergjoch (1 hr).

Now climb the ridge heading south-east, first over rocks, then up the broad snow ridge to a rocky rise. Turn this on the left or climb it directly (II) and follow a snow ridge to the summit of the Hohberghorn (4219m). Continue east-south-east on the snow ridge down into the Stecknadeljoch (4142m, 2 hrs from Hohbergjoch). The rocky pinnacle ridge above is passed on the right on rising ledges (II– and I) to reach the summit of the Stecknadelhorn (4241m, 2–3 hrs from the Hohbergjoch). Descend over rock to a snow saddle and over a snow ridge to a gendarme. Climb this direct (II+) or turn it (often bare ice) to reach a snow notch behind. From there it is a short distance further along the ridge to the summit of the Nadelhorn (4327m, 3–4 hrs from Hohbergjoch). For descent, see Nadelhorn.

Other worthwhile routes: *The complete Nadelgrat*, from the Dom Hut over the Lenzspitze and the Nadelhorn and on to the Dürrenhorn (AD, a whole day's expedition, or more).

Dürrenhorn North Ridge from the Galenjoch (AD, III/II, brittle, long approach or descent.

Hohberghorn North-East Face (AD, 350mH, up to 50° ice).

Hohberghorn and/or Stecknadelhorn from west (PD, 5 hrs from the Dom Hut via the Festijoch and the Stecknadeljoch Couloir (afternoon stone-fall) is a technically easier but not the usual approach).

Guidebook: *Valais Alps East* (Alpine Club, 1999).

Nadelhorn 4327m

This peak, the highest of the group, sends out three prominent ridges. Between them, rocky gneiss faces of steep gullies and ribs fall to the south-east and south-west, while the concave North Face is more icy. The first ascent was made in September 1858 by the labourers Joseph Zimmermann, Alois Supersaxo and Baptist Epiney, led by the guide Franz Andermatten, in order to erect a trig point. They are approached by the Windjoch and the elegant North-East Ridge which today is still the Normal Route.

Maps: LKS 1328 *Randa*, also LKS 5006 *Matterhorn-Mischabel*. See Lenzspitze and Dom sketches on p.79 and p.85.

Travel: By rail to Stalden, from there by bus 18km via Saas Grund up to Saas Fee (1792m; exclusive tourist resort, now

Difficulties: PD. On the rocky sections of the ridge, some pitches of II–, mostly I, mixed, with snow to 40°.
Effort: To the Mischabel Hut from Saas Fee 1550mH ascent (4–5 hrs), from Hannigalp 1000mH (3–4 hrs). Summit climb 1000mH.
Dangers: An objectively safe route. On the Hohbalm Glacier there are some crevasses (easily outflanked) and sometimes cornices on the final ridge.
Pleasures: The ridge is an ideal line, practical as guide-line for route-finding, helpful for belaying, free of stone-fall and with the great symbolic power of a direct line to the highest point in the sky.

pedestrianised (multi-storey garage at the outskirts of the town).
Hut climb: Pass through the town and from Leeboden, ascend westwards to the avalanche barrier at the Torrenbach. Go through a tunnel and over the stream. After that, to the broad track which leads, with a daunting number of bends, up the slope of the Trift to P.2448 on the South-East Ridge of the Distelhorn.

Continue directly up the ridge (now equipped, previously the path went left) to the Mischabel Huts (3340m, SAC, AACZ, 120 B, managed in summer, Tel. 027-9571317).

The route from the cableway terminus at Hannigalpe takes an indistinct ski descent south and after 150 metres moves right on a narrow path descending slightly to the valley of the Torrenbach. This is crossed by a bridge beyond which the path goes under the East Face of the Distelhorn to P.2448 to join the main Saas Fee path.

Summit route: From the huts, ascend the Hohbalm Glacier moraine ridge until at about 3600m it becomes more level and tamer. Traverse the glacier northwards (good view of the Lenzspitze's N.E. Face) and then ascend a steeper snow-slope (crevasses), keeping below the Ulrichshorn, before trending left to climb to the Windjoch (3850m; 1–2 hrs from the Mischabel Huts).

Follow the initially broad, but soon narrowing snow ridge. Continue above over rocky rises (turnable in part on right), then keep directly on the ridge line to the summit block with slight deviations on the left near the top (3–4 hrs from the huts).

View: Lenzspitze and the mighty Dom are close at hand to the south but interrupt the distant view. There is a panorama of the Weisshorn group to the west and to the north a more distant view of the Bernese Oberland. The Weissmies group is to the east.

Descent by the Normal Route: From the summit, descent north-east (crampon scratches) keeping near the ridge edge which is followed down to the Windjoch. Descend from this on the south side and cross the level Hohbalm Glacier to its south side. There, on the rock/scree ridge, go left down to the Mischabel Huts.

Other worthwhile routes: *Nadelgrat, from Dürrenhorn* (p.72). *South-East Ridge from the Lenzspitze over the Nadeljoch,* first and most beautiful part of the entire Nadelgrat – AD, III in dry condition but, if icy, it becomes hard, 4 hrs from the Lenzspitze). Guidebook: *Valais Alps East* (Alpine Club, 1999).

Lenzspitze 4294m

The most southerly summit of the Nadelgrat is, like the Nadelhorn, a three-sided gneiss pyramid. From the Saas side, it is conspicuous by the steep ice sheet of its North-East Face. The first ascent was made in 1870 by Clinton Dent with Alexander

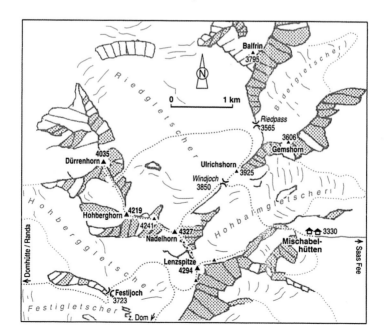

and Franz Burgener who climbed to the of the ice sheet to the Nadeljoch and thence up the North-West Ridge. Today's customary Normal Routes are the East-North-East Ridge, first done in 1882 by W.W. Graham, Ambros Supersaxo and Theodor Andenmatten, and the South Ridge from the Lenzjoch which R.F. Ball, Ambros Supersaxo and L. Zurbriggen climbed in 1888. The usual escape is to traverse the pinnacled ridge to the Nadelhorn (southern Nadelgrat – only advisable in good conditions and reliable weather) and descend Nadelhorn's North-East Ridge.

Difficulties: East-North-East Ridge (AD, with sustained mixed climbing at II and I and several pitches of III). South-West Ridge from the Lenzjoch (PD with II+ and II). The traverse to the Nadelhorn along the southern Nadelgrat (AD, an exposed alpine ridge with constant up and down passages with some pitches of III, all of which can become troublesome if heavily iced).
Effort: From the Mischabel Huts to the summit 950mH ascent (4–5 hrs), from the Dom Hut 1350mH (5–6 hrs). The traverse over the Nadelhorn c.200mH (2–3 hrs), then 1000mH descent (2 hrs).
Dangers: Beware of cornices on the ridges. In the upper part of the North-East Ridge and on the South-West Ridge there is some brittle rock, but generally both are objectively safe climbs in good conditions, but in high winds or storms they can become very tricky. In really bad weather even strong parties will find it hard to cope with such exposed ridges at this height!
Pleasures: Rock pitches of the N.E.Ridge and the Nadelgrat give delectable sections of firm climbing harder than anything on the northern Nadelgrat.

Maps, travel, hut climbs: See Nadelhorn and Dom.
Summit route by the East-North-East Ridge: From the Mischabel Huts head west along a path up rounded rocks past the branching of the track to the Windjoch, and keep on the ridge to P.3815. (This point can also be reached by first ascending the Hohbalm Glacier and then gaining the ridge by a snow gully.)

After a horizontal section, the ridge steepens. Climb the first steep rise on the north side and then continue along the sharp, often corniced, ridge to the first tower. Climb a slab until one can traverse right to a crack which leads to a ledge, then go obliquely left towards a recess and up steps to the ridge above. The ridge continues more easily to a notch and to the foot of Grand

Gendarme which overhangs on the south-side. Avoid the flank and climb its prominent big slab on the left (piton). On the other side, climb or abseil down the difficult five-metre crack. Continue along the following horizontal section of ridge to the third rise. This is taken on its edge, steeply but on good holds and then zig-zags, partly on the knife-edge, partly beside it, to the snow ridge. This joins the South Ridge and leads on to the summit.

On descent, the steeper parts of the rock pinnacles or little tops can be abseiled (possibly renewing slings!).

The South Ridge from the Dom Hut: This follows the same approach as the Normal Route to the Dom until below the Lenzjoch. Go up a steepening snow slope trending left to cross the bergschrund and then climb up to the notch left (north) of the lowest col, left of several pinnacles. The ridge is first of all predominantly on snow, but this becomes more rocky leading up to a big, pointed gendarme that is turned on the right (Saas side) and the ridge regained. Continue with decreasing difficulty and finally ascend to the summit by a gully on the west side.

Traverse to the Nadelhorn: Descend the North-West Ridge on snow (in parts delicate, beware of cornices) and some rock to the Nadeljoch (4213m). After that, continue on the rocky ridge, either by steady up and down work over the ridge towers on good holds, or by turning the towers. From the Nadeljoch traverse the first tower on its south edge on the right (east) as far as the overhang, and go up a slab on good small holds to the notch. Traverse the second tower at half height on the east and up a little wall to the ridge. Descend over slabs to the next notch. Continue on the ridge. The next, bigger, gendarme is climbed direct and then descended to a low notch. From this go directly on the knife-edge to the summit of the Nadelhorn. For descent, see Nadelhorn, p.78).

4000m tops: The N. Ridge Gendarme (c.4240m), the S. Ridge Gendarme (c.4200m) and the ENE Ridge Gendarme (4091m).

Other worthwhile routes: *North-East Face (Dreieselswand)* (D, a classic ice face with sections of 55°, 4–6 hrs, 500mH).

Dom 4545m

The highest mountain lying wholly inside Switzerland. From the east and south-west it is seen as the highest in a row of pointed rock peaks, but from the north-west it appears as a pure snow peak, easily lost amidst the clouds in certain conditions. The name seems logical on account of its height, prominent shape or its majestic icy north face. It was named, however, after the surveyor Domherr Berchthold. Its first ascent (11 Sept. 1858) was made by the Rev. J. Llewellyn-Davies, Johann Zumtaugwald, Johann Krönig and Hieronymous Brantschen by the North-West Ridge or Festigrat. The easiest climb is, by contrast, the North Face, a grinding snow plod, but still an impressive undertaking.

Difficulties: PD. On approach to the Festijoch there are some pitches to II, but otherwise a glacier ascent, practically without technical difficulties. The Festigrat is PD+ with snow or ice up to 50°.
Effort: Hut climb 1510mH (5–6 hrs, best tackled in the early morning shade), summit climb 1650mH (5–7 hrs).
Dangers: The Dom is noted for its high altitude storms. On the traverse of the Hohberg Glacier move quickly keeping a sensible distance from the sérac zone, where there is often ice debris. Otherwise, the customary glacier precautions are advisable. In mist and in storm or with driving snow covering tracks, route-finding can quickly become very problematical.
Pleasures: A very remote area with no cableways and therefore people are, through the efforts of the ascent, correspondingly hand-picked.

Maps: LKS 1328 *Randa*, also LKS 5006 *Matterhorn-Mischabel*. See also Lenzspitze topo.

Travel: By rail up the Matter valley to Randa, a quiet tourist resort. 23km from Visp (Rhône valley) by car, bus or train.

Hut climb: From Randa church go north-east to the Dorfbach. Before this, climb up through the wood on the south side and cross the torrent at about 1900m and ascend to the tree-line. Continue up the bends, over pasture slopes to a rock barrier. Ascend this over steps, gullies and ledges (some wire ropes) to a small rock plateau and up to the north moraine of the Festi Glacier which is followed to the Dom Hut (2940m, SAC Section

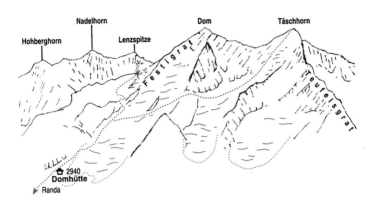

Hohberghorn · Nadelhorn · Lenzspitze · Dom · Täschhorn

Festigrat

Teufelsgrat

⌂ 2940
Domhütte
Randa

Uto, 75 B, managed: mid-July – end of August, Tel. 027-9672634).
Summit route: From the hut, continue along the moraine to
the Festi Glacier. Ascend the north edge of this heading for the
area below the Festijoch (1 hour). Before this, cut up the hill west
of the fall line (cairned) over the spine of a small black tower to
gain the main Hohberg/Festi ridge. Traverse steep rocks on the
south side to a small notch, then cross to the north side and follow
an exposed, rising ledge (II) to a stance and then down to the
Festijoch (3723m, 2–3 hrs from the Dom Hut. This col can also
be gained directly from the Festi Glacier (II and I).

Now descend somewhat northwards (short section of steep

The North Face of the Dom with the Festigrat (the sunlit edge) on the right.

The Festijoch and the Festigrat

ice and a bergschrund) to the Hohberg Glacier. Keeping a respectful distance from the sérac zone, traverse swiftly across to under the faces of the Hohberghorn and Stecknadelhorn. From this safer region, climb up the glacier to below the Lenzjoch. Now head southwards over the interminable glacier slopes in the direction of the saddle between the western fore-summit and the main summit of the Dom. From the saddle continue to the highest point (5–7 hrs from the hut).

View: Looking north allows an inspection of the gneiss flanks of the Nadelgrat, to the south the Täschhorn looks impressive, Weissmies is to the east, the paraphernalia of the summer ski circus surrounds the Allalinhorn to the south-east. Weisshorn dominates to the west, and the Matterhorn to the south-west.

Adjacent peaks: The western fore-summit P.4479 is quickly climbed from the Normal Route. The North-East Ridge Summit P.4468 is reachable with a somewhat bigger detour from the Normal Route but without undue difficulty.

Other routes: *Festigrat* (from the Festijoch go directly up the little marked N.W. Ridge, PD+, II, in the higher section keeping left of the edge, mostly on snow, 3 hrs from the Festijoch).

North-East Ridge (above the Lenzjoch, the lower part to P.4468 has difficulties up to IV+, after that there is easier snow work, TD, 3–5 hrs from the Lenzjoch).

South Ridge (III, usually done as part of the Täschhorn/Dom traverse which is long and committing and at a great height).

West Ridge (IV, big but seldom climbed, 8 hrs).

Guidebook: *Valais Alps East* (Alpine Club, 1999).

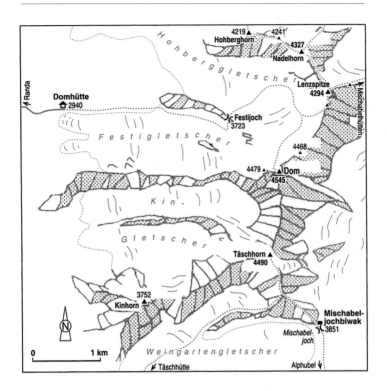

Täschhorn 4490m

Seen from the south, the Täschhorn tends to upstage the higher Dom, not only because it hides it, but because its rugged South-West Face holds the attention. There is no comparable face in this part of the Alps. Its first ascent in 1906 by Valentine Ryan and Geoffrey Winthrop Young with their guides Franz and Josef Lochmatter and Josef Knubel, remains a major alpine event in which Franz Lochmatter's lead of the crucial pitches placed him in the pantheon of the finest guides (as related in *On High Hills*).

This is one of the more difficult 4000 metre peaks. All the climbs are demanding in one way or another: the North-West Face, the 1862 first ascent route (by the Rev. John Llewellyn-Davies, Rev. J.W. Hayward guided by Johann and Stephan Zumtaugwald), has difficulties on the ice. The elegant South-East

Ridge (or Mischabelgrat), climbed in 1876 by Rev. James Jackson guided by Christian and Ulrich Almer, is long, demanding and exposed. Since the building of the Mischabeljoch bivouac, it is now one of the finest 'Normal Routes' in the Alps. The South-West Ridge (Teufelsgrat), which is almost 2km long, climbed in 1887 by Albert Frederick Mummery and his wife, guided by Alexander Burgener and Joseph Andenmatten, is AD+ but unfortunately not of high quality (though well described by Mary Mummery in *My Climbs in the Alps and Caucasus*).

Difficulties: The South-East Ridge is AD with pitches of III, though generally easier, but long. The start is somewhat brittle and on the middle part of the snow ridge and particularly on the snow shoulder there are cornices. The ideal conditions are not too snowy and not too dry (when the ridge becomes unstable). The North-West Face (AD) is a steep glacier with very variable difficulties according to conditions, often with passages of steep ice climbing, as well as rock up to II+. In addition there can be route-finding problems because the mountain is not frequently climbed by this way and one cannot count on having a track to follow – a particularly relevant consideration if the face is to be used for descent. Indeed there is no easy descent from this peak, an important factor if bad weather threatens.
Effort: The climb to the Täsch Hut involves 1300mH (4 hrs), then 1700mH ascent to the summit (7–9 hrs). From the Dom Hut by the Festi-Kin-Lücke and North-West Face 1700mH allow 6 hrs.
Dangers: Crevasses on the Weingarten Glacier, plus those noted above.
Pleasures: On the summit block there is enjoyable climbing on firm gneiss in a fantastic position on a remote and difficult 4000er.

Maps: LKS 1328 *Randa*, also LKS 5006 *Matterhorn-Mischabel*.
Travel: By rail from Visp (Rhône Valley) up the Matter Valley (31km) to Täsch (1449m, tourist resort, campsites and a large car-park at the road end – the upper valley having restricted access).
Hut climbs: From Täsch, north of the Täschbach, take the path up to Täschberg (1696m) and continue to Eggenstadel (1950m). Before reaching the bridge take a path up the steep slope north of the stream to the upper Täschalp. Here there is accommodation at Ottavan, (2214m, private, 15B) reached by car up the back road from Täsch, or by a long traversing route from the south using the mountain station of Sunegga (2288m). Continue steeply on the broad track rising up the north side of the valley to the Täsch Hut at the foot of the Alphubel's Rotgrat (2701m, SAC-Section Uto,

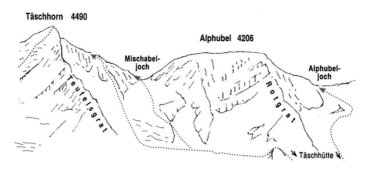

60 B, managed from June to September, Tel. 027-9673913).

Summit route from the Täsch Hut: *by the South-West Rib and the upper South-East Ridge.* Head north-westwards from the hut along a good track that passes under the rocks of the Rotgrat. Beyond that, climb eastwards up the Talli Cwm. Before reaching P.3195 work north and cross the Wissgrat and descend a stone staircase to the broad moraine fields of the Weingarten Glacier. Continue north between the southern part of the glacier and a lake and pass below P.3242 and P.3223 at the foot of two ridges descending from the Alphubel and cross below a crevassed section of the glacier to gain the foot of a spur descending west from the Täschhorn's South-East Ridge. Climb this, first over debris and snow, then steeper but without any major difficulty, passing P.3633, to finally join the South-East Ridge about halfway between the Mischabeljoch and the summit, somewhat south of P.4175.

Climb the broad ridge to a couloir descending to the east. Here the ridge becomes a snow edge, the east side of which is heavily corniced. At a steep snow/ice shoulder traverse along a ledge on the west side and climb steep ice to regain the ridge crest. Two pitches on ice or snow lead to the foot of the final pyramid. Move up right to rocks which give enjoyable climbing to the summit.

The lower, more friable, section of the South-East Ridge can also be climbed with moderate difficulties direct from the Mischabeljoch Bivouac, but in good weather this may be unpleasantly crowded. If a traverse to the Dom is planned it is best to start from here. This is conveniently reached (making use of the Metro or the cableway) by an approach over the Alphubel (see Alphubel chapter), but note that the descent of the Alphubel's

North Ridge (AD) can be nasty if the snow conditions are poor, as good belays are rare. The Täsch approach reaches the crevassed upper Weingarten Glacier by a route using the notch at P.3481.

Summit climb from the Dom Hut: *by the North-West Face.* A fine route, best tackled in good snow conditions to minimise the crevasse and step-cutting problems. Follow the same approach as for the Normal Route to the Dom to below the Festijoch. Now traverse the Festi Glacier under the rock island with P.3781 and up a steepening slope (55° often icy, bergschrund often large) to the Festi-Kin-Lücke (3734m, 2–3 hrs from the Dom Hut; in good snow conditions one can start the traverse earlier at 3400m, and ascend south-eastwards). Move up the lower part of the West Ridge of the Dom for about 100mH (to where the ground below the Dom Hut is again visible), then work obliquely downwards on ledges to the northern Kin Glacier and make a rising traverse across the snow basin to the North-West Face of the Täschhorn (3–4 hrs from the Dom Hut). The face is a very confusing glacier with constantly changing topography making detailed description pointless. Work a way up as conditions dictate but in the final section move right to finish up the Teufelsgrat.

View: To the north is the nearby Dom with its rock and ice faces. To south-east the lower Alphubel and Allalinhorn and to the south the whole of the head of the Zermatt Valley. To the east is the Weissmies group and to the west the Weisshorn group.

Adjacent peaks: The North Ridge Summit P.4404 is passed on the ridge traverse to the Dom. The similarly minor South-East Ridge Summit P.4175 is traversed on the ascent described.

Other worthwhile routes: *The Täschhorn-Dom traverse* (AD+, III and II, but mostly narrow and airy, in part corniced, very long and high, 3–5 hrs summit to summit). An alpine classic and also useful as it gives access to the easier descent of the Dom which may be preferred to either of the Täschhorn routes.

South-West Ridge or *Teufelsgrat* (D, IV, very long, 12–15 hrs).

South-West Face (TD+, 900mH, 10–15 hrs). Though not beautiful – 'a horror show' – it remains prestigious, being rarely climbed.

Guidebook: *Valais Alps East* (Alpine Club, 1999).

The view from Täschhorn's summit, looking down past climbers on the South-East Ridge to the Mischabeljoch and the Alphubel.

North Pennine Alps – Allalin Group

From Saas and the Matter valley The almost rectilinear ridge crest of the Mischabel dominates the scene, but further south the character of the changes – glacier basins extend further and the crest line is more rounded and glacier worn.

The peaks are also more easily accessed using mountain railways or cableways and are thus suitable for quick ascents.

Alphubel 4206m

The Alphubel has two different aspects: from the east a gigantic and apparently tedious snow hump, from the west a rugged rock peak with walls and buttressed ridges. Yet the east side is not as harmless as it appears as crevasse complications on the Fee Glacier make alpinists work hard during ascents from that quarter.

But on this side the peak can be approached by the tunnel

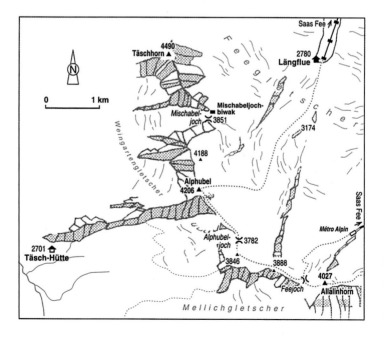

railway (Métro) and cableway to the Mittelallalin, or by the more direct cableway to Längflue. The Metro, though higher, has the disadvantage that there are no overnight possibilities (apart from a bivouac) and thus an early departure is impossible. For that reason, the Längflue ascent is described, followed by a traverse to the Feejoch and thence down to Mittelallalin is described.

The Alphubel was first climbed from Täsch (Alphubeljoch/ South-East Ridge) in 1860 by Leslie Stephen, Thomas Hinchliff, Melchior Anderegg and Peter Perren. This route, or the Rotgrat, is the best for those who wish to avoid the cableway distraction.

Difficulties: PD. Normally the east side is a snow plod, also useful as a ski excursion, but in late season, crevasses must be reckoned with. On the ridge from the Feejoch there are few crevasse problems, but instead there is a 50-metre mixed passage (II) to surmount on the climb to the Feechopf. In addition the upper part of the South-East Ridge (Eisnase 45°) is often icy. In bad visibility the route-finding on the south-east route is more difficult and the high point on the summit plateau hard to locate.
Effort: Hut climb to the Längflue 1170mH (but with the seductive cable way nearby scarcely anyone does this). From Längflue – 1330mH (4–5 hrs) snaking through the crevasses to the summit. Descent to Mittelallalin and to the Métro alpin 860mH, plus 110mH in the opposite direction (2–3 hrs).
Dangers: To cope with the crevasses on the Fee Glacier a very early start allows a return by the same route. In bad visibility, and if wind covers the track, there can be serious route-finding problems.
Pleasures: The south-east route offers wonderful views on descent or ascent in total contrast to the skiing bedlam of the upper Fee Glacier.

Maps, travel, guidebooks: See Nadelhorn and Täschhorn.
Hut climb: Pass through Saas Fee and its conspicuous, and hideously intrusive, red tennis courts. Pass the valley station of the Felskinn Railway and move on to an old central moraine of the Fee Glacier (Gletscheralp) under the cableway up to the Spielboden (2447m, midway station of the cableway from Saas Fee). Continue up the path to a rock step and thence over rubble to the mountain station of the cableway and the Längflue Hut (2870m, private, 220B, managed all year, Tel. 027-9572132).
Summit route from Längflue: Head south-south-westwards and southwards across the Fee Glacier past the rock island

P.3173.7, passing through some crevasse zones. Always keep a respectful distance from the mighty slanting rock wall of the Alphubel's North-East Spur which is often impressively animated by ice avalanches. From about 3600m one ascends directly over the steepening eastern slopes, often with a big crevasse at 4000m, to the extensive summit plateau and the highest point

Descent: *by Alphubeljoch/Feejoch to Mittelallalin.* Reverse the Normal Route from the main summit, eastwards until under the uppermost steep slope and then make a long, descending traverse south. Alternatively a direct descent down the often icy South-East Ridge is usually harder. Both routes lead to the Alphubeljoch (3782m). Head south over the flat top of P.3846, then go east to a saddle and up the slope to the prominent Feechopf (3888m). Continue carefully on the ridge (II) down to the Feejoch (3826m) from where a broad track leads down to the Métro at Mittelallalin. Fast parties can make a detour from the Feejoch to take in the Allalinhorn.

Adjacent peaks: The North Summit P.4188 is a flat top some 500m north of the highest point. 300m further P.4128, sometimes called North-East Summit, is only a snow shoulder.

Other worthwhile routes: *South-East Ridge* from the west (easy except for the now icy and bulging (Eisnäse) summit slope, 1500mH ascent, 4–5 hrs from the Täsch Hut; first ascent route). *West Ridge* (*Rotgrat*) (AD, III and II, firm rock and mixed, 5–7 hrs from the Täsch Hut).
North Ridge (AD, III–, 1–2 hrs from the col – serious in descent).
North Summit, West Ridge (D+, IV+, not wholly perfect rock but objectively safe, 8–9 hrs from the Täsch Hut).

**On Allalinhorn's Hohlaubgrat:
climbing the steep slope to P.3597.**

Allalinhorn 4027m

The mountain railway has turned this into a very easy proposition. Its upper part, built in a tunnel (Métro alpin), is at least scenically acceptable. It is also maintenance friendly. Nevertheless, the concentration of so many people in one spot is ecologically undesirable and the ski circus, with noisy piste-making vehicles and a glacier basin blocked by lift masts, is brutal in the extreme. The track of the Normal Route leads through this area, only on the last few hundred metres assuming the true character of a high alpine ascent. For that reason many people prefer to climb the mountain by the scenically grand Hohlaubgrat. Another tranquil route is by the South-West Ridge (an earlier Normal Route) from the Allalinpass, by which the Saas pastor Johann Josef Imboden, one of his relatives, Edward Levi Ames and Franz Josef Andenmatten made the first ascent in 1856. The Hohlaubgrat was first done in descent in 1882 by Heinrich Dubi with Alphons and Peter Supersaxo and first ascended in 1887 by Harold Ward Topham and G.H. Rendall with Aloys Supersaxo.

Maps and Travel: See Nadelhorn; also LKS 1329 *Saas*.

Difficulties: PD. The Normal Route is only on snow (short pitches on crevasses to 50°, on the often icy summit slope 40°). On the Hohlaubgrat PD+, before reaching the summit there is a 30mH rock step (II), otherwise easy scrambling (I) and sections of snow/ice to 40°.

Effort: On the Normal Route, from Mittelallalin (Métro), there is 580mH ascent on broad track (2 hrs); to climb up to there from the valley on foot under the cableway and over the ski circus would not only demand severe physical effort, but also a high tolerance to aesthetic ugliness. On the unspoiled (apart from 3 iron stakes) Hohlaubgrat from the Britannia Hut, 1050mH ascent (4–5 hrs).

Dangers: On the first part of the Normal Route the main risk is of being run down by skiers. On ascent to the Feejoch there are some crevasses. There is also subjective danger, in particular the temptation to the inexperienced to make the ascent without the necessary acclimatization and equipment.

Pleasures: For many people this is the only 4000er which they ever climb, or the last which they feel capable of.

At P.3837 on the Hohlaubgrat with (right) a view up the ridge to the summit block

Hut climb: The Normal Route from Mittelallalin doesn't need an overnight stop. For the Hohlaubgrat, start at Felskinn station (2991m). Go east across the glacier to the Egginerjoch and continue at roughly the same height to the Britannia Hut on the saddle between the Hinterallalin and the Kleiner Allalin (3030m, SAC, 113 B, managed February to October, Tel. 027-9572288).

Summit route from the Mittelallalin over the Feejoch: Cross the pistes heading south-west of the prominent spur on the initially steep glacier (crevasses with steep upper lips), then head up to the Feejoch (3826m). The summit slope is reached in a wide arc and the summit ridge gained from the south-west.

Summit route from the Britannia Hut: *by the East Ridge* or *Hohlaubgrat*. Descend a path heading obliquely south-west, down to the Hohlaub Glacier. Ascend this keeping right (north-

west) to turn a crevasse zone and then move left (south), gently rising to the rocky ridge. Continue on the ridge. In dry conditions this is entertaining but without difficulties (I).

After a steeper section taken on the left, keep close to the increasingly higher south-east cliffs (where the rock dries off soonest) to a steep snow or ice slope which goes above this to P.3597. Make a short but definite descent into a saddle. (This point can be reached by a less interesting and more tiring ascent up the glacier). Continue up a long steep slope (often corniced on the left) to the east shoulder (P.3837), and over three short steep rises, with views down the South Face, to the summit block. Climb a crack with good rough holds and over some steps (iron posts) to the eastern end of the final ridge and a little further to the summit.

View: A marvellous panorama with Mischabel group to the

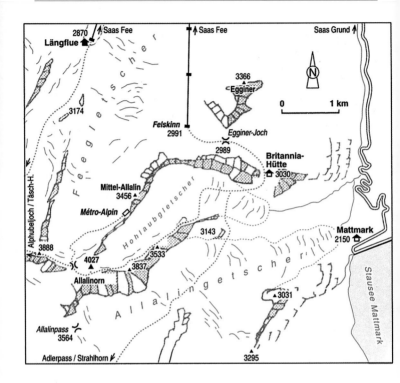

north-west and the nearby Rimpfischhorn and Strahlhorn to the south, as well as the aforementioned disfigurement to the north.
Descent by the Normal Route: From the eastern end of the summit ridge at first descend south-westwards, but soon trend more to the right (west) and go down to the Feejoch. From there descend the steep glacier on the north side and then, on more gentle slopes, move right to the ski circus and the Métro (1 hr).
Other worthwhile routes: *South-West Ridge* (PD, from the Allalinpass – reachable from the Britannia Hut or from the Täsch Hut in 3 hrs, 500mH, 2 hrs, pitches of II).
North-East Ridge (AD+, ice to 50°, 580mH, 3 hrs).
North-East Face (TD, hard ice route left of the ridge, with steep séracs and climbing from 60° to 90°, 430mH, 8 hrs).
South Face (AD+, IV, mixed, 600mH, 4 hrs).
Guidebook: *Valais Alps East* (Alpine Club, 1999).

Rimpfischhorn
Grand Gendarme 4108m

The prominent pointed tower at the start of the rocky part of the North Ridge of the Rimpfischhorn is so obviously separated by a deep notch that it should qualify as independent in the UIAA list – its slender form adding to its character and challenge.

The easiest approach (2–3 hrs) is from the Britannia Hut to working up the Allalin Glacier to the Allalin Pass from (see Strahlhorn, p.101). From the Pass go south-south-west along a broad snow ridge which at the top turns into a narrow snow ridge and finally an airy ridge of rock to gain the top (90 mins from the Allalin pass). The climb can also be done as a prelude to an ascent of the North Ridge during which, after two abseils down the south edge of the Grand Gendarme (in ascent, IV), you climb a series of smaller tops to the summit of the Rimpfischhorn.

Rimpfischhorn 4199m

The pinnacled summit ridge, like the crest of a prehistoric giant reptile, is flanked to south-east and east by an almost pure rock face, on the west by a mixed face. The length of the approach, together with the climbing on the summit block, makes this one

---

Difficulties: PD+. On the summit block there is exposed climbing, II+, otherwise II and I. In the couloir above the Rimpfischsattel there is ice climbing up to 50°, but up to that point a long plod, with just 200mH of easy climbing (II and I, possibly also interspersed with snow) to P.4009.
Effort: From Blauherd station of the Zermatt/Unterrothorn railway involves about 80mH descent and ascent (30 mins) to reach the hut. From Zermatt to hut 1000mH, (3 hrs). Hut to summit is 1600mH (5–6 hrs).
Dangers: The ascent is objectively only mildly dangerous as it leads over an almost (!) crevasse-free snow ridge to the summit block. The summit rocks are often icy and in those conditions are very unfriendly.
Pleasures: Getting to grips with a beautifully shaped, rugged summit with a gradual increase in difficulty and exposure towards the summit. On the ridge edge of the fore-summit, 'gorgeous rock awaits'.

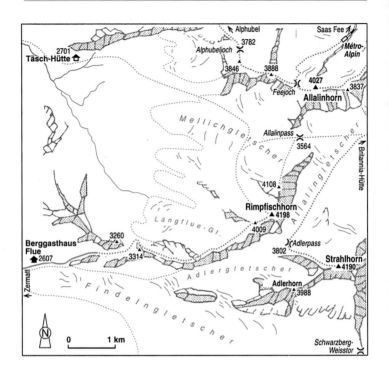

of the more exacting peaks of the region, even when one permits oneself the shortening of the hut climb by using the little railway. The first ascent was made in 1859, by Leslie Stephen, Robert Liveing, Melchior Anderegg and Johann Zumtaugwald by today's Normal Route.

Maps: LKS 1348 *Zermatt*, LKS 5006 *Matterhorn-Mischabel*.
Travel: To Zermatt (1606m), see Dufourspitze.
Hut climb: From Zermatt head south to Winkelmatten. Then begin climbing to the east, first close to the northern bank of the Findelbach. Later, keeping to the left, cross over the Gornergrat rack railway track and on forest path in many bends up to Findeln (2051m). Climb obliquely via Eggen (2177m) eastwards up the slopes of the Findelalp to the Stellisee (2537m) and continue to the Berggasthaus Flue (2618m, private, 20 + 30B, managed in the ski and summer season, Tel. 027-672551).

Flue can also be reached from Zermatt by the funicular railway to Sunnegga (2288m), and then by cableway to Blauherd (2560m) and thence south-east down to the Stellisee.

Summit route by the East Ridge: From Flue, head east for about 1km to small moraine lakes. The path now goes obliquely left up over pasture/debris slopes of the Usseri Rimpfischwang and finally through a block labyrinth and over marl slopes or snow up to the Pfulwe saddle (3155m, between Spitzi Flue and Pfulwe). Traverse to the north of Pfulwe (3314m) to reach a not very prominent shoulder over a somewhat low snow-field, and from this make a rising traverse over the North-East Face (crevasses) to the Längfluejoch (3270m). (This point can also be reached from the head of the valley above Täschalpe by a south-easterly line over moraines and the lower Längflue Glacier.)

Continue up the broad rock-studded ridge and then on the not very defined ridge edge (II and I) up to the snowy West Summit P.4009 and the Rimpfischsattel beyond (3985m, 4 hrs from Flue). P.4009 can be reached from the Britannia Hut (or the Täsch Hut) via the Allalinpass then taking a line across the slopes below the North-West Face (5 hrs).

From P.4009 go east up an icy snow slope to a couloir between two rock ribs (best taken close to the right-flanking rocks). After about 50m of climbing quit the tempting direct line which leads to a tiring thrash and traverse left (north) over ledges and a recess to a notch on the West Ridge of the fore-summit. Climb directly up the stepped ridge edge on good firm holds, using the right flank at one point on a slab (II+), to gain the fore-summit. Descend to the notch beyond, and follow the exposed ridge to the summit (1–2 hrs from the Rimpfischsattel).

View: Well placed for both the Zermatt and Saas panoramas. To the north is the Mischabel group and Allalinhorn, to the east, the very white Strahlhorn, to the south the Monte Rosa massif, with good views of the north-west slope of the Nordend and Liskamm's icy N.W. Face. Breithorn and Matterhorn (south-west) and Weisshorn (north-west) complete the scene.

Subsidiary summits: The West Summit P.4009 is climbed during the ascent. Apart from the Grand Gendarme P.4108, on the jagged North Ridge there are another five lesser tops at

The view south from the summit of the Rimpfischhorn past the southern fore-summit (with the south shoulder summit – lower left) across the upper basin of the Gorner Glacier to the Monte Rosa and Liskamm massifs.

4120m, c.4130m, c.4140m, c.4160m and finally the north fore-summit about 4175m. The southern fore-summit at c.4180m and the more distant south shoulder summit at c.4150m complete Rimpfischorn's quota (two summits/eight 4000m tops).

Other routes: *North Ridge* (AD, pitches of III, the gendarme by the south edge direct is IV, from the Allalinpass 4–5 hrs).

East Face (D, pitches of IV, mostly III, mixed; from the Adlerpass 3–4 hrs; the best route if combining this mountain with an ascent to the Strahlhorn).

North-West Face (D, small but fine, 300mH, ice to 55º).

Guidebook: *Valais Alps East* (Alpine Club, 1999).

Strahlhorn 4190m

From the Moro Pass and the Ofen valley, the East Face of this peak is conspicuous as a mighty rock triangle, but the Normal Route over the glacier-covered north side is a snow plod. No wonder that here even to moderate skiers think hard about a ski ascent (even if ski ascents right to the top are usual only in very good conditions). The first ascent was made in 1854 by the three brothers James Grenville Smyth, Christopher Smyth and Edmund Smyth, led by Franz Joseph Andenmatten and Ulrich Lauener.

The ascent from the west to the Adlerpass is, in winter, part of the last big stage of the Haute Route. In the summer, however, it has recently developed a reputation for its increasingly chaotic crevasse systems.

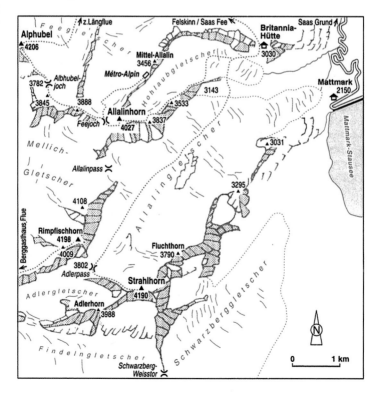

Strahlhorn (left) and Rimpfischhorn (right) with its Grande Gendarme

Difficulties: PD. Technically a pure plod. In mist, if the track is lost, route-finding is difficult. This is because the twists and turns needed to avoid the ice-falls on the Allalin Glacier prevent a straight compass bearing to the foot of the South-East Face of the Rimpfischhorn.
Effort: The hut climb utilizing the cableway to the Felskinn takes about 30 mins, and the summit climb is 1250mH (4–5 hrs).
Dangers: Extensive glacier work with well-camouflaged crevasse risks.
Pleasures: Only really enjoyable on skis.

Maps: LKS 1348 *Zermatt* and LKS 1328 *Randa*, also LKS 5006 *Matterhorn-Mischabel*.

Hut climb: To the Britannia Hut, see Allalinhorn (p.94); to Flue, see Rimpfischhorn (p.98).

Summit route via the Adler pass and the West Ridge: From the Britannia Hut head west on the path down the slope to the Hohlaub Glacier. Cross this at about 3000m to the foot of the Hohlaubgrat descending from the Allalinhorn (P.3143). Now on the Allalin Glacier, ascend parallel to the faces breaking off south-eastwards from the Hohlaubgrat. Cross the flatter glacier

– prominent on the right – seen from the Hohlaubgrat on the Allalinhorn

bottom under the junction of the ice stream descending from the Allalinpass and then pass under the east walls of the Rimpfisch-horn (crevasses!) to gain the Adlerpass (3789m, from Flue 4 hrs). Continue on the initially defined, then broader, North-West Ridge over P.3957 and P.4128 to the summit.

Adjacent peaks: Points P.4128 and P.4143 are only ridge up-swings and cannot really be described as tops.

Other worthwhile routes: *North-East Ridge* (AD, possibly combined with the Fluchthorn; snow climb, on the summit block rock to II, 1250/1330mH, 4–5 hrs from the Britannia Hut). *West-South-West Ridge* (AD, in summer mostly problematical on the Adler Glacier, best combined with the Adlerhorn 3988m; 1600mH, 6 hrs from Gasthaus Flue).

South Face (AD+, in part II, mostly mixed, and snow, from the Schwarzberg-Weisstor over rock face, snow terrace and summit wall. Conveniently reached from the Sella Hut over Neues Weisstor, 1200mH, 5 hrs, alternatively from the Gasthaus Flue. 1600mH, 6–7 hrs).

Guidebook: *Valais Alps East* (Alpine Club, 1999).

West Pennine Alps

These mountains between the Matter valley and Val d'Hérens are in a more natural state than those of the more popular peaks to the east. No mountain railways or cableways disfigure the slopes and no rush of weekend traffic. The huts are high and the paths long and there is a welcome absence of ski villages marring their lower slopes.

Bishorn 4153m

The Bishorn is situated to the north of the Weisshorn and, with a drop of only 120m between them, is not very independent. Even though it is one of the less exacting 4000ers on the climb above the hut, the overall expediting remains demanding as the entire approach must still be done on foot and the valley is far below. The summit is often visited in both winter and summer, thanks to the modest difficulties of its North-West Face. Its first ascent date is formally recorded as 1884 by G.S. Barnes and R. Chessyre-Walker guided by Joseph Imboden and J.M. Chanton though such a modest peak may well have been climbed earlier.

> **Difficulties:** F. A snow plod, with a little climbing (I) on the summit ridge.
> **Effort:** The hut climb is a hard 1580mH (5 hrs), summit ascent 900mH (2–3 hrs, a departure at 5 or 6 a.m. suffices).
> **Dangers:** The glaciers always have crevasses. On ascent to the summit ridge look out for cornices above the North-East Face.
> **Pleasures:** The singular view from the summit ridge of the nearby show-piece, the Weisshorn.

Maps: LKS 1327 *Evolène* and LKS 1328 *Randa*, also LKS 5006 *Matterhorn-Mischabel*.

Travel: By rail through the Rhône valley to Sierre, from there by bus or car 28km through the Val D'Anniviers to Zinal (1680m, a tourist resort with moderate development and refreshingly original surroundings, campsite).

Hut climb: From the southern end of the village, before reaching the campsite at the hamlet of Les Doberts, head east on a prominent zig-zag track up to Alpe Tracuit (Chiesso, 2061m).

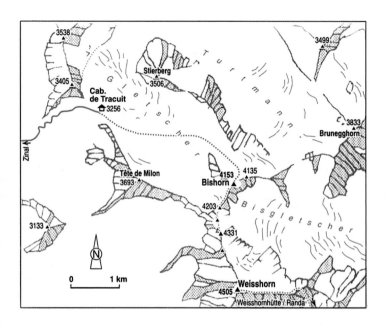

Continue in wide bends above, then turn southwards to work up into the valley of the Torrent du Barmé and then north-east to Alm Combautanna (2578m). Continue over sparser slopes to the Tracuit Hut by the Col Tracuit just before reaching the Turtmann Glacier (3256m, SAC Chaussy, 140 B, managed from mid-June to mid-September, Tel. 027-4751500).

Summit route by the North-West Face: From the hut head east over the Turtmann Glacier to its eastern arm, keeping away from the drop to its north-east (potential avalanches). Go steadily up the North-West Face to the col between the two summits and turn right and ascend the summit ridge which is often corniced.

View: To the south the nearby Weisshorn dominates, to the east is the Mischabel group and to the north the Bernese Oberland.

Adjacent peaks: The east summit – Pointe Burnaby (4135m).

Other worthwhile routes: *North-East Face* (TD, a fine ice face with passages of 70°–90° 650mH, 4–6 hrs from the bergschrund). Best approached from the Turtmann Hut.

South-West Ridge from the Weisshornjoch (PD, II, 3 hrs).

Specialist guidebook: *Valais Alps East* (Alpine Club, 1999).

Weisshorn 4505m

Here is a magnificent pyramid, from the north-east a white triangle, from the south-east and south-west rocky with snow couloirs, but after new snow-fall the whole edifice looks icily white. It has three knife-edged ridges at the meeting of the steep faces, giving it all the aura of the ideal peak. Though lacking the arresting presence of the Matterhorn in its dominating position above a big valley town, it is more finely sculpted, unfolding its full splendour only to those who gain its heights.

The peak was first climbed in 1861 by the Irish physicist John Tyndall with J.J. Bennen and Ulrich Wenger by today's Normal Route route up the East Ridge. The Schalligrat (South Ridge), the most exacting of the three, was climbed in 1895 by

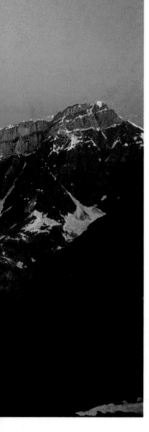

The Weisshorn and Bishorn north faces and Brunegghorn from below the Festijoch. The East Ridge of the Weisshorn faces the camera.

Edward Broome, Joseph Biner and Ambros Imboden and in 1898 the entire North Ridge was traversed by Hans Biehly and Heinrich Burgener. The rocky Younggrat to the Grand Gendarme of the North Ridge was climbed in 1900 by Geoffrey Winthrop Young with the Zinal guides Louis and Benoit Theytaz (later spoilt by a "thankfully" short-lived fixed rope route). The South-East Face fell in 1906 to Young, Joseph Knubel, Valentine Ryan and Josef and Gabriel Lochmatter. Young, Knubel and the American alpinist (and Saxony sandstone pioneer) Oliver Perry-Smith climbed the North-East Face in 1909.

The East Ridge retains most of its original problems, and with its long approach is among the most demanding Alpine summits.

Difficulties: AD. Rock: some III, but mostly II/I and a 45°snow ridge.
Effort: A wretched 1500mH hut climb (5 hrs) and then a 1600mH summit climb (6–7 hrs) on which it is advised not to start too early on account of route-finding problems on the approach to P.3916.
Dangers: On the glacier take the customary crevasse precautions and on the ridge beware of cornices. A helmet is advisable as there is some stone-fall danger from other parties, especially below Frühstucksplatz (breakfast site). On that section avoid the gullies and keep to the rock ribs.
Pleasures: One of the most beautiful peaks in the Alps (or indeed the world) situated in an unspoilt and wild part of the range.

Maps: LKS 1328 *Randa*, also LKS 5006 *Matterhorn-Mischabel*.
Travel: From Visp (Rhône valley) by rail/car 23km to Randa.

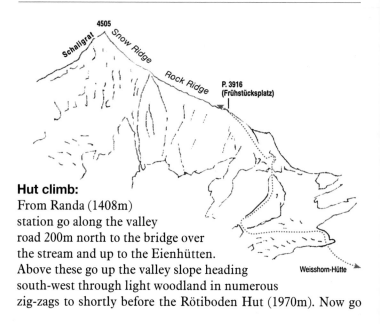

4505

Schaligrat

Snow Ridge

Rock Ridge

P. 3916
(Frühstücksplatz)

Weisshorn-Hütte

Hut climb:

From Randa (1408m)
station go along the valley
road 200m north to the bridge over
the stream and up to the Eienhütten.
Above these go up the valley slope heading
south-west through light woodland in numerous
zig-zags to shortly before the Rötiboden Hut (1970m). Now go

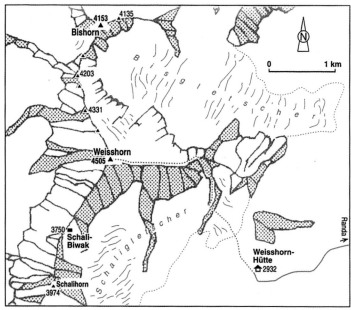

4153 **4135**
Bishorn

4203

4331

Weisshorn
4505

B

s

g

e

s

c

h

e

l

3750
Schali-
Biwak

Schalhorn
3974

Schaligletscher

Weisshorn-
Hütte
2932

Randa

N

0   1 km

right and ascend to the Jatz-Alpe (c.2280m). The path goes west over grass slopes, crossing two streams and climbing obliquely over further slopes to the Weisshorn Hut (2932m, SAC Basel, 40 B, managed from mid-July to mid-Sept, Tel. 027-9671262).

Summit Route by the East Ridge: Head north-west on a path leading to the most easterly basin of the Schali Glacier. Traverse this obliquely leftwards (west) to a rock rib, which descends from the East Ridge. Climb the prominent snow couloir (just right of P.3145), starting on the right but soon moving to the rocks on the left to gain the top of the rib. Climb the snow slopes on the left beside the rib to the rock barrier at its upper end. At this point move right, over exposed snow and slabs (II, harder if bare) to gain a snow or debris shoulder. Climb (ideally in daylight) a short snow and debris ridge to a rock wall which is taken straight up for a few metres before following a ledge leading downwards to the left to a terrace with prominent cairn. From here, zig-zag several hundred metres up the edge of a rubble spur to the lower rocks of the East Ridge (P.3916, Frühstücksplatz, 3 hrs from hut).

On the East Ridge of the Weisshorn

Climb the airy ridge with numerous steps and gendarmes. Most of them are climbed direct, but on the difficult Loch-matterturm, just above the Frühstucksplatz (iron posts) is turned by a traverse on the left (south). The highest tower is traversed on the right (1 hour from P.3916). After this a knife-edged snow arête (sometimes corniced) leads to the upper, steep snow ridge which is followed (small bergschrund) to the summit rocks.

View: The Mischabel group is to the east across the Matter valley. To the south are the summits at the head of the Zermatt valley and to the south-west is Dent Blanche.

Adjacent peaks: The highest East Ridge Gendarme (P.4178) is usually turned during the ascent. The lower Lochmatterturm c.4050m (where the guide met his death) can be climbed direct on the south. The North Ridge's Grand Gendarme (4331m) merits summit status but Pts. 4362, 4203 and 4108 are less assertive.

Other routes: *North Ridge* (AD+, III+, mixed, snow 45°, 450mH from Weisshornjoch, 8 hrs from Tracuit Hut).

South Ridge (Schaligrat) (D, fine rock-climbing to IV, 750mH from the Schali Bivouac, with adventurous approaches to this; from there 5–7 hrs to the summit).

North-East Rib (D, a classic ice route, 7–10 hrs).

Guidebook: *Valais Alps East* (Alpine Club, 1999).

Weisshorn: Grand Gendarme 4331m

The prominent rock tower on the Weisshorn's North Ridge (70m col depth) forms a proud secondary objective which has (incredibly) not been included in the UIAA list of 4000ers despite fulfilling all the conditions. The first ascent took place in 1898 by A.G.Cooke and his guides by the Normal Route (a route quickly repeated by Biehly and Burgener during their complete ascent of the North Ridge of the Weisshorn). The peak's individual status was reinforced in 1900 by the first ascent of the Younggrat (see p107), the classic rock route on the West Face.

Difficulties: AD+ (with lengthy passages of III+ and III. Only viable at this grade in really good conditions.

Effort: The Normal Route to the Bishorn (1580+900mH) and thence up the North Ridge (400mH ascent and a 150mH descent as well) 5–6 hrs from the Tracuit Hut). Add to this the descent either by the ascent route or by a traverse of the Weisshorn descending its East Ridge.

Dangers: Not easy to quit if caught out by really bad weather.

Highlights: One of the most remote summits in the Alps.

Route: Take the Normal Route on the Bishorn (p.105). From its summit descend to the south by a snow ridge to Weisshornjoch (4058m). Continue along the snow ridge to P.4203 (1 hr. from the Bishorn) – the lower North Ridge Gendarme. Now abseil down steep steps (III), move along a shoulder and descend another difficult step (III or abseil) and traverse the less difficult, but broken upper small gendarme to the foot of the big steep rise of the Grand Gendarme. It's best here to ascend about 5m and then traverse 6m left on the east flank and there climb a difficult chimney-like dihedral (III+) to gain the ridge which soon leads to the summit. The continuation of the North Ridge (reached by a descending traverse on the east flank of the Gendarme) to the summit of the Weisshorn is less difficult.

Other routes: *North Ridge/Younggrat* (D, elegant rock climb up to IV when clear of snow, the iron stakes of an old projected Tourist Route assist belaying. 6 hrs from the Cabanne d'Ar Pitetta).

Zinalrothorn 4221m

This slender peak of firm gneiss presents a series of entertaining rock ridges. When Leslie Stephen and Florence Crauford Grove guided by Jakob and Melchior Anderegg made the first ascent in 1864, they followed the exposed and windswept North Ridge. Today's Normal Route by the lower South-East Ridge and Gabel notch was devised in 1872 by Clinton Dent, George Passingham with the guides Alexander Burgener, Ferdinand Imseng and Franz Andermatten. The distinctly more difficult (high quality) South-West Ridge *intégral* or 'Rothorngrat' fell to C.R. Gross with Rudolf Taugwalder in 1901. Geoffrey Winthrop Young's party climbed the right side of the East Face in 1907 and its more direct line fell to André Roch, Robert Gréloz and Ruedi Schmidt in 1945. The South-East Ridge ('Kanzelgrat') was climbed in 1928 by Emile Robert Blanchet and Kaspar Mooser.

The absence of mountain railways and cableways ensures that the full challenge of this fine peak is largely preserved.

Maps: LKS 1327 *Evolène*, LKS 1348 *Zermatt*, LKS 1328 *Randa*, also LKS 5006 *Matterhorn-Mischabel*.

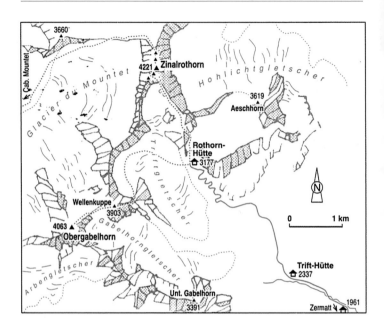

Travel: To Zermatt, see Dufourspitze/Monte Rosa (page 124).

Hut climb: From Zermatt station walk through the town then climb up the north side of the Triftbach. Later, move to the south of the stream and go up the side of the Triftschlucht (steep) to Gasthaus Edelweiss (1961m). Continue across the slope of the scenic gorge (regaining the north bank) to the Trifthotel (2337m).

Climb on a broad track over pastures and slopes to the Vieliboden and on to the picturesque pool of the Triftsee (2579m). Zig-zag up the northern moraine of the Trift Glacier and then on to the Rothorn Hut situated in front of the rock spur Eseltschuggen, an outlier of the Zinalrothorn's South-East Ridge

---

Difficulties: AD–. In part exposed rock-climbing to III–, mostly II and I. When icy or in new snow, these sections become very difficult.
Effort: Hut climb 1700mH (5 hrs), summit climb 1050mH (4–5 hrs).
Dangers: On the lower part of the ridge, beware of cornices. In the couloir and on the summit ridge there are often tricky iced-up sections.
Pleasures: Enjoyable climbing, notably on the spectacular summit ridge.

Zinal Rothorn's South-East Ridge with the Gabel Notch on the left.

(3178m, SAC Ober-Aargau, 104B, managed from end of June to mid-Sept, Tel. 027-9672043).
Summit climb by the South-East Ridge: Go north from the hut along the west side of the Rothorn Glacier until below a snow

break splitting the rock wall on the left. Ascend this to the foot of a rock step climbed by a chimney/gully starting from the lowest point. From the top of the step continue up mixed ground then snow slopes to gain the ridge (breakfast place). Head north along the ridge, first up rock (trending left) and then by a snow ridge to a point just west of P.3786 where a subsidiary ridge comes in from the east.

Go north-west up the narrowing ridge, first over rock, then on snow (cornices) to P.3912. At this point, below the steep part of the Kanzelgrat, climb two rock steps, then traverse left, first into a couloir and then up and across rocks and snow beds on the South Face to a snow couloir on the face below the Gabel Notch. Climb the couloir or the left bordering rocks (II+) to the prominent Gabel Notch right of the twin-topped gendarme (3 hrs from the hut).

Go directly up the ridge for 50m to a stance at the foot of a steep rise. Here, descend left through a cleft to the Biner Slab, which is often iced. Climb this by a slanting crack (peg), or turn it on the west side, and then climb a rock rib (III) to regain the ridge (or on the left if the rib is icy). Make an exposed traverse of a gendarme on the left (west) to the fore-summit ('Kanzel'). Turn this on the right (above the impressive East Face) on a wide ledge and over a last piece of ridge to the summit (1–2 hrs from Gabel Notch).

View: An extensive panorama, but is low enough to make several of the nearby peaks appear huge. To the north the Weisshorn towers up behind the Schalihorn. To the west the Mountet Glacier basin of the Zinal Glacier is dominated by the Dent Blanche and the Grand Cornier. To the south-west are the Trifthorn and Wellenkuppe and Obergabelhorn and beyond the Wellenkuppe, the Matterhorn looks particularly splendid, and east of that the

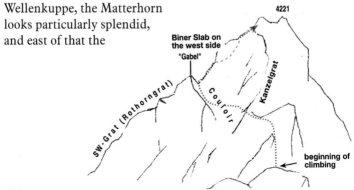

Approach to the Gabel Notch (left) and on the Biner Slab.

Breithorn, Liskamm and Monte Rosa. Finally, to the east, are the Allalinhorn group and the Mischabel peaks.

Adjacent peaks: On the South-West Ridge, the fore-summit or Kanzel is 4210m (15m col depth) and the prominent fork-shaped gendarme above the Gabel is 4120m (15m). On the North Ridge there is the striking Bosse at c.4150m (15m) and the narrow pinnacle edge of the c.4100m Sphinx (10m) and rather lower down is the prominent P.4017 (Epaule) on a kink in the ridge.

Other worthwhile routes: *North Ridge* (AD, III+ and II, 1400mH, 5 hrs from Mountet Hut).

South-West Ridge or *Rothorngrat* (D, IV and III+, one of the finest ridge climbs in the Alps with excellent rock. 370mH, 3–4 hrs from Ober-Rotjoch, 1100mH, 7 hrs from Rothorn Hut).

South-East Ridge Intégral or *Kanzelgrat* (TD–, V and IV+, a more difficult and direct finish to the Normal Route that avoids the loose couloir and Biner Slab, 4–5 hrs from starting climb).

East Face Direct (TD, to V+, 8 hrs from foot of face).

Guidebook: *Valais Alps East* (The Alpine Club, 1999).

Obergabelhorn 4063m

This is a symmetrical, four-sided pyramid, with a North-East Face bristling with ice and a sunny South Face. In a ranking of the most beautiful mountains in the Alps, many consider this the finest, ahead of the Weisshorn and Matterhorn.

The first ascent was in 1865 by Adolphus Moore, Horace Walker and Jakob Anderegg from the Gabelhorn Glacier to the east. Only a day later, Lord Francis Douglas guided by Peter Taugwalder and Josef Viennin reached the summit by the NNW Ridge ('Coeurgrat'), just a week before Douglas's death on the Matterhorn. The noted WSW Ridge ('Arbengrat') fell in 1874 to Henry Seymour Hoare, Eustace Hulton with Johann von Bergen, Josef Moser and Peter Rubi. The unjustly neglected SE Ridge ('Gabelhorngrat') was climbed in 1877 by Edward Davidson and James Hartley with Johann Jaun and Peter Rubi. Today's Normal Route by the North-East Ridge was first done in 1890 by Ludwig Norman-Neruda with Christian Klucker. This became popular after 1918, when the Kluckerturm was tamed by a fixed rope. The best line on the South Face was discovered in 1892 by Percy Farrer with Daniel Maquignaz. The North Face was first climbed by Hans Kiener and Rudolf Schwazgruber in 1930.

Difficulties: AD. Rock-climbing on the Wellenkuppe to II+ (now loose and more serious), on the traverse to the Obergabelhorn there are some sections of III (on the Kluckerturm), but mostly it is II and I, mixed, and a snow ridge with ice slopes up to 50°. The difficulty varies considerably with the state of the track and whether steps have been cut.
Effort: Hut climb 1700mH (5 hrs), summit climb 850mH (5–6 hrs).
Dangers: Typical glacier problems on the approach to the Wellenkuppe and cornices on the connecting ridge to the Obergabelhorn.
Pleasures: An intricate ascent of a beautiful Alpine peak.

Obergabelhorn from the north. The Normal Route follows the left skyline – the icy step of the Kluckerturm on the left. The Arbengrat takes the right skyline and the Couergrat is in the centre.

Maps, sketches, travel, hut climb: See Zinalrothorn.

Summit climb by the North-East Ridge: From the Rothorn Hut head north-west and make a wide left arc under the uppermost ice-fall of the Trift Glacier (crevasses!) and rising up under the Trifthorn gain access to a snow shoulder on the ENE Ridge of the Wellenkuppe (c.3650m). Turn the first ridge rise on the left (south) between rock and a snow patch and, after crossing a small couloir, go up to the ridge on easier rocks. Follow this for 100m to a rocky crest which can be turned on the left on snow. After that, continue on the slabby ridge (now loose as the 'ice mortar' has melted) over a last rise to the summit of the **Wellenkuppe** (3903m).

Head west to a saddle on the soon narrowing snow ridge (cornices) to the foot of the Grand Gendarme ('Kluckerturm').

On the Obergabelhorn's Arbengrat with the Matterhorn beyond

Climb icy slabs and ribs (III, old fixed stanchions) to the fixed cable and pull strenuously up the remaining 20m to the top of the gendarme (or free on the left IV+). Beyond the gendarme, on the steep face of the snow ridge, heavily corniced on the south side, cross first into a small saddle then go steeply up to the summit ridge to the rocky summit block, keeping just right of the ridge edge throughout on snowy rock with good holds.

View: To the south are the Matterhorn and Dent d'Hérens in all their majesty, to the west to the equally splendid Dent Blanche and to the north-east is the Zinalrothorn. All these peaks, with their greater height, are especially impressive.

Adjacent peaks: Grand Gendarme (P.3870) on the N.E. Ridge.

Other worthwhile routes: *WSW Ridge/Arbengrat* (AD, to III+, 1200mH, 6 hrs from the Mountet Hut. Useful for descent to complete a traverse by a southerly discent via the Arben Bivouac Hut, but take care to locate the correct descent point above the Arbenjoch (going down from the col itself is unpleasant) or cross Mont Durand *en route* to the Schönbiel Hut).
NNW Ridge/Coeurgrat (AD, III, mixed, and ice to 50°, 6 hrs from the Mountet Hut, highly praised when fully snow covered).
South-East Ridge (AD+, 850mH, 4 hrs from the Arben Bivouac).
South Face (AD, IV and III, firm gneiss, 6 hrs from Arben Biv).
North Face (TD–, ice/snow to 55° and a steeper mixed finish.
Guidebook: *Valais Alps East* (Alpine Club, 1999).

Dent Blanche 4356m

A mighty, free-standing, slightly tilted, gneiss pyramid. The long, exposed ridges are set on the four points of the compass. Between them complex broken faces fall away.

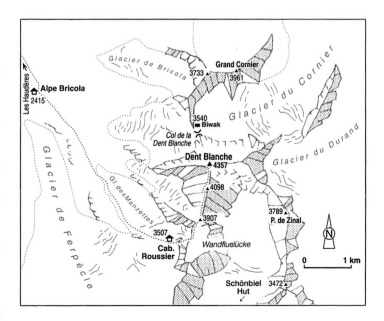

The first ascent was made in 1862 by Thomas Kennedy, Woolmar Wigram, Jean-Baptiste Croz and Johann Krönig. They took the South Ridge which, although very demanding, remains the Normal Route, made easier these days because of a very high hut. The beautiful but increasingly precarious East Ridge ('Viereselsgrat'), has no such amenity. It was first climbed in 1882 by John Stafford Anderson and George Baker with Ulrich Almer and Aloys Pollinger. In 1889 Pollinger, guiding Walter Gröbli, also bagged the technically more difficult Ferpècle Ridge (having descended it in 1882). The steep rocky North Ridge was climbed twice in 1928 by indirect lines: the first (veering right) by Ivor Richards and Dorothy Pilley guided by Joseph and Anthoine

Difficulties: AD. Rock to III, mixed, on snow to 35°.
Effort: Hut climb 1700mH (5–7 hrs), summit climb of 850mH (3–6 hrs).
Dangers: On the ridge can be corniced as it is very exposed to the wind which can greatly complicate the long stretches of tricky climbing. In iced up conditions (not infrequent) they become quite difficult.
Pleasures: A regal summit set in a stately and isolated position.

Looking up Dent Blanche's South Ridge to the Grand Gendarme

George; the second (veering left onto the North Face) was done three weeks later by Dr. Maud Cairney with Théophile and Hilaire Theytaz. The North Face, one of the great alpine ice walls, was captured in 1930 by Karl Schneider and Franz Singer.

Maps: LKS 1327 *Evolène* and LKS 1347 *Matterhorn*, also LKS 5006 *Matterhorn-Mischabel*.

Travel: By rail to Sion in the Rhône valley, from there 33km by post bus to Les Haudères (1450m, a quiet tourist resort with a campsite). Another 7km by car via La Forclaz and Salay gains the Ferpècle car-park (beyond Salay, before the bridge).

Hut climb: Continue up the road to the water works. Before reaching the stream, go left through the wood and climb steadily on good path south-east over pasture slopes to Alpe Bricola (2415m; original old stone huts and a closed hotel). Move on in the same direction over sparser terrain above the Ferpècle glacier. Finally work up south-east onto the northern moraine of the Manzettes Glacier which descends from the west side of the Dent Blanche. Traverse laboriously south across the moraines and the glacier tongue, to gain the southern edge, working up over snow parallel to the slabs and block ridge of the Roc Noir. Further up, still heading in the same direction, climb over an ice top to the Dent Blanche Hut placed at the foot of a rock ridge (Dent Blanche or Roussier Hut, 3507m, SAC Jaman, 40B, managed: mid-July – early September, Tel. 027-2831085). This hut can be approached from the Schönbiel Hut by a loose mixed route over the Wandfluelücke (II, 1000mH plus a 200m descent, 3–4 hours).

Summit climb by the South Ridge: Go up the rocky ridge immediately behind the hut and then up an ice slope to the wide saddle of the Wandfluelücke (3703m). Continue to the north over easy block ridge to the snow top of P.3907. The increasingly rugged ridge continues up to the foot of the prominent Grand Gendarme. Either climb this directly (IV) or pass it by an oblique line to the left (west) over slabs for about 50m and then by a sort of gully to the notch right of a prominent lateral pinnacle. From this notch take a shallow, icy couloir (III, 3 iron posts for belays and abseiling) steeply up to the notch behind the Grand Gendarme. The next towers can be crossed directly, but it is still easier to turn the second one on the right (east) and the third one on the left (west) over often icy slabs. Before reaching the last

Dent Blanche from the west – the South Ridge is the right skyline, The North Ridge is on the left and the longer Ferpècle Arête in the centre.

tower traverse 20m to the left and climb a 8m wall following a (often icy) groove up to the ridge again. After that continue along a snow ridge (occasional cornices) to the summit cross.

View: Fantastic panorama from Mont Blanc and Grand Combin to Monte Rosa, Weisshorn and Mischabel group including unusual views of the Matterhorn and the Dent d'Hérens.

Adjacent peaks: The non-independent but prominent Grand Gendarme (4098m) on the South Ridge is quickly reached from the narrow col above by difficult climbing.

Other worthwhile routes: *East Ridge* or *Viereselsgrat* (D, III+ and III, mixed, serious, long, delicate and exposed yet still popular, 1500mH, 11–15 hrs from the Mountet Hut).

West Ridge or *Ferpècle Arête* (D+, rock-climbing to IV+, IV and III, mixed 850mH, 7 hrs from start of climb).

North Ridge (TD+, rock to V+, mixed, fierce, dangerous, 950mH, 12–15 hrs from the foot of the face).

Guidebook: *Valais Alps West* (Alpine Club, 1998).

Pennine Alps, Frontier Crest: Monte Rosa Group

The watershed, likewise the frontier, takes the main crest of the Alps between Switzerland and Italy. Here the high summits lie impressively strung in a row: to the east the broad Monte Rosa massif, after that the narrower and almost rectilinear middle section and finally, far removed, to the west, the Grand Combin.

Nordend 4609m

As part of the Monte Rosa massif, the third highest summit has, with a drop to the col height of just 94 metres, only limited independence. Its ascent is inconvenient to combine with an ascent of the main summit so its Normal Route has an independent long-distance approach that frequently involves glacier navigation to gain the Silbersattel as it is not often done and the wind quickly obliterates old tracks.

In the 1850s several parties reached the Silbersattel but were rebuffed on the ridge by the then apparently considerable bergschrunds, and it was not until 1861 that the first ascent was made by Edward and T.F. Buxton and John Jermyn Cowell with the guides Michel Payot and Binder.

Another viable route of ascent is from the Jägerhorn direction

Difficulties: PD+. A glacier climb of variable difficulty as it is often without track! The summit block has sections of II and I.

Effort: Hut climb from the Gornergrat railway – 300mH descent and 250mH ascent (2 hrs, from Zermatt on foot 4–5 hrs, summit climb 1820mH, 6–7 hrs).

Dangers: The firmness of the crevasse bridges in the upper part is a factor, as they have been untested. The cornices on the summit ridge, overhanging the two-and-a-half thousand metre East Face, should also be treated with circumspection. On descent the glacier should be quit no later than 1 p.m!

Pleasures: A beautiful, seldom visited summit that provides a full palette of route-finding thrills and pioneering exploration.

Nordend seen from Dufourspitze. The route takes the right-hand ridge.

by the North-East Ridge (Cresta di Santa Catarina) first climbed in 1906 by Irishman Valentine Ryan with his guides Franz and Josef Lochmatter – another fine prize for the Ryan/Lochmatter team made without any aid from pitons, a factor that should sober anyone making a modern ascent of this superb and remote route.

Maps, travel, hut climbs: See Dufourspitze (p.127).

Summit climb: From the Monte Rosa Hut (2795m) as for Normal Route to the Dufourspitze as far as the hollow before the slope of the 'Satteltole' (c.4100m). Now leave the generally tracked route and continue left (east) into the glacier basin between Nordend on the left and Dufourspitze on the right. Work through a system of big crevasses and over a bergschrund up to the Silbersattel (4515m). Continue along the west side of the corniced South Ridge, traversing a small ridge hump (P.4542) and finally climbing rocks (II and I) to the summit.

View: The curved course of the whole summit ridge allows a stupendous view to the south-east down the highest ice face in the Alps. Dufourspitze dominates to the south.

Adjacent peaks: P.4542, traversed during the ascent.

Other worthwhile routes: *North-West Buttress* (AD, II, mixed, snow to 40° from the Monte Rosa Glacier north of P.3696, snow and a reddish rock rib to P.4071, 1800mH from the hut, and 1000mH from start of climb, from there 7–8 hrs to summit). *Morshead Spur* (AD, pitches of IV, otherwise II and mixed, from

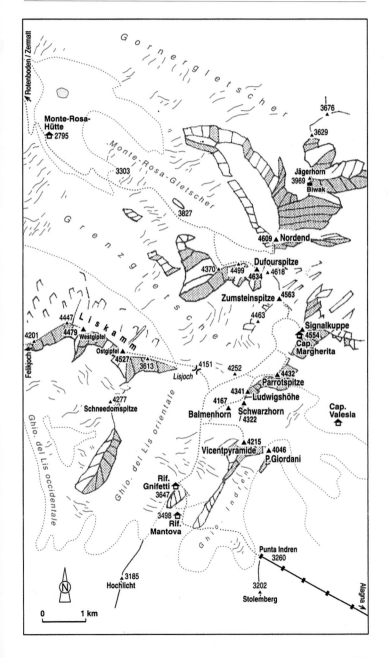

P.4200 at the foot of the West Face go direct to the north-west snow slope; 2–3 hrs from start of climb).

North-East Ridge or *Cresta di Santa Catarina* (TD–, IV with one section of V, mostly mixed, 700mH from the Città di Gallarate Bivouac on the Jägerhorn, from there a difficult 450mH, 5–7 hrs from the bivouac to the summit, large-scale classic ascent).

East Face, Brioschi Route (D+, IV and III and ice to 60°, 2300mH, from the Marinelli Hut 1580mH, from there 9–12 hrs, a marvellous climb up a wild and remote ice face, but now increasingly problematic due to global warming).

Traverse to Dufourspitze (AD, pitches of III, mixed, over Grenzgipfel and summit ridge, 2 hrs from the Silbersattel. Fixed ropes have now reduced the difficulties between the Silbersattel and the col east of Ostspitze).

Guidebook: *Valais Alps East* (Alpine Club, 1999).

Dufourspitze 4634m

Monte Rosa is the greatest mountain massif in the Alps. Mont Blanc rises higher but, in terms of mountain mass (ground above 4000m), it is easily beaten by Monte Rosa and its satellites.

The ascent of the Normal Route to its highest summit – the Dufourspitze – is also considerably more demanding than Mont Blanc's Normal Route, because the main difficulties occur on the summit ridge. The first ascent was made in 1855 (following a variety of near ascents of nearby rock pinnacles during the previous eight years) by a considerable caravan, paid for by Charles Hudson (who was to perish on the Matterhorn ten years later) with John Birkbeck, Edward Stephenson and the brothers James and Christopher Smythe with the Lauterbrunnen guide Ulrich Lauener and the locals Johann and Matthias Zumtaugwald. The summit was named after the publisher of the first precise Swiss map.

The Marinelli Couloir – the first route up the Himalayan-scale 2500m East Face – was climbed in 1872 by the international party led by Ferdinand Imseng (Switzerland) with Richard and William Pendlebury and Charles Taylor (Great Britain), Gabriel Spechtenhauser (Austria) and Giovanni Oberto (Italy).

Difficulties: PD. A long glacier-plod as a prelude to summit ridge with climbing to II+, mostly I, mixed, on exposed rock, rounded by crampon scratches, with ice to 40°.

Effort: To the hut from the Gornergrat railway, 300mH descent, 250mH ascent (2 hrs, if walking from Zermatt an additional 1220mH taking in total 5–6 hrs), summit climb 1880mH (5–7 hrs).

Dangers: On the glacier there is normally a broad trail, but in mist and with the track drifted over there can be serious route-finding difficulties with corresponding crevasse dangers. Initially, on the summit ridge, there are few natural belay possibilities, but on the harder summit block there are useful pinnacles and spikes. On the summit ridge especially, good windproof clothing is often of decisive importance. The long descent over the glacier should be completed by about 1 p.m., before the snow becomes bad and the crevasse bridges soften.

Pleasures: An ascent that must be 'toiled for' and thus provides especially deep satisfaction. In addition, there is a fantastic panorama.

Maps: LKS 1348 *Zermatt*; LKS 5006 *Matterhorn-Mischabel*.
Travel: By rail via Visp (Rhône valley) – Stalden – Täsch and the Matter valley to Zermatt (1606m, full of tradition, an exclusive tourist resort with all the trimmings, including a Naturfreundeheim (Friends of Nature Hostel) and an alpine museum with all sorts of ghoulish objects. Cars must be left in a big car-park in Täsch and the journey completed by train.

Dufourspitze seen from Satteltole. Sattel (4359m) is on the right.

Approaching the summit of the Dufourspitze. The Gorner Glacier below flows down to the west towards Zermatt with the Matterhorn and Dent Blanche the prominent peaks in the distance.

Hut climb: From the Rotenboden station (2815m) of the Gornergrat railway take the track south past the Riffelsee and Riffelhorn and into a hollow, then down a gradually descending path to the dry Gorner Glacier. Traverse the bare ice (markers), crossing the

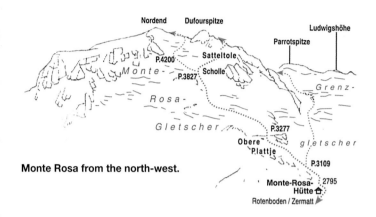

Monte Rosa from the north-west.

block wall of the central moraine then up by the lightly crevassed ice of the adjoining Grenz Glacier to the polished rocks of the eastern glacier bank. Before reaching a crevasse system, move on to the rocks and climb up a good path in long zig-zags to the bank moraine and the Monte Rosa Hut (2795m, SAC, 128 B, managed from mid-March to mid-September, Tel. 0278-9672175).

Summit route by the East Ridge: From the hut take the lateral moraine for a spell, then follow cairns over the polished rocks and the debris of the Unterer Plattje and on up a steep step to the Obere Plattje (3200m).

Move up onto the Monte Rosa Glacier, soon trending left through a crevasse system and then up by the glacier trough keeping south of the straggling rock island of P.3827. Climbing steeply up the 'Scholle' to reach the foot of the broad slope of the 'Satteltole'. Head up this to a final steep section leading to Sattel at P.4359 on the West Ridge of the Dufourspitze.

Now work east along the ridge, at first on an icy knife-edge, then over broken rock to the rocky ridge hump (P.4499). On the other side, descend a little and continue up a snow slope and rock to the fore-summit. A rocky ridge with pinnacles and blocks leads down into a notch and steeply up cracks and steps, with good holds scratched by many crampons, in the final part keeping left of the ridge edge to eventually pull onto the summit.

View: Lower summits all around, but nearby there is a whole collection of satellites, especially on the frontier crest running from the Signalkuppe westwards to the Liskamm. The glacier scenery is particularly impressive with the scale of the Grenz and Monte Rosa Glaciers emphasised from this viewpoint. To the west the Matterhorn and Weisshorn groups stand in sharp profile.

Adjacent peaks: The Grenzgipfel P.4618, 150m away (the easterly corner point of the summit ridge), is occasionally even done as an independent summit (and despite its closeness still offers problems). In between there is another ridge tower, Gratturm, c.4630m. These two elevations can be climbed on the traverse of the ridge to the Zumsteinspitze and Signalkuppe. On the West Ridge, besides the fore-summit (c.4600m), about 60m away from the highest point, the Upper West Ridge Summit P.4499 and, west of the saddle, the Lower West Ridge Summit (c.4380m) can be distinguished, the two first having been traversed on the Normal Route, the last quickly reached from the saddle P.4359.

Other worthwhile routes: *Descent over the Grenzgipfel to the Zumsteinspitze and the Signalkuppe* (AD, III and II, 3 hrs to Marghérita Hut, and about the same time in the reverse direction).

Ascent from the Silbersattel along the frontier summit to the Dufourspitze (AD, III and II, mixed, often made harder by ice and snow, 2 hrs to the main summit).

South Rib or *Cresta Rey* (AD, III– and II, an ideal line, steep rock, dries quickly, long glacier approach, then 400mH from start of climb, 3 hrs).

East Face or *Marinelli Couloir* (D+, at 2400mH the mightiest ice face in the Alps, around 50°–55°, by direct exit over the rock rib to the Grenzgipfel also climbing to III+, very menaced by falling ice, especially in mild weather, 9–12 hrs from the Marinelli Hut). Climate change has now rendered this route loose and serious during the summer months.

Guidebook: *Valais Alps East* (Alpine Club, 1999).

Zumsteinspitze 4563m

This rock pyramid sits neatly between Dufourspitze and Signal-kuppe – but in what a situation! Seen from the north-east, it crowns the mighty East Face of Monte Rosa and from the west it stands at the source of the wild Grenz Glacier. With a col depth of over 100 metres it also secures the right to be described as an independent summit with a straightforward ascent from the nearby Marghérita Hut. It is worth remembering that when Joseph Zumstein and his retinue undertook the first ascent on 1 August 1820 from the snow plateau of the Colle Gnifetti, after climbing the Grenz Glacier, this was still one of the most remote places in the Alps and the first of the Monte Rosa summits to be climbed.

> **Difficulties:** F. Easy going on snow with, just before the summit, a few metres at 40° with some rock.
> **Effort:** Anyone who has the ascent of the Signalkuppe behind him/her, will knock off 111mH from the Colle Gnifetti at any convenient moment.
> **Dangers:** In bad visibility on the Colle Gnifetti, very careful route-finding essential.
> **Pleasures:** Another really high summit 'done'. And what a view.

Maps, travel, hut climb: See Signalkuppe.
Summit climb from the Marghérita Hut: Go down to the Colle Gnifetti in a few minutes. From there, climb north-westwards, finally on small ridge to the summit.
View: You seem close enough to touch the summit block of the Dufourspitze to the north, to the east is the 2400-metre drop into the Macugnaga valley, to the south the Signalkuppe and behind that the expanses of the plain of the River Po and to the west the mountains of the central chain, from the mini-4000ers like Parrotspitze, Ludwigshöhe and Schwarzhorn over the bulky Liskamm to the Breithorn and Matterhorn and Dent Blanche.
Adjacent peaks: The snowy hump P.4463 at the base of the South-West Ridge is easily reached from the Colle Gnifetti.
Other worthwhile routes: *North Ridge from the frontier saddle* (corniced ridge with rock steps of II, mixed, 30 mins).
Traverse from the Dufourspitze across the frontier saddle (AD, III and II, 2 hrs).

The view from the Marghérita Hut over the snowy Zumsteinspite t
with the pointed summit of Nordend to its right. In the distant i

Signalkuppe
(Punta Gnifetti) 4556m

This summit, which is somewhat lower than the Zumsteinspitze,
nevertheless upstages it as the prominent topographical junction
between the frontier crest and the ridge crest running north over
the Nordend-Strahlhorn-Mischabel group to Stalden. Seen from
the plain and the foothills, the rugged rock bastion of the Signalkuppe appears as the dominating elevation. The name Punta
Gnifetti recalls the pastor Giovanni Gnifetti, from the hamlet of
Alagna at the foot of the mountain, and his seven guides and porters
who in 1842 found today's customary ascent over the Lisjoch.

The building and 1893 inauguration of the eponymous hut
by the Italian Queen Marghérita fundamentally altered the
mountaineering situation. This was accentuated in 1980 by its
replacement by a gigantic, two-storied wooden box covered with
sheet copper. Though this highest placed construction in Europe
offers a high-level refuge in unsettled weather, it also removes all

The rocky bulk of Dufourspitze (the second highest peak in the Alps)
ne Mischabel group backed by the skyline of the Bernese Alps.

the qualities of mountain solitude that this high top should right-
fully possess. The intrusion is reinforced as the hut lacks an
adequate sewage disposal system and it is a squalid distraction to
have to contend with sundry excreta on the approach slopes.

Difficulties: A glacier plod to great height.

Effort: The 2100mH to Punta Indren are almost never climbed (buy a
ticket for the railway from Alagna). From there it is 400mH to the
Gnifetti Hut and a further 900mH up the glistening concave mirror of
the glacier basin to the summit. A further, very unexpected effort for all
under-acclimatized people is spending a night at this unusually high
hut – you have been warned!

Dangers: Route-finding is problematic in bad visibility and if the track
gets covered. There is a delicate crevasse zone just above the Gnifetti
Hut. On the traverse below the Parrotspitze and Signalkuppe there is a
slight danger from sérac-fall.

Pleasures: One moans freely about the crowd in the hut but, for all
that, this is a place in which one can take in the magic of a
breathtaking evening at very high altitude and morning moods at
leisure, without all the rigmarole and paraphernalia of bivouacing.

Maps: LKS 1348 *Zermatt (Signalkuppe-Parrotspitze-Liskamm)* though the first part of the described route is not shown as this Swiss map ends at the Italian-Swiss border. LKS 1:50,000 sheets 284 *Mischabel*, 294 *Gressone*. LKS 5006 *Matterhorn-Mischabel* (extends further south to just take in Piramide Vincent). For sketches, see Dufourspitze and Ludwigshöhe.

Travel: From the south, by rail to Varallo (456m) via Borgosesia. By car go from the Simplon Pass via Domodossola and Omegna/Lago d'Orta-Passo La Colma (942m), then 35km up the Sesia valley (bus) to Alagna (1190m, tourist resort, camping).

Hut climb: From Alagna, nowadays scarcely anyone resists the temptation of the cableway. To ascend on foot, from the upper end of the town go via the Rusa district, up through the wood beneath the cableway, then climb the whole Olenbach valley to the Colle D'Olen (2864m, 4 hrs). Turn the north-lying Corno del Camoscio on the east (path) and after that continue on the crest almost as far as Monte Oliveto/Stolemberg. The summit block of this is turned on the west on a path heading downwards to the Col de la Pisse. Continue northwards on a ridge (past a ruined hut) and opposite a cairn cross a notch to the Indren Glacier. Ascend this to the Punta Indren (3260m, mountain station of the cableway – on foot from there 6 hrs).

Traverse north-west across the ski-ravaged glacier, then over a rock and rubble step obliquely up the path to moraine slopes.

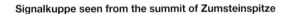

Signalkuppe seen from the summit of Zumsteinspitze

These lead to the Cittá di Mantova Hut (3498m, BV Gressoney, 112B, managed: end of March – mid-April, mid-June – mid-September, Tel. 0163-91039), 1hr from Punta Indren.

Continue up over the moraine slopes, then traverse the reduced tongue of the Garstelet Glacier and over a rocky face to the Gnifetti Hut lying between the small Garstelet Glacier and contorted ice stream of the Lis Orientale Glacier (3647m,; CAI, 277B, managed: mid-April – mid-September, Tel. 0163-78 015).

Summit route from the Gnifetti Hut: Go north-east up the glacier which is disrupted by deep crevasses where the Garstelet Glacier branches off. Then head up west of Piramide Vincent, towards the Lisjoch. Before reaching this, just after passing the rock island of the Balmenhorn and the Schwarzhorn/Corno Nero, work up to the east to gain the flat saddle between the Ludwigshöhe and the glacier top P.4252. Now traverse under the North Faces of the Ludwigshöhe and Parrotspitze into a wide basin and work up obliquely left (north-west) under the Signal-kuppe to Colle Gnifetti. From there climb obliquely and easily south-east to the summit of the Signalkuppe.

Summit route from the Monte Rosa Hut: First of all go to the Monte Rosa Hut (see Dufourspitze, p.129). From there, as to the Dufourspitze, up the path over the Plattje, then go south-east past P.3109 and move right to the Grenz Glacier. Ascend this (many crevasses) to P.3472 at the foot of a rock island and pass this close to its south side to go up to P.3699. Continue up south-eastwards to below the Parrotspitze. Here one joins the route from the Gnifetti Hut (6–7 hrs from the Monte Rosa Hut).

View: To the west are the small Monte Rosa 4000ers and after that Liskamm, Matterhorn, Dent Blanche and Zinalrothorn. Close at hand to the north are Dufourspitze, Zumsteinspitze and Nordend (with the upper part of the East Face), as well as the more distant Mischabel group and Strahlhorn. From the narrow terrace of the south side there is an exciting view down the rocky South Face and over the foothills to the expanses of the plain of the River Po. The breathtaking easterly view down the Signalgrat is best seen from the lavatory window of the hut.

Adjacent peaks: On the East Ridge there is, close under the hut, a prominent gendarme and P.3769 near the Passo Signal.

Other worthwhile routes: *South-West Ridge* (I and snow to 45°, 250mH from the Seserjoch, 1 hr).
East Ridge (*Cresta Signal* or *Topham Ridge*) (III and II, mixed, almost 1000mH, 6 hrs from Resegotti Bivouac, with very long approach of 2000mH, 7 hrs from Alagna) – a notable first ascent in 1887 by Harold Topham with Aloys Supersaxo and a porter.

Parrotspitze 4436m

The independent summit south-west of the Signalkuppe, with a col depth of 140 metres, is mostly only climbed in connection with this during a traverse. From the west, it appears as a snow pyramid with sharp cut summit ridge, from the south as a puzzlingly dark rock mountain. The formality of the first ascent was made in 1863 by Reginald MacDonald, Florence Crauford Grove, Montagu Woodmass and (probably) William Hall with their guides Melchior Anderegg and Peter Perren though the difficult E–W Seserjoch crossing by Rev. Hereford Brooke George, A.W. Moore, Florence Crauford Grove with Christian Almer and Mattias Zumtaugwald passed close to the summit. (Note: The 1869 W–E Seserjoch crossing (in mistake for the Lisjoch) by Ellen and Anna Pigeon with Pierre Martin and a porter was one of the more remarkable unintended alpine feats).

Difficulties: PD. An exposed snow ridge.
Effort: In addition to the Signalkuppe climb allow 170mH, 1 hr.
Dangers: Observe the usual cautions, particularly on the summit ridge.
Pleasures: Elegant summit ridge from which to observe the scene of the exciting events linked to the 1862 and 1869 crossings of the Seserjoch.

Maps, sketches, travel, approaches: See Signalkuppe.
Summit climb: From the ascent track to the Signalkuppe, and before reaching this, move up to the Seserjoch (4296m),and then follow the North-East Ridge to the summit.
Other worthwhile routes: *West Ridge* (a snow knife-edge, to 40°, 1 hr conveniently added on the Gnifetti Hut ascent).
North-North-West Face (50° snow/ice, 200mH, small but nice).

Ludwigshöhe 4341m

A less independent, snowed-over hump to the south-west of the Parrotspitze and separated from this by the Piodejoch. Mostly visited only in combination with the neighbouring summits on the descent (or ascent) from the Signalkuppe. First climbed by the surveyor Ludwig van Welden and several companions in 1822.

> **Difficulties:** F. Snow to 40°.
> **Effort:** Slight, 48mH and 20 mins extra.
> **Pleasures:** Another 4000er crossed off on the crest of a splendid massif.

Approach: See Signalkuppe, then a pleasurable, easy diversion.
Adjacent peaks: The glacier hump P.4252 to the north-west requires only eight metres of climbing in the opposite direction.

Schwarzhorn (Corno Nero) 4322m

Though lacking independence this is still a well-positioned rock peak south of the Ludwigshöhe. The 1873 first ascent was by Marco Maglioni and Albert de Rothschild with guides and porters.

> **Difficulties:** PD. Short but hearty, snow to 50° and some rock.
> **Effort:** Additional height difference from the route to the Signalkuppe about 30mH, 30 mins extra (from the Gnifetti Hut 720mH, 2–3 hrs).
> **Pleasures:** An attractive belvedere.

Maps and approach: See Signalkuppe.
Ascent: Over the steep but short North-West Face or the rocky South-West Ridge (I) to the summit.
Adjacent peaks: The Balmenhorn 4167m was demoted to a top in the UIAA 1994 list. Prior to that Karl Blodig had given it peak status. A 4000er it may be, mountain it is not. There are a couple of dozen adjacent peaks exactly like this nunatak. This rock pinnacle rises scarcely a dozen metres above the surrounding slopes, is decorated with a gigantic statue of Christ and a filthy bivouac box. From Gnifetti Hut 560mH (1–2 hrs).

Piramide Vincent 4215m

This summit lying south of the main crest beyond the Schwarzhorn is indeed lower but far more independent than the elevations
on this part of the main crest. Due to the proximity of the Gnifetti
Hut, it offers an ideal acclimatization excursion or a short climb
in unsettled weather. The first ascent was made in 1819 by the
then owner of the gold mines around Alagna, Johann Nikolaus
Vincent, with two of his mountain folk and a hunter.

Difficulties: PD. Simple snow slopes.
Effort: From the Gnifetti Hut, 600mH ascent (2 hrs).
Dangers: On the glacier the customary caution is advisable, especially
in the crevasse system immediately behind the hut.
Pleasures: A beautiful prelude to bigger things, be it in days to follow or
on the same day, with the traverse also of the summits to the Signalkuppe,
which look appetizing from this outlier. Alternatively it is a summit to
complete the traverse when already somewhat tired but giving a good
opportunity for a retrospective view of the day's achievements.

Maps, travel, hut climb: See Signalkuppe.
Summit climb: As for the Signalkuppe to below the Balmenhorn.
Turn right and work east to the Colle Vincent and from there take
the north slope to the summit.
View: The peak offers a good view of the main crest.

Punta Giordani 4046m

It is difficult to understand why this obscure shoulder/col on the
South-East Ridge of the Piramide Vincent is included in the new
UIAA list given a mere 5 metre rise on the ridge. The Punta
Giordani is best reached from the Rif. Gnifetti by taking the
South-West Ridge of the Piramide Vincent and then moving
right on ledges to the Indren Glacier which is then climbed to
gain the summit (2 hrs). Alternatively a descent from Piramide
Vincent during a traverse or a 2 hour/886mH ascent from the
Punta Indren station over the Bors glacier and the South-East
Ridge completes the job for assiduous 4000m peak collectors.

Pennine Alps:
Central Frontier Crest

The 20km section of the frontier crest above Zermatt from the Liskamm to the Dent d'Herens carries a parade of mountains with very differing claims and very different development.

Schneedomspitze (Il Naso) 4272m

A modest-looking cone west of the Lisjoch defining the end of the South Ridge of the Liskamm East. In contrast to the somewhat underwhelming Punta Giordani this peak at least has a prominence equal to other minor new summits in the UIAA list.

> **Grade:** F+. Snow trudge. Bergschrund often difficult.
> **Effort:** To the hut 400mH. Summit climb 960mH (2–3 hrs).
> **Dangers:** On the glacier, crevasses especially close together above the Gnifetti hut and in the basin – often without tracks – of the eastern Lis glacier. If there is no track there can be considerable orientation problems here in unsettled weather.
> **Highlights:** Normally one of the easiest 4000ers.

Maps, access and hut ascent: see Signalkuppe, p.132.
Summit ascent: Follow the Signalkuppe route until just before the Balmenhorn and from there head in a westerly direction, at first descending a little, across the glacier basin (crevasses) to the foot of the rocks. Cross the bergschrund there and trend left up to the broad south ridge which leads to the summit.

Liskamm East 4527m

This mighty five-kilometre ridge is a goal to be taken very seriously, particularly as it is notorious for large cornices. The East Summit is 50 metres higher than the West Summit, about a kilometre away with a pronounced col between. The faces are very different: the South somewhat rugged and quite small, rising just a few hundred metres above the névé basin of the Ghiacciaio del

Lis; the North, a steep, hostile wall of ice, at its highest 1100m above the crevasse and sérac labyrinths of the Grenz Glacier.

The first ascent of the main peak was made by the South-East Ridge in 1861 by J.F. Hardy, A.C. Ramsey, F. Gibson, T. Rennison, J.A. Hudson, W.E. Hall, C.H. Pilkington and R.M. Stevenson. Their guides were J.P. Cachet, F. Lochmatter, K. Kerr, S. Zumtaugwald and P. and J. Perren. Three years later Leslie Stephen, Edward Buxton, Jakob Anderegg and Franz Biner traversed the entire summit ridge (from west to east). The South-West Ridge was the scene of tragedy in 1877 when two Englishmen and three guides fell to their deaths when a cornice broke, thereby founding the mountain's dark reputation. The ideal line, and objectively safe, is by the North Rib of the East Summit, first done in 1890 by Ludwig Norman-Neruda with Christian Klucker and Josef Reinstadler.

Difficulties: AD. Snow or ice to 45°, very exposed. Here less technical ability is required than endurance, constant surefootedness and good mountain judgement.

Effort: Hut climb from Punta Indren 350mH (from the valley 2420m), summit climb 920mH (4–5 hrs) with 350mH (2–3 hrs) on the snow ridge.

Dangers: A mountain rightly infamous for its (especially between the East and West peaks) double-sided cornices. For that reason it is essential to move on a long rope and to stay below the cornice fracture line being circumspect about previous tracks taking care to assess whether they follow a sensible line. When in doubt be prepared to use ice screw protection. Particular caution is needed in bad visibility!

Pleasures: A high level traverse of one the finest ice peaks in the Alps.

Maps, travel, hut climb: To the Gnifetti Hut – see Signalkuppe.
Summit climb by the East Ridge: First of all proceed as for Signalkuppe, but go directly to the Lisjoch (4151m). Climb south of a rock hump (P.4177) and up over the snow knife-edge to the East Shoulder Summit/Cima di Scoperta (P.4335). Continue along the almost horizontal ridge keeping well down on the north side (tremendous cornices to the south) to the summit block. There, still on the north side, make another steep climb (often on bare ice) up to the connecting point between the East Ridge and the rocky South Ridge. Go right along the narrow ridge over rock and snow to reach the summit.
View: To the north-east the Monte Rosa peaks overlook the ice

Liskamm from Monte Rosa. Liskamm East is on the left – Il Naso on its rocky southern flank – with Liskamm West at the right end of the ridge. The peak's great feature is its fabulous icy North Face (700m–1100m) taken by the classic Klucker, Welzenbach and Blanchet routes on East Peak, the harder Liskamm West routes (Stefan/Diemberger and Hiebeler/Pokorski) and the elegant North-West Ridge (right).

wastes of the Gorner, Monte Rosa and Grenz Glaciers. To the south are the Italian foothills. To the west, beyond the West Summit are Castor, Pollux and the Breithorn. To the north-west the Weisshorn is the most dominant peak.

Adjacent peaks: The truly independent West Summit P.4479 can be reached by the traverse or (independently) from the Felikjoch via its South-West Ridge which also allows the South West Ridge Summit P.4201 and the Western Fore-Summit P.4417 to be 'ticked'. There is a further minor ridge hump east of the West Summit on the connecting ridge (about 4450m).

Other worthwhile routes: *Traverse* (AD with pitches of II, a long, narrow, snow and rock ridge, cornices on both sides, 2 hrs summit to summit, 4–5 hrs Lisjoch to Felikjoch or vice versa.

Swiss Approach: From the Monte Rosa Hut over the Grenz Glacier to the Lisjoch (long glacier route, 5–6 hrs, crevasses, usually without track and best left alone in bad visibility!

North Face of the East Summit – Norman-Neruda Route or *Klucker Rib* (D, III, ice to 50°, 3–6 hrs from the foot of the face).

Guidebook: *Valais Alps East* (The Alpine Club, 1999).

Liskamm West 4479m

Elevated to a separate peak in the UIAA listings, Liskamm West fully justifies its new status not only for its col depth but also for its huge North Face ice climbs, amongst the biggest in the Alps. Its first ascent was made in 1864 by the afore-mentioned Stephen, Buxton, Anderegg, Biner party. The WSW Ridge (these days from the Quintino Sella Hut) was climbed in 1867 by Frederick Morsehead, Charles Mathews, Christian Almer and Andreas Maurer. Another interesting early route was the first essay onto the North Face on a blustery morning in 1902 by Mrs Rhona Roberts Thomson, Christian Klucker and Christian Zippert who followed the elegant (and relatively safe) 1150m North-West Ridge (a Valais Brenva Spur). It was nearly 60 years before the the North Face proper was climbed, by two major ice routes: in 1960 (on the left) by Wolfgang Stefan and Kurt Diemberger and 1961 (centre right) by Toni Hiebeler and Heinz Pokorski.

Looking east from Breithorn to the Monte Rosa group (left), Breithorn Central with Liskamm behind (centre), and Pollux and Castor (right).

Access, hut, etc.: see Castor, p.144. **Map:** see Breithorn, p.151.
Summit route from the Quinto Sella Hut: The same as the Castor approach to the Felikjoch. From the col follow a long at broad snow ridge to P.4201, then a narrower ridge section (can be corniced in early season) to a steep shoulder. Depending on conditions this can be taken direct or with a long, exposed, rising traverse to the left, to reach the easier angled ridge leading to the final summit rise. Now either keep on the snow ridge, or move onto rocks on the south-eastern flank, to the western fore-summit P.4447 and on to the summit.
Other worthwhile routes: *North West Ridge* AD+. A quality ice climb, with sometimes an awkward bergschrund, but few objective dangers.
Castor approach: A fast party can add the ascent after climbing Castor from the Klein Matterhorn.
Breithorn to Lisjoch Traverse: By using the Cesare e Georgio Rosso Bivouac Hut at the eastern end of the Breithorn, this classic

---

Grade: PD. Glacier and snow ridge up to 40°. Often icy near the summit.
Effort: Climb to hut 1970mH (by cable car 960mH, see Castor), summit ascent 900mH (3–4 hrs).
Dangers: On tracks and in good weather little danger. Cornices can develop near summit. After fresh snow/cold winds difficulties accumulate.
Highlights: One of the highest technically less difficult alpine summits.

traverse incorporates Liskamm West in a superb two-day expedition (see p.147) but the West/East traverse ends with the south-facing descent slopes of Liskamm East which can be bare ice, or soft snow lying on ice, late in the day. Below this, in poor visibility, even the glacier descent to the Gnifetti Hut can present serious route-finding problems.

View: Similar to Liskamm East, but with better Breithorn views.

Castor 4228m

The higher of the Zwillinge (Twins) rises above the Felikjoch as a symmetrical, white pyramid. In contrast with the size of Liskamm and Breithorn the pair look modest. The challenge lies less in the summit climb but more in solving the approach problems so as to arrive early enough to make a dual ascent in safety. The first ascent of Castor by the South-East Ridge was made in 1861 by William Mathews and F.W. Jacomb guided by Michel Croz.

Difficulties: PD. Snow or ice to 35°.

Effort: Hut climb to the Quintino Sella Hut from Gressoney la Trinité 1970mH (6 hrs, or using the chair lift to the Colle Bettaforca 920mH – 3 hrs, summit climb 650mH (2–3 hrs). Alternative way from the cableway terminus Klein Matterhorn 700mH (4 hrs).

Dangers: The typical glacier and snow slope problems. The south-west slopes are occasionally avalanche prone.

Pleasures: For people who seek an easy ascent, here is one!

Maps: From Switzerland LKS 5006 *Matterhorn-Mischabel*; from Italy – 1:50,000 LKS 294 *Gressoney*. General diagram see p.151.

Travel: From the south by rail to Pont St Martin in the Aosta valley, then 35km by road (post bus or car) to Gressoney la Trinité (1624m, tourist resort, still in part a German-speaking enclave of the Valais) or by rail to Verès in the Aosta valley and then 31km on a little road to San Giacomo (1689m, hamlet at the end of the Valle d'Ayas). From Zermatt use the Klein Matterhorn cableway.

Hut climb: *From Gressoney la Trinité to the Quintino Sella Hut*: First of all, follow the footpath on the eastern bank of the Lis, after ten minutes cross the stream and on the other side up to the

Kapelle St Anna. Continue over alpine pastures to Alm Sitten and up to the Bettliner Pass/Fourcla Bettaforca (2672m, on foot 3 hrs; to here from San Giacomo in 3 hrs; also chair lift from Stával, 3km up the valley from Gressoney). Now go north on a path over debris and rock ridges (climbing aids) for a further 3 hrs to the Quintino Sella Hut sited south of Punta Perazzi on the rock ridge between Piccola Ghiacciaio di Verra and Ghiacciaio di Felik (3587m, CAI Bella, 140 B, managed: late June – mid-September, Tel. 0125-366113).

Summit climb: From the Sella Hut on the Felik Glacier, head north-east round Punta Perazzi and, keeping right, ascend to the Felikjoch on a broad ridge descending from P.4093. Leave the lowest point of the col on the right. Go up left on the South-East Ridge of Castor, with few technical difficulties but being alert for cornices, crossing the South-East Summit (Felikhorn or Punta Felik, 4174m) and a fore-summit to gain the highest point.

From Klein Matterhorn station: Go to the Zwillingsjoch (2–3 hrs, see Pollux). Continue south-east zig-zagging up the South-West Face to a col between the north summit and the summit (400mH, 2 hrs, when there is danger of avalanches on the west flank, take the North-West Ridge. AD)

View: Dominated by the nearby Liskamm and also fine glaciers.

Adjacent peaks: South-East fore-summit (c.4185m) and the Felikhorn (4174m) as well as the Felikjoch-Kuppe (P.4093) – also a North Summit P.4205 reached easily from the summit.

Other worthwhile routes: *South-West Ridge* (D, on firm rock to IV, approach via a saddle north of Pt. Perazzi (sometimes difficult). Can be done from the Mezzalama Hut, 720mH, 5 hrs). *Felikjoch / Zwillingsjoch* Gained by glacier routes from the north.

Guidebook: *Valais Alps East* (Alpine Club, 1999).

Pollux 4092m

The smaller neighbour of Castor, most pleasantly approached by the Klein Matterhorn cableway or the Mezzalama Hut, was first climbed in 1864 by Jules Jacot guided by Peter Taugwalder snr.

Difficulties: PD. Pitches of II, mostly I and snow to 50°; often delicate.
Effort: From the Klein Matterhorn station 600mH, 3–4 hrs to the summit.
On the way back allow the same time or longer on a softening glacier.
Dangers: The customary use of the cableway to the very high starting
point can induce unacclimatized people to over-tax themselves. Once
started it is essential to move rapidly to allow a return to be made in
reasonable snow conditions. On the glacier the customary caution is
advisable, particularly on the return. In bad visibility and if the track is
lost this becomes an exciting expedition. See map on p.151.
Pleasures: Anyone who can put aside the fact that by this route only a
fraction of the whole mountain is climbed, enjoys the additional summit
in his/her collection. Those who prefer a full ascent can take the North
Ridge or traverse the summit in the course of the strenuous extended
traverse from Monte Rosa over the Liskamm and the Breithorn.

Maps: LKS 1348 *Zermatt*, LKS 5006 *Matterhorn-Mischabel*.
Travel: To Zermatt, see Dufourspitze. From Zermatt, cableway
to Klein Matterhorn, Tel. 028-671316 or 671252. From the south
5 hrs from San Giacomo/St Jacques (see Castor) to the Mezzalama
Hut (3036m, CAI, 34 B) and from there 3 hrs to the Zwillingsjoch.
Summit climb: From the terminus (3820m, no overnighting), go
down to the saddle (3796m) and then head east on the broad track
towards the Breithorn. Now head eastwards over the Breithornpass
(3824m) and along under the Breithorn's southern flank, below
the crevasse zones of the upper Ghiacciaio di Verra and then below
the rock island with the Rosso Bivouac (3750m) and the slope to
the easily reachable Schwarztor. Pass under the south-west rock
spur of Pollux and move round and up to the Zwillingsjoch (Passo
di Verra, 3845m; 2–3 hrs from the cableway). Climb the, often icy,
steep slope on the left (west) to the loose rocks of the South-East
Ridge, which leads very airily to the summit (1 hr from the col).
View: Impressive aspects of Liskamm, Castor and the eastern
summits of the Breithorn, plus the surrounding glaciers.
Other worthwhile routes: *North-West Ridge* (PD, ice 45°, rock,
wire rope pitch, 360mH, 1–2 hrs from the Schwarztor).
North Ridge (AD, 50°, 1350mH, 5 hrs from the Monte Rosa Hut).
Guidebook: *Valais Alps Central* (Alpine Club, 1999).

The view from Pollux to the Breithorn massif. Roccia Nera is nearby
with the Breithorn East twins further right. Breithorn Central's rock
steps dominate the middle of the ridge.

Schwarzfluh (Roccia Nera) 4075m
Breithorn Twin (East) 4106m

The eastern pillar of the Breithorn ridge with a sheer rock face above the Schwarztor. Although linked to the Breithorn Twins by a near level snow ridge (just 20m col depth), it is UIAA noted because of its separate identity and demanding north face route. Breithorn Twin (East) the lower of the two Breithorn East peaks can be climbed during the Roccia Nera ascent

Grade: PD. A snow/ice climb up to 45° to the ridge and Roccia Nera. PD+ for the climb to Breithorn Twin East (awkward rock pitches to finish).
Effort: 350mH from the Schwarztor or the Bivouac Hut, 700mH from Rif. Guida Ayas (see Pollux, p.145). From Klein Matterhorn, descent of 150mH and climb of 350mH (3 hrs to summit) – with 150mH on return (2–3 hours).
Dangers: Routine crevasse/avalanche risks on glaciers and snow slopes with large cornices further along the ridge.

Summit route: Take the Pollux approach (p.146) to the Cesare e Giorgio Rosso Bivouac Hut. Climb the snow slopes to the summit ridge (Roccia Nera is easily reached with a short diversion). Take the snow ridge leading west (cornices) to a rock ridge which leads to the summit. Grade III rock climbing leads on to the West Twin.

Looking down Breithorn Central's East Ridge to the sharp summit of Breithorn Twin (West) with the east top to its right. The Younggrat is in profile (left) with Monte Rosa beyond.

Breithorn Twin (West) 4139m

Breithorn's main eastern summit can be tackled from the col east of Breithorn Central (instead of from Roccia Nera). The first Breithorn traverse (east/west) was made in 1884 by Viereselgrat pioneers J. Stafford Anderson, Ulrich Almer and Aloys Pollinger (possible first ascent). Almer was also involved in the 1897 North Face ascent with H.J. Mothersele, C.S. Acherson, Christian Kaufmann and Christian Jossi. 1910 saw the first ascent of North Ridge by Geoffrey Winthrop Young, C.D. Robertson, R.J. Mayor guided by Joseph Knubel and Moritz Ruppen.

> **Grade:** PD–. Mainly snow but craggy at the end.
> **Effort:** 300mH from the Klein Matterhorn, 745mH from the Ayas Hut.
> **Dangers:** The snow ridge from the notch can hair-raise in poor conditions.
> **Pleasures:** A short but spectacular ascent.

Summit route: Use the Klein Matterhorn / Pollux approach at first, but when below the rock buttresses of Breithorn Central, cross the bergschrund and ascend rock and snow to the deep col to its east. Traverse the southern flank of the sharp linking snow ridge to a shoulder and thence on rock to the summit.
Other worthwhile routes: *North Ridge / Younggrat* (D, up to IV, 1250mH, 9–10 hrs from the Gandegg hut).

Breithorn Central 4159m

> **Grade:** F+. Pure snow ascent, at 35°.
> **Effort:** 350mH from the Klein Matterhorn.
> **Dangers:** Big cornices on the north side of the summit ridge.
> **Highlights:** One of the easiest 4000ers but frequently in virgin condition.

Summit route: From the Breithorn Pass go north into a snow basin and steeply up to the col. Climb east along the snow ridge to Breithorn Central (keeping well clear of the cornices). On the return Breithorn West can be reached along a fine snow arête.
Other worthwhile routes: *Traverse from the East Summit* (PD+, has III+ pitches on Central's rocky East Ridge).

On the East Ridge of Breithorn Central.

Breithorn 4164m

This magnificient mountain wall holds the attention from the north and west. Since the 1813 first ascent by the easier southern side by Henry Maynard, Joseph-Marie Couttet, Jean Gras, Jean-Baptiste and Jean-Jacques Erin, the approach has greatly changed. The area between Matterhorn and Breithorn is now so filled with cableways

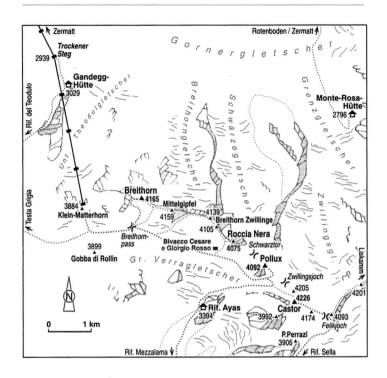

that most climbers use them. The mountain is thus very crowded.

Maps: LKS 1348 *Zermatt*, LKS 5006 *Matterhorn-Mischabel*.

Travel: To Zermatt, see Dufourspitze (p.126). From Zermatt, take the cableway to Klein Matterhorn's underground station (3820m, Tel. 027-9668100). From the south by rail to Châtillon in the Aosta valley, then 26km by road to Breuil (Cervinia, 2006m, tourist resort) and thence by cableway to the Testa Grigia (3480m).

Hut climb: Those not using the cableway to Trockener Steg will take the steep path to Hermettji, then up left spur of the Furgg-

---

Difficulties: PD–. Taken overall, perhaps the easiest of the main 4000m peaks. However, with snow slopes of 35°, often icy, crampons are essential.
Effort: 350mH climb from the mountain station (1–2 hrs).
Dangers: Routine crevasse and avalanche risks. In bad visibility and loss of tracks, one can very easily go astray.
Pleasures: After such a crowded climb any other ascent is pure bliss.

---

bach valley to Trockener Steg and on to the Gandegg Hut – 4 hrs
from Zermatt (3029m, private, 30 B, managed, Tel. 028-672196). For
the Normal Route follow the eastern edge of the Oberer Theodul
Glacier, then cross it to the Theodul Hut – 6 hrs (3327m, CAI, 86 B,
managed: April – September, Tel. 0166-949400). Continue up the
glacier to the Testa Grigia (accomodation). Go south-east up the
glacier and then north-east (crevasses) on the climb to the plateau
and Klein Matterhorn route (1½ hours from Testa Grigia).

Summit climb: From the cableway station (3820m, no overnight
stops) descend to the saddle (3796m) by the Breithorn Plateau. Go
east to the Breithorn Pass and then work up and across the steep
south-west slope to the South-West Ridge and on to the summit.

Adjacent peaks: The Central Summit (4159m) is easily reached.

Other worthwhile routes: *Breithorn Ridge* (AD, III, mixed,
usually done east/west, 8–9 hrs from the Rosso Bivouac).

North Ridge or *Triftjigrat* (AD, rock III, II, mixed, longer passages
of ice to 55°, 1150mH, 8 hrs from the Gandegg Hut).

Breithorn East: North Ridge or *Younggrat* (D, to IV, more taxing
than the Triftjigrat, 1250mH, 9–10 hrs from the Gandegg Hut).

Guidebook: *Valais Alps East* (Alpine Club, 1999).

**Liskamm (left), Castor and Pollux (centre), the Breithorn summits and
the Breithorn Pass (right) in an evening view from the Rothorn Hut.**

Matterhorn 4478m

The Matterhorn (Cervin or Monte Cervino) is the epitome of the majestic peak, among the most famous mountains in the world but correspondingly overcrowded. This does not deter most climbers, and even those who think they can resist its popularity usually change their views when they actually see the mountain.

The drama of its first ascent underpins its fame. The race, into which the final attempts degenerated, was decided by Edward Whymper and his equally driven companions, Lord Francis Douglas, Charles Hudson, Douglas Hadow and the guides Michel Croz and Peter (father and son) Taugwalder on 14 July 1865 by their successful *ascent* of the North-East (Hörnli) Ridge. But after an accident on the *descent*, only Whymper and the Taugwalders returned. The harder Italian Ridge was mastered three days later by Whymper's former ally Jean-Antoine Carrel with Abbé Gorret, Jean Baptiste Bich and Jean-Augustin Meynet but only Carrel and Bich did the devious finish above Pic Tyndall (by a traverse to the Zmutt Ridge). A direct finish was done in 1867 by Jean Joseph and Pierre Maquignaz and soon equipped with ropes and a short ladder (a process that also 'tamed' the Hörnli Ridge). The still largely unequipped Zmutt Ridge was

Difficulties: AD– Despite the fixed ropes and other equipping this is still one of the hardest Normal Routes on a 4000m peak more for its length, the care demanded on the constant rocky terrain, and the mountain's exposure to weather changes. Even with the use of the fixed ropes, there are still passages III–, mostly II (very sustained) and I (if the fixed ropes are not used, there are pitches of IV and IV+, at great height and hence more strenuous). In the summit area there are also difficulties on mixed ground.

The rock on the ridge provides good holds and is enjoyable to climb in dry conditions, but on the faces it is slabby and less secure. Route-finding is easy following the polished rock, but in wet or snow it is less obvious and the smoothness creates difficulties which make the Hörnli route very taxing for climbers of average ability, because of its sheer length.

Effort: If the cableway is not used the Schwarzsee climb is 950mH (2–3 hrs). From the Schwarzsee to the Hörnli Hut is 700mH (2 hrs), the summit climb is 1200mH (c.1700m of climbing, 5–6 hrs). At least 5 hours should be allowed for descent (in poor conditions much longer) on which steady simultaneous movement by all members of the team is a skill that, ideally, should have been perfected in advance.

Dangers: There have been approximately 500 deaths on the Matterhorn and this fact sends a clear message. The main danger is the hectic state into which many people drive themselves prompted by the muddle brought about in moving and belaying on the harder passages. As most climbers move together, roped, but generally unbelayed (good natural belays being scarce), there are many opportunities for mishap, particularly during the numerous unavoidable passing manouevres.

A second substantial danger is the sheer length of the climb which, especially with the onset of bad weather, makes route-finding harder and ensnares many, particularly those who are climbing at their limit. Although most of the original loose rock has now been cleaned there are still loose sections, so stone-fall risk, even though localised, is another big problem.

Further difficulties are added by the 'polished' fixed ropes which are only anchored to the rock at long intervals and are bad to grip with gloves on account of their thickness. Regarding equipment, it is not wise to economise on warm clothing, windproofs or crampons. The Solvay Hut (4003m) placed in a convenient notch on the ridge on the east side, is exclusively assigned as emergency quarters for bad weather or accidents. Several experienced parties have been forced into prolonged stops at the Solvay to await a weather change allowing a safer descent.

Pleasures: Even though the detailed climbing is not of high quality, the ambience of this great symbolic peak and its position is still fascinating. Providing the weather is settled, a well trained party may elect to start in daylight when the route-finding and climbing will be more pleasurable. The only problem with this strategy is that of passing the many descending climbers with the corresponding stonefall and hurly burly.

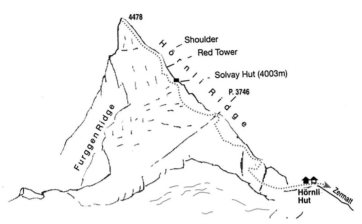

4478
Shoulder
Red Tower
Solvay Hut (4003m)
P. 3746
Hörnli Ridge
Furggen Ridge
Hörnli
Hut
Zermatt

The East Face of the Matterhorn with the Hörnli Ridge on the right and the Italian Ridge on the left, its finish hidden behind the final pyramid. The steep Furggen Ridge finish takes the high left skyline.

On the Hörnli Ridge: in the slabby recess below the Solvay Refuge.

climbed in 1879 by Albert Mummery with Alexander Burgener, Johann Petrus and Augustin Gentinetta, and the North Face ascent by Franz and Toni Schmid (1931) also made headlines.

Maps: LKS 1348 *Zermatt*, LKS 1347 *Matterhorn*, LKS 5006 *Matterhorn-Mischabel*.

Travel: The valley base is Zermatt, see Dufourspitze p.126.

Hut climb: From Zermatt railway station walk through the town and head up the valley to Winkelmatten. From there cableways lead to the Schwarzsee. Those resisting this temptation should follow the western bank of the Mattervisp to the junction of the Zmuttbach. Follow that for about 600m, then cross the bridge to the Zum See district (1766m). Take the Stafelalp path, but go left at the first fork on the path to Hermettji (2053m). Here, continue right (many bends) up the ridge to the Schwarzsee Hotel (2584m) and the Schwarzsee (2–3 hrs). Continue west on the broad path (grassy humps, moraine debris) to the dark rock wall of the Hirli. Before reaching that, first ascend left then cut back right to gain the ridge. The path leads up, with numerous short bends, to gain the shoulder with the Hotel Belvedere and the Hörnli Hut

(3260m, SAC Section Monte Rosa, 60B, usually overcrowded; managed: mid-June – mid-September, Tel.027-9672769).

Summit route by the Hörnli Ridge: Generally the route stays to the left (east side) of the ridge and only above the Solvay Hut does one keep more generally to the ridge edge. If one plans a nighttime start, a reconnaissance of the lower section of the route is advisable.

From the Hörnli Hut, follow a horizontal ridge to a step. Move up this obliquely left (fixed rope) and traverse left (tracks) to a shoulder on the East Face. Ascend a little further in the direction of the ridge then traverse left to the East Face. There, cross a couloir and traverse further to a second couloir. Go up that for about 25m and then move on to a rock rib on the left (right of a third couloir) and follow this back to the ridge.

On the ridge, climb about 100mH on good holds (tracks, crampon scratches) as far as a ledge of yellowish rock. Follow this left on the face to its end. Zig-zag directly up to the ridge to a rock

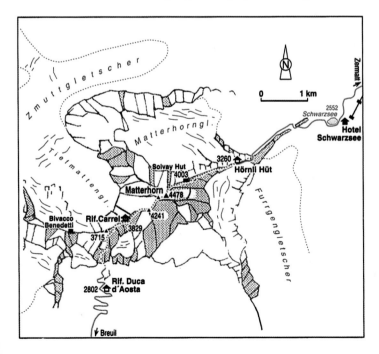

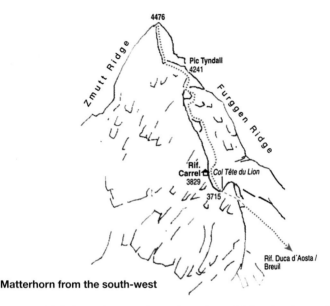

4476

Pic Tyndall
4241

Zmutt Ridge

Furggen Ridge

'Rif.
Carrel
3829

Col Tête du Lion

3715

Rif. Duca d'Aosta /
Breuil

Matterhorn from the south-west

tower which bars the way (remains of an old hut in front of it, 3818m, 2 hrs from the Hörnli Hut). Make another long detour left up across the face to a slabby recess, cross a rock band and continue up left until below the Solvay Refuge. Climb up on increasingly steeper rock to reach the near vertical 'Moseley Slab' (III–, iron peg for belay) which goes directly up to the Solvay Hut (4003m, 3 hrs from the start). Move left round the hut and go up a slabby gangway set between steeper rocks and soon move back up (the Upper Moseley Slab, III–) to regain the ridge, which is followed over blocks. Turn the Red Tower on the left and after that go up the ridge to the 'Shoulder' (mostly snow and ice with iron belay pegs).

Climb a short snow and ice ridge and the crest of the ridge above to gain the steep summit block. Keep on the edge using steep cracks and steps, on which thick, greasy fixed ropes obtrude as aids to heaving oneself up inelegantly. Thus one reaches the often icy summit slope and soon afterwards gain the highest point (at the eastern end of the Summit Ridge).

South-West or Italian Ridge (AD, III and fixed ropes (without these, IV), a better climb than the Hörnli Ridge, but overall more tiring and for that reason is often done in descent).

The Hörnli Ridge in blustery, post-squall, summer conditions:
looking down to the Shoulder from the first fixed rope.

From Breuil (2006m) go to the Duca degli Abruzzi Hut
(2802m, 2–3 hrs). Take the path to the Croce di Carrel and go up
a gully heading obliquely left over a rock barrier to a rock ridge.
Traverse to and climb the eastern edge of the snow-field under
constant threat of stone-fall to a rock rib under the summit block
of the Tête du Lion. Go right on ledge, crossing some gullies

(stone-fall, delicate), to the Col du Lion (3580m). Keeping on the south side of the ridge, climb a succession of slabby rocks using fixed ropes to reach and climb the 'Seiler Slab' and above the vertical 12m 'Whymper Chimney' (chain), followed by more slabs (fixed ropes) leading to the Savoia Hut (only for emergencies) and the Rifugio Carrel (3829m, 40B, radio telephone; 4–5 hrs from Aosta Hut).

Turn the pinnacle ridge above on the south side (many fixed ropes) passing the 'Mauvais Pas' (a toe ledge) and 'Linceul' (a small patch of ice) to a wall with another fixed rope ('Corde Tyndall') which leads to the ridge. Continue up that, turning most obstacles on the left, to the Pic Tyndall (4241m, 3 hrs). Move across the almost horizontal ridge, and cross a deep notch ('Enjambée'), to gain the summit block. Follow the obvious line of the ropes and up a rope ladder ('Echelle Jordan') to the West (Italian) Summit. A short climb along the summit ridge (with notch) leads to the main summit (5 hrs from the Carrel Hut).

View: Overwhelming – from Mont Blanc, Dent d'Hérens and Grand Combin in the west to the northern giants of Dent Blanche, Obergabelhorn, Zinalrothorn and Weisshorn to the Mischabel group with Dom, Täschhorn, Alphubel, Allalinhorn, Rimpfischhorn and Strahlhorn and further to Monte Rosa, to the Liskamm and the Breithorn in the east.

To the south the distant view is unexceptional but the view down the mountain itself leaves nothing to be desired.

Adjacent peaks: The not very prominent West Summit (with an iron cross) is at 4476m. Pic Tyndall (4241m) is traversed on the ascent of the Italian Ridge.

Other worthwhile routes: *North-West / Zmutt Ridge* (D, IV– and III, mixed, seldom in good condition, snow or ice to 50°, the great classic Matterhorn ridge, 1200mH, 7–9 hrs from the Hörnli Hut – the Lonza Hut, erected in 1997 at the foot of the ridge, was soon damaged by avalanche).

South-East / Furggen Ridge (D+/TD, IV, direct up to VI, unstable rock; 1150mH from start of climb, 8–12 hrs).

North Face (TD, steep ice and IV, or V, delicate unstable rock, one of the great alpine north faces , 1100mH, 10–12 hrs).

Guidebooks: *Valais Alps West* (Alpine Club, 1998).

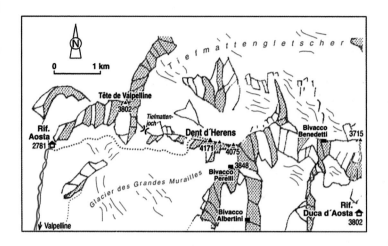

Dent d'Hérens 4171m

Upstaged by the Matterhorn, this remote mountain is beautifully formed with rewarding routes. In 1863 the South West Face (its Normal Route) was climbed by Florence Crauford Grove, William Hall, Reginald MacDonald and Montagu Woodmass guided by Melchior Anderegg, Peter Perren and Jean-Pierre Cachat. The West Ridge was climbed in 1901 by Giles Puller, the three Maquinaz brothers and Louis Carrell. (Note: Because of glacier retreat the South West Face is now difficult to access in mid season and the West Ridge is becoming the favoured route from the south – its friable approach and difficult lower rocks now equipped with fixed ropes.) The 2km East Ridge was climbed in 1906 by Valentine Ryan with Franz and Joseph Lochmatter. They descended the icy WNW Face with abseils

Difficulties: PD Mainly a long glacier climb, then some rock climbing to II, finally along a narrow, exposed summit ridge.
Effort: Hut climb 800mH (5–6 hrs), summit climb 1400mH (5–6 hrs).
Dangers: The customary rules of caution on glaciers must be particularly carefully observed, especially since one can scarcely count on outside help.
Pleasures: A solitary and serious mountain.

down steep lower séracs. A year later Joseph Lochmatter *climbed* that face with J.W. Wyatt, Rev. W.C. Compton and Léon Truffer followed by W.H. Glover, Peter Perren and Joseph Marie Julen. This established the easiest route from Switzerland. The North Face, one of the first extreme ice climbs, was overcome in 1925 by Willo Welzenbach and Eugen Allwein.

Maps: LKS 1347 *Matterhorn*; LKS 5006 *Matterhorn-Mischabel*.

Travel: By rail or motorway to Aosta. From the main road leading to the Great St Bernard, and after about 4km fork to Valpelline (960m) and up to Bionaz (1606m; post bus, 29km from Aosta).

Hut climb: The lane is still suitable for motors for another 6km to the reservoir dam of Lac di Place Moulin. From there a one hour walk along the lakeside leads to Prarayer (2005m, hotel, only open in summer). Now follow the track (paying careful attention to the markings) up the long valley to the Aosta Hut (2781m, CAI Section Aosta, 24 B, managed at times: mid-June – end of August, Tel. 0165-73006). This can also be reached from Zermatt in 5–6

The WNW Face of Dent d'Hérens seen from Tête de Valpelline. The Normal Route (SW Face) is gained by the Grandes Murailles Glacier on the right. The Tiefenmattenjoch is low on the right linked to the summit by the West Ridge. The North Face is in profile on the left with the Matterhorn beyond.

hrs by the Schönbiel Hut over Col de Valpelline or from Val d'Arolla by the Bertol Hut over Col des Bouquetins.

Summit route: Descend from the hut and then head east on a moraine path to the northern part of the Grandes Murailles Glacier. Avoid a crevasse zone on the left and then cross under the Tiefenmattenjoch (or up to it if climbing the West Ridge) and ascend below the flank of the West Ridge (keep clear because of stone-fall) heading towards the foot of the SSW Ridge before cutting back left to about 3800m. Cross the rimaye and climb the South West Face over snow and easy rocks (keeping left) to gain the easier upper West Ridge. Continue up blocks and steps, then a narrow pinnacle ridge to the summit.

View: The Matterhorn towers up to the east, its Italian and Zmutt Ridges prominent. By contrast, Dent Blanche to the north appears distant. To the west is Mont Collon at the head of the Arolla valley.

Adjacent peaks: The Épaule (4075m) on the East Ridge.

Other routes: *West Ridge* (AD–, III+ and III, mixed, 1400mH from Aosta Hut, 600mH, 3 hrs, from the col – friable in the lower sections).

West-North-West Face (AD, to 45°, occasionally extreme crevasses; 1500mH from Schönbiel Hut, with 850mH on the face).

East Ridge (D, IV and III, 700mH, sections unstable with very long stretches of climbing, 8–10 hrs from the Col Tournanche).

North Face (TD+, ice to 90°, rock to IV, menaced by falling ice, 1300mH, 10–15 hrs).

Guidebook: *Valais Alps West* (Alpine Club, 1998).

Pennine Alps West:

Far to the west of the other Pennine 4000ers, the Grand Combin is really a separate mountain massif – close to the St Bernard Pass and the Italian and French frontiers.

Grand Combin de Grafeneire 4314m

The Grand Combin is a truly alpine mountain. One reaches the huts by long approaches up delightful quiet valleys, and even then there is still a considerable distance to go to the summit. Also the easiest of its ascents have their problems, especially Benjamin and Maurice Felley's and Jouvence Bruchez's 1857 'Corridor' route. This is threatened by a wall of séracs which regularly disgorge ice avalanches making an ascent akin to Russian Roulette. The Felley/Bruchez group only reached the fore-summit – the Aiguille du Croissant – the main summit being reached two years later by Charles St Clair Deville, Daniel, Emmanuel and Gaspard Balleys and Basile Dorsaz.

Difficulties: Snow to 45° on the Col du Meitin approach from the south which can be serious. The North-West Face (AD+) has snow/ice to 50° (sometimes steeper on the séracs). The rock-climbing on the West Ridge, (PD+/AD–) has friable parts of III and II, but mostly mixed. The South Face (PD+) has some unstable rock at II and mixed/snow climbing to 45°.
Effort: Hut climb from Bourg St Pierre to Valsorey Hut 1400mH (5 hrs). Summit climb by North-West Face is 1450mH (5 hrs) and on return 200mH to recross the col; by the West Ridge or South Face 1300mH (5–6 hrs).
Dangers: The North-West Face has some danger of falling ice, but far less than on the 'Corridor'. On the South Face and on the approach to the Col du Meitin stone-fall is possible in fine weather and late in the day. On all the routes there are long passages of ascent and descent on steep ground to overcome, so considerable endurance and constant surefootedness are necessary. The West Ridge offers an (almost) glacier-free ascent. On the glaciers, observe customary crevasse precautions, on the summit ridges in the vicinity of the summit, beware of the gigantic cornices on the south side.
Pleasures: Being underway on a really untouched range.

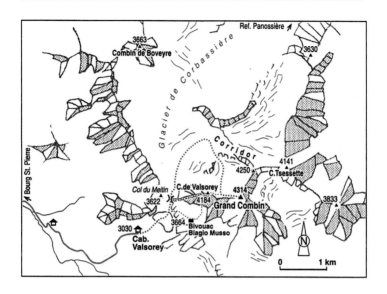

The Corridor's dangers prompt the choice of harder routes with less objective risk. The West Ridge (1884), climbed by Charles Boisviel with Daniel Balleys and Seraphin Henry, and Emile Blanchet and Kaspar Mooser's North-West Face (1933) are two alternatives that became popular after the destruction (by avalanche) of the Panossière Hut (since rebuilt) in 1988. When approaching these routes from the south the traverse of the slopes under the Col du Meitin adds the problem of sporadic stonefall.

Maps: LKS 5003 *Mont Blanc-Grand Combin*.

Travel: By rail to Aosta or Orsières (via Martigny). From Aosta by bus over the Great St Bernard Pass to Bourg St Pierre (1632m; small place on the main road, businesses; the village can also be reached more conveniently from Orsierres or Martigny (37km).

Hut climb: From above the filling station in Bourge St Pierre take a narrow track, or a small road, up into the side valley of the Valsorey stream. Where the road leads back left, continue by the stream, then soon climb the northern slope to an alm hut (1834m). Continue on the track on the north slope of the valley. At the bridge (Vélan Hut path branches off) stay on the north bank and soon reach the Chalet d'Amont (2197m). Continue to a rocky wall, breached by a constructed path. After that, trend

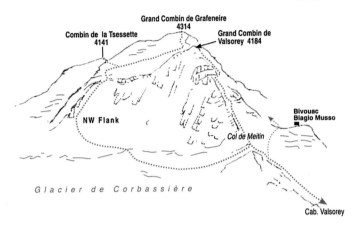

round to the east on the slope leading to the high pastures and then up a long block and debris slope to the Valsorey Hut which is placed on a spur (3030m, SAC Chaux de Fonds, 60 B, managed: April – September, in June weekends only, Tel. 027-7871122).

Summit climb to the Col du Meitin: From the Valsorey Hut, go north-east over moraines to the small Glacier du Meitin and steeply up a snow gully (or on the easy rocks right or left of it) to the not very prominent Col du Meitin (c.3610m, 2 hrs from the hut; a little to the west is the Combin du Meitin, 3622m).

North-West Face: From the Col du Meitin, descend north into the upper basin of the Glacier de Corbassière keeping distance from the ice debris and avalanche remains, before crossing the rimaye and traversing up the North-West Face to the flatter slopes of the spur above P.3406 (also from the Panossière Hut by the Glacier de Corbassière – 3 hrs). Move up right of the rocks onto the steep snow/ice going directly up to a break in the sérac barrier above. Steep climbing leads through this (with or without ice, according to conditions) to the lower edge of the summit plateau (P.3987). Ascend, in a slanting line to the right to gain the saddle east of the Combin de Valsorey. Then head left (east) over the slopes (gigantic cornices on the right over the South Face!) to the transmitter installed on the summit and keeping left of that, gain the highest point (Combin de Grafeneire, 4314m). This route is perhaps best in good snow conditions when the West Ridge may be iced up. In lean conditions, the ridge would be the best choice.

Grand Combin from the Glacier de Corbassière. The 'Corridor' slants up left under the sunlit ice cliffs. The North-West Flank takes the shadowy slopes right of the cliffs. The summit is above the Corridor with Combin de Valsorey forming the end of the rocky West Ridge rising above the Col du Meitin on the right.

West Ridge: From the Col du Meitin there is initially some scrambling to the first of the three big steps. These are overcome very near the edge with the harder sections turned on the right (several possibilities). The overhang at the end of the first step is turned on the right and after that the ridge is regained by a groove. On the second step, the difficulties can also be avoided on the right using a couloir with whitish rock. After that there is a horizontal section (shoulder). The third step is climbed direct or turned on the right. Finally, scramble up the shattered ridge to reach the summit of the Combin de Valsorey (4184m). To the east of this move easily down into the wide saddle (4132m) to join the final part of the North-West Face route to the main summit.

South Face to Combin de Valsorey: When below the snow gully on the Col du Meitin climb, move out right and climb steep slopes to the Plateau du Couloir (3664m, bivouac hut) below the South Face of Combin de Valsorey. From there climb the broken face (brittle rock, mixed) either keeping left to the shoulder of the West Ridge or trending right to the saddle east of the Valsorey.

View: The Combin dominates the nearby peaks but Mont Vélan (south-west) and Mont Blanc du Cheilon (east) catch the eye.

Adjacent peaks: On the North Ridge is Aiguille du Croissant (4250m, 15m col depth).

Other worthwhile routes: *North-West Face to the Combin de Valsorey* (D/D+, ice to 60°, 700mH, 5–7 hrs from the rimaye).

From the north-east by the Corridor (PD, technically easy but only for people who wish to live dangerously; from the Panossière Hut 1650mH, 6–8 hrs, of that more than 1 hr in an area acutely menaced by falling ice – descent option for speedy climbers).

The South-East Ridge (PD+, a fine route, some friable rock; from the Amiante Hut 1335mH 6–8 hrs, or the Valsorey Hut 7–9 hrs).

Guidebook: *Valais Alps West* (Alpine Club, 1998).

Combin de Valsorey 4184m

Now ranked as independent by the UIAA (52m col depth), this peak forms the western corner point of the Grand Combin. It is part of the West Ridge and South Face climbs, but is also quickly and easily accessible across snow and boulders after climbing the North-West Face.

Combin de la Tsessette 4141m

This striking north-eastern summit of the Combin (55m col depth) is reached from the exit from the sérac barrier of the North-West Face. Make a long traverse eastwards and a diagonal descent across the steep slope of the Mûr de Côte to the col P.4090 and thence head along the ridge to the east. The prominent western summit (4121m, 31m col depth) can be traversed or reached on a diversion from the main routes. This adds 1 hour, plus return time, from the North-West Face exit.

Mont Blanc Massif East

The Mont Blanc group is not the most extensive massif in the Alps, but has many of the highest peaks. It consists in the main of splendid granite, a rock that decorates the peaks with a diversity of wild, coloured sculptural forms and also provides wonderful rock climbing in the highest and most splendid situations. The main disadvantage is that with its height and position as a focal point at the western end of the Alps it suffers from sudden violent weather changes.

Aiguille Verte 4122m

Elegance and difficulty determine the aura of this big peak which, with its many filigree ridges, stands in sharp contrast to the more lumpen ice masses of Mont Blanc or the rock bastions of the Jorasses. These three mountain groups stand in marvellous juxtaposition. That this slender, snow-glittering form hanging ethereally above the gothic rock splendour of its satellite the Dru, should be called 'Green Needle' is a puzzle. Perhaps it indicates that to the people of the Chamonix valley the green bases of the mountains were more nourishing and for that reason more important than the icy splendour above them in the clouds.

The summit was reached for the first time on 29 June 1865 by Edward Whymper and his Swiss guides Christian Almer and Franz Biener, who took the South (Whymper) Couloir. It triggered a storm of doubt in the guides' guild of Chamonix, who were indignant that a local guide had not been hired. Certainly some local guides were capable of such ascents, as Michel Croz, M.A. Ducroz and the Zermatt guide Peter Perren proved a week later with Thomas Stuart Kennedy, Charles Hudson and G.C. Hodgkinson on the first ascent of the Moine Ridge.

The splendid ice climbs of the north side offered a challenge for ice specialists. Already by 1876 the North (Cordier) Couloir was climbed by Henri Cordier, Thomas Middlemore, John Oakley Maund with Jakob Anderegg, Johann Jaun and Andreas

> **Difficulties:** Whymper Couloir (best with a generous snow cover in early summer) AD. The difficulties depend on conditions. This is a large-scale, snow and ice route with sections of 55° and an average inclination of 48°. In lean conditions the ice climbing can be very hard at the rimaye (on descent this is often problematic with a big jump or awkward abseil manouevres). A well-established line of steps can make a considerable difference to the speed of ascent. Moine Ridge (preferably when very dry) AD. Some mixed climbing, with rock-climbing sustained at II with passages of III.
> **Effort:** The mountain railway speeds the ascent to Montenvers. From there hut climb 900mH (3–4 hrs), summit climb 1450mH (6–9 hrs from hut).
> **Dangers:** On the generally easy Mer de Glace take care on the access ice ribs above Montenvers and also be cautious when crossing the broad melt water gullies. On the Glacier de Talèfre, especially on the upper part, beware of crevasses. On the summit ridge watch carefully for cornices. The Whymper Couloir faces south and in good weather warms up correspondingly quickly, thus a very early departure and rapid completion of the climb is essential before the snow becomes rotten and the stones begin to fall. When the ice is very bare, the danger of stone-fall increases and then the less dangerous Moine Ridge is preferable. By either route the ascent of the mountain is a serious undertaking not to be underestimated.
> **Pleasures:** All climbs on the Verte are big, high alpine undertakings.

Maurer. The long ascent over the Montets Ridge was made in 1925 by Pierre Dalloz, Jacques Lagarde and Henri de Ségogne. The gigantic (1100m) Couturier Couloir was climbed in 1929 by Georges Charlet, A. Couttet and André Devassoux with the American Bradford Washburn by a devious line that was straightened three years later by Marcel Couturier with Armand Charlet and Jules Simond. Charlet, with his client D. Platanov, also claimed the high and icy North-West or Nant Blanc Face in 1935. The ESE Ridge over the Aiguille du Jardin and Grande Rocheuse was first traversed in 1904 by Emile Fontaine with Jean Ravanel and Léon Tournier. The West Ridge fell in 1926 to Armand Charlet and M. Bozon with Mlle G. de Longchamp.
Map: IGN 3630 OT 1:25,000, *Massif du Mont Blanc*.
Travel: By rail or car to Chamonix (1030m; a bustling, cosmo-politan, tourist resort with all conceivable attractions. Also a

Looking steeply up the Talefrè Glacier to the Aiguille Verte. The Whymper Couloir slants up to the summit from the right with Grande Rocheuse above it. Further right are Aiguille du Jardin and Col de l'Aiguille Verte. The Moine Ridge is the left skyline.

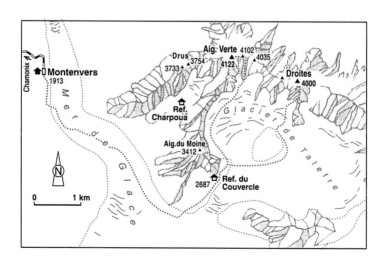

focal point for international mountaineers who gather to tackle the great routes. The Bureau des Hautes Montagnes offers a comprehensive information service about routes and weather conditions, ENSA (Ecole Nationale de Ski et d'Alpinisme), campsites to suit all purses but always packed as are car-parks, saloons, mountain railways, huts, water sports centres. The Mont Blanc Tunnel, closed for three years after a fire, is now reopened to both cars and trucks but with long waits at busy periods.

Hut climb: From Chamonix take the rack railway or nearby footpaths to Montenvers (1876m). Descend southwards (finally using ladders over ice-polished slabs) to reach the Mer de Glace. Ascend at first on the western edge, then move up to the middle of the glacier for about 3km. At the junction with the Leschaux Glacier, turn left and work across to the north bank. After traversing the debris-covered ice sections and moraines (coloured barrel markers) gain and climb a series of iron ladders that ascend the cliffs on the left (north). Follow the rising path, high above the ice-fall of the Glacier de Talèfre, over grass and moraine to the Couvercle Hut, at the foot of the Aiguille du Moine. (2687m, CAF Paris, 30 + 120 B, self-service room, managed in summer, Tel. 450-531694. Just above the new hut the old hut is built on the historic bivouac site under a huge roofing slab.)

Summit climbs: From the Couvercle Hut take the path over the moraines to the western edge of the Glacier de Talèfre. Climb the glacier in a wide arc under the rock walls of the Aiguille du Moine and the connecting pinnacled ridge, to the foot of the Aiguille Verte (2 hrs). There are now two possibilities:

To reach the Whymper Couloir ascend to the uppermost part of the glacier. The couloir descends from the notch on the ridge between the Aiguille Verte and Grande Rocheuse. Cross the rimaye on the right under the rocks of the Grande Rocheuse and first of all ascend a small parallel couloir. Then move left on to a rocky ridge and further above traverse to a side branch of the main couloir. Cross this too and then ascend a rock rib on the right (eastern) side of the main couloir. Where this runs out, move obliquely left and go directly up to the saddle in front of the Grande Rocheuse or continue left up mixed ground to the East Ridge which leads (cornices!) to the summit.

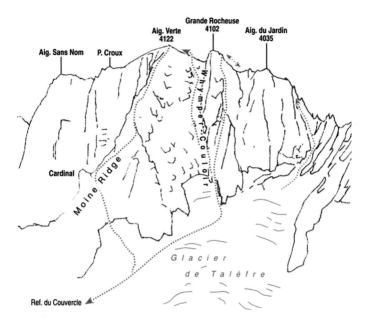

For the Moine Ridge, turn left at 3350m, before reaching the Aiguille Verte, and cross the rimaye below a conspicious, right-slanting, snow couloir at the back of a bay, right of the prominent rock pinnacle of The Cardinal. From the foot of the couloir move up ledges, heading up for about 200m to the notch between the Cardinal and Aiguille Verte (3600m). On the ridge turn back in the direction of the Aiguille Verte. First keeping right, zig-zag up ledges and go up to the small notch of an adjacent ridge (by a five-metre gendarme at the upper end of the couloir mentioned earlier). Continue up the adjacent ridge and after that ascend obliquely right over slabs and snow patches until one can see into the Whymper Couloir. Now climb directly back to the ridge, first up a chimney/gully then zig-zagging over slabs to reach the ridge by a less assertive gendarme. Go up on the right (east) of the ridge, turning a final tower on the east, to the summit.

View: A magnificent vantage point for studying the Chamonix Aiguilles and beyond the great snowy bulk of Mont Blanc. To the south the Grandes Jorasses and the Dent du Geant catch the eye and to the north-east the Aiguille du Chardonnet and the Aiguille du Argentiere and beyond them the great peaks of Switzerland

Descent: If the snow in the Whymper Couloir is already dangerous, the objectively safer South Spur of the Grande Rocheuse might be considered. This is, nevertheless, very steep and, without local knowledge or a track, will be difficult to locate. One can of course descend the Moine Ridge. If the couloir is still preferred, it is best to wait until the evening to descend on hardening snow (some abseil points are installed).

Adjacent peaks: On the West Ridge the Pointe Croux (4023m) is an insignificant gendarme which can be reached from the summit with a descent and re-ascent in about an hour. Beyond that is the Aiguille Sans Nom (3982m), a sort of buttress summit. Strictly speaking, the Grande Rocheuse and Aiguille du Jardin (col depths 70m and 37m) are the eastern fore-summits of the Aiguille Verte but both are considered independent 4000ers.

Other worthwhile routes: *North-West Ridge* or *Arête des Grands Montets* (D, rock-climbing to IV, mixed, long and high, finally with snow or ice to 50°, 900mH and c.1.7km length, 8–12 hrs from Grands Montets téléphérique.

East-South-East or *Jardin Ridge* (D, a long ridge climb that crosses both Aiguille du Jardin and Grande Rocheuse with two pitches IV, 10–14 hrs from the Couvercle Hut).

North-East Face or *Couturier Couloir* (D, major ice route, 55°, it is rare for the whole couloir to be in good condition – the summit slopes can have slab avalanche risks even in summer, 1100mH, 4–7 hrs from rimaye, 6–9 hrs from Argentière Hut).

North-West or *Nant Blanc Face* (D+, a sustained mixed climb on rock to IV and ice to 55°, 950mH from the rimaye, 8–10 hrs).

West or *Sans Nom Ridge* (D+, climbing to IV, mostly mixed, an especially beautiful and very long route, 10–12 hrs from the Charpoua Hut).

Guidebook: *Mont Blanc Massif*, Vol. II (Alpine Club, 1990).

Grande Rocheuse 4102m

The prominent ridge summit east of the Aiguille Verte but only separated by a col depth of about 70 metres. The summit can be taken in during a Whymper Couloir ascent with about an hour's extra effort. The alternative is the adjacent and less dangerous South Pillar (a useful route to know as it can also serve as a descent from the Aiguille Verte). The peak was first climbed in September 1865 by Robert Fowler with Michel Ducroz and Michel Balmat starting up the Whymper Couloir and then taking South Pillar which led them to the summit *en route* to the Aiguille Verte.

> **Difficulties:** AD. Pitches of III, but mostly II.
> **Effort:** Hut climb and summit climb, see Aiguille Verte.
> **Dangers:** See Aiguille Verte, but the stone-fall danger is only on the lower section of the route.
> **Pleasures:** A summit to take in on the way to Aiguille Verte.

Maps, sketches, travel, hut climb: See Aiguille Verte.
Summit climb by the South Pillar: Begin as for the Whymper Couloir as far as the upper end of the rock rib left of the initial couloir. Now cross the adjacent couloir on the right and go straight up the rocks of the pillar to a gendarme (3820m). Pass this on the left (west) and 150m higher, turn a second gendarme on the right and follow the ridge of the pillar to the steep summit wall. Keeping left at first, climb chimneys and then move more to the right and go up to the summit ridge about 50m east of the main summit.

Aiguille du Jardin 4035m

This is the broader ridge summit south-east of the Grande Rocheuse and separated from it by the Col Armand Charlet. The first ascent of this pinnacle, which rises only 40m above the col, was made in 1904 by Emile Fontaine with Jean Ravanel and Léon Tournier during an ascent of the Jardin Ridge to the Aiguille Verte. In 1932 when the peak was climbed solo by the seventy-two year old Karl Blodig, via the steep (up to 54°) North-East Couloir.

Blodig was protecting his claim as the first to have climbed 'all' the 4000m peaks, and thus had to 'bag' these newly hailed summits.

Difficulties: D. Several passages IV, mostly III and II. A large-scale, high alpine ridge-traverse with some route-finding difficulties.
Effort: From the Couvercle Hut a climb of 1400mH with a complicated line.
Dangers: A long climb over glacier followed by a rock ascent (unstable in places).
Pleasures: One of the oddest 4000s for the obsessive peak bagger.

Maps, sketches, travel, hut climb: See Aiguille Verte.
Summit route: As for Whymper Couloir as far as under the face. Now traverse under the Grande Rocheuse and Aiguille du Jardin and then climb the right-flanking rib (east) of the snow gully that leads up to the Col de l'Aiguille Verte (3796m), or follow the gully itself if conditions are suitable. At three-quarters height, cross the snow gully to the left to a broad rock gully. Go up this keeping left (I) and continue parallel to the East Ridge. The gully then steepens to a rotten chimney (IV). This leads to a gendarme on a ridge rib further left. Climb the firm rock of this rib (III and IV), keeping left higher up, to the main ridge. This whole exercise allows one to turn the difficult lower towers of the East Ridge. Now, keeping to the edge, go up an exposed buttress then a less steep section to a snow shoulder. From there it is a short distance to the summit.
Adjacent peaks: On the short North-West Ridge is the gendarme Pointe Éveline (4026m). There is also a small gendarme of 4015m standing 17m above the Col Armand Charlet.

Les Droites 4000m

A broad wedge of rock and ice which reaches 4000m exactly at its East Summit. It is well-known for its fierce North Face, falling to the Argentière basin, which has a row of the most extreme mixed routes in the Alps. The first ascent of the East Summit was made in 1876 by Henri Cordier, Thomas Middlemore, John Oakley Maund with Johann Jaun and Andreas Maurer. The almost endless climbing on the 2000-metre North-East spur was done in 1937 by Charles Authenac and Ferdinand Tournier, and straightened in 1946 by André Contamine, Louis Lachenal, Pierre Leroux and Lionel Terray. The notoriously steep, mixed North Face, with ice to over 70°, was first conquered in 1955 by Philippe Corneau and Maurice Davaille with five bivouacs. Its reputation for fierce difficulty has subsequently been reduced a little by rapidly improved ice gear and a string of daring solo ascents, but it still remains an exacting and serious expedition.

Difficulties: AD. Climbing to III, mixed, often with an awkward rimaye.
Effort: From the Couvercle Hut a 700mH approach and 600mH of climbing (6–7 hrs from the hut to the summit).
Dangers: Observe all precautions, although the approach is short, the glacier and rimaye can be awful. The rock is brittle in places.
Pleasures: Very untouched, fierce surroundings.

Maps, sketches, travel, hut climb: See Aiguille Verte.
Summit climb by the South Ridge of the East Peak: From the Couvercle Hut go north-east over the Glacier de Talèfre, to pass the moraine island 'Jardin de Talèfre' on its west side (also possible on the east side). The South Ridge of the East Peak lies east of the upper end of the 'Jardin'. The lower, ridge-like part is avoided on its west side. After overcoming the rimaye climb a dièdre-like snow couloir on the flank, or by the rocks on its right boundary. After reaching the knife-edge of the spur, continue up an easy rock ridge to a steep wall. Climb this near the ridge over steps to reach a steep snow-field. Work up and across this (left) and finish by a snow ridge which leads to the summit ridge a little to the east of the highest point.
View: To the south-west is Mont Blanc and the pinnacled ridges of the Chamonix Aiguilles. Nearby, to the west is Aiguille Verte and its satellites. To the south the Jorasses dominate and below and to the east the Argentière basin, famed for its fine ice routes.
Adjacent peaks: The West Summit (3994m) is 500m away.
Other worthwhile routes: *Traverse to the West Summit* (AD, III, mixed, 4–5 hrs).
North-East Spur (TD+, VI, V+ and V, one of the finest mixed climbs in the Alps, 1200mH, c.2000m of climbing, 12–20 hrs).

The North Face of the Grandes Jorasses from the Talefrè Glacier.

Grandes Jorasses:
Pointe Walker 4208m

This majestic ridge crest east of the bulky Mont Blanc massif though not of such great height, surpasses it in its northern and western aspects, with its wildness and elegance. The south side, though not elegant, is certainly wild, being defended by disrupted glaciers and thrusting bastions of distorted rock. The ultimate in remoteness is surely the gigantic slab triangle of the East Face dominating the wildly crevassed Frébouze Glacier. The showpiece of the whole Mont Blanc range remains the huge granite wall on the north side with its slender buttresses. The greatest of these is the Walker Spur, the highest and most unbroken buttress on the face. It ends directly at the highest point and offers the most ideal extreme route in the Alps, continuously difficult, without escape possibilities, but with comparatively few objective dangers in good weather. Its fine position and its sustained unspoiled climbing, high above the Leschaux Glacier completes the aura of a great classic climb set far from the bustle of civilization.

Even the easiest climb on the Grandes Jorasses is a demanding

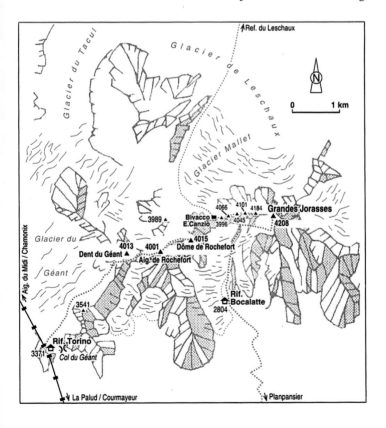

undertaking. It was mastered in 1865 (a few weeks before the Matterhorn tragedy) by Edward Whymper with Michel Croz, Christian Almer and Franz Biener. They climbed the lower Pointe Whymper because their ascent was made principally to gain the ridge to view the Aiguille Verte. The highest point was reached three years later by Horace Walker with Melchior Anderegg, Johann Jaun and Julien Grange by the Normal Route.

The North-East (Hirondelles) Ridge was first explored in 1911 when H.O. Jones and Geoffrey Winthrop Young with Joseph Knubel and Laurent Croux descended it as a preliminary to their plan to traverse the whole ridge. It was first ascended in 1927 by a big Italian party led by Adolphe Rey and Alphonse Chenoz. The South-East Ridge (Tronchey Arête), which leads from the valley slopes in a long line of steps and towers, was first climbed directly in 1936 by Titta Gilberti and Elisio Croux.

The epic attempts to conquer the North Face fill the alpine history books. It was first climbed in 1935 (after some forty attempts by various parties) by Rudolf Peters and Martin Meier who followed the Croz Spur in the middle of the face. The first ascent of the Walker Spur was made by Riccardo Cassin, Gino Esposito and Ugo Tizzoni in 1938. Although many more difficult routes have since been added to this great face none improved on the Walker Spur in terms of climbing quality, line and scale.

Maps: IGN 3630 OT 1:25,000, *Massif du Mont Blanc*.

Travel: By rail to the Aosta valley at Pré-St Didier. From there, 5km by bus to Courmayeur (1264m; the principal town on the south side of Mont Blanc, with all amenities, or on the north side through the Arve valley to Chamonix. From there by bus or car through the Mont Blanc tunnel to Entrèves (1306m, 2.5km from Courmayeur) and then by bus or car north-eastwards up the Val

---

Difficulties: AD–. Predominantly ice, to 45°, in part rock to II.

Effort: Hut climb 1200mH (4 hrs), summit climb 1400mH (6–7 hrs).

Dangers: In the snow basin before the summit block, there is danger of avalanches and falling ice (recently several parties were wiped out by a sérac fall at this point). Otherwise take the customary precautions against crevasses and watch out for big cornices on the summit ridge.

Pleasures: One of the great alpine peaks, steeped in historic associations.

Dent du Géant, the Rochefort Ridge and the Grandes Jorasses – with the glacier basin of the Normal Route obvious below Pointe Walker.

Ferret 3.5 km to Planpincieux (or, Planpansier, 1579m, camping). **Hut climb:** Take the path starting left of the church and head northwards up through sparse woods and over grassy slopes to the edge of the Torrent de Marguera gorge. Go along the gorge to a rock wall and at its foot, cross right over the stream. After that climb a steep, rugged rock rib and gully to the upper end of the steep step. Now go up less steep slopes to the moraine between Glacier de Planpancieux (west) and Glacier des Grandes Jorasses (east). Climb the moraine ridge and higher up go left and over a slabby step (II, chains, ladders) obliquely up to the Grandes Jorasses Hut (Rifugio Boccalatte), hung on the rocks above the Glacier de Planpincieux (2804m, CAI Torino, 30 B, managed: mid-July – end of August, ask in valley about current condition). **Summit climb from the south:** From the hut go up over debris and snow to the rock ridge which separates Glacier Planpincieux and the Glacier des Grandes Jorasses. Ascend snow on the left (north) under these rocks (on the eastern edge of the Glacier de Planpincieux). From the upper end of the rock ridge, keeping somewhat left (north) go up the very crevassed glacier, for about 300m to the lower end of the Rocher du Reposoir (1½ hrs from the hut) a spur of Pointe Hélène. Climb the ridge on good holds (II and some III), usually exactly on its knife-edge, to its upper end – 3 hrs from the hut. Now cross the steep glacier arm to the right (often threatened by avalanches in new snow or rotten afternoon snow) to the broad rock rib which descends from Pointe Whymper. Climb this, keeping left of the wildly disrupted Jorasses Glacier, up a sort of gully until one can traverse right into the flat glacier trough. Traverse swiftly east (ice cliffs above and ice debris in the trough emphasise the urgency). Move up the snow slope right of the ice cliffs and finally gain the ridge (keeping a respectful distance from the cornices overhanging to the right!) which leads directly to the summit of Pointe Walker.

Alternative finishes: After crossing the glacier arm, one can continue directly up the rib to Pointe Whymper and from there reach the highest point by the summit ridge. Though objectively safer and easier to find, this way is more difficult but takes about the same time. On balance it is best reserved for the descent.

From the top of the Rocher du Reposoir a direct ascent can be made (AD snow and mixed) to the summit ridge at Pointe Hélène or Pointe Croz (new UIAA summits – a fast party might also take in Pointe Marguérite) and then head east along the summit ridge to Pointes Whymper and Walker.

View: The view to the west, over the Dôme de Rochefort and Dent du Géant, is dominated by Mont Blanc. The Chamonix Aiguilles are stretched out to the north-west with the Aiguille Verte massif further to the right. To the north-east are the lower Petites Jorasses and Aiguille de Leschaux, Mont Gruetta, and Mont Dolent and in the far distance the Grand Combin. Gran Paradiso and the Grivola are the most prominent peaks to the south-west.

Other worthwhile routes: *Hirondelles Ridge* (D+, IV with a pitch of V, 750mH, 6–10 hrs from the Col des Hirondelles).

Tronchey Arête (TD, sustained at IV with pitches of V in the upper part, 1600m long plus 1100mH, 10–12 hrs from Jacchia Bivouac).

Walker Spur (ED, VI, V+ and V, seldom easier than IV, in part mixed, ice to 55°–60°, 1200mH, 14–18 hrs from the rimaye).

Croz Spur (TD+, pitches of V+ but mostly IV and III, mixed, ice to 60°, 1100mH, 13–16 hrs from foot of face).
East Face (ED, sections of VI and V with pitches of A1, on compact rock, 12–14 hrs from the Col des Hirondelles).
Guidebook: *Mont Blanc Massif*, Vol. 1 (Alpine Club, 1990).

Pointe Whymper 4184m

Now a UIAA summit, this is easily taken in during the descent by a crossing from Pointe Walker (30 mins., beware of cornices!)

Pointe Croz 4101m

With a 20m col depth this barely passes muster as a UIAA summit. It was climbed in 1909 by a route up the South Face (a variant on the Abruzzi route) by the German quartet of Fräulein Eleonore Hasenclever, Wilhelm Klemm, Felix König and Richard Weitzenboch, though it may have been reached during earlier ridge traverse explorations. It can be reached from Pointe Whymper by an AD climb taking 1–2 hrs (see 'alternative finishes' opposite).

Pointe Hélène 4045m
Pointe Marguérite 4066m

These peaks were first climbed in 1898 by the Duke of the Abruzzi with Joseph Ollier, Laurent Croux and Cesar and Felix Ollier taking a route up the South Face from the Rocher du Reposoir. The peaks were named after the Duchesses of Abruzzi and Aosta.

If already on the ridge, Pointe Hélène, the next peak west of Pointe Croz can be gained from there in a 1–2 hr round trip (AD) but if continuing to Pointe Marguérita there is hard exposed climbing along a sharp rock ridge (III and IV) – 2 hrs more.

Pointe Young (3996m), the final West Ridge peak was first climbed from the Col du Grandes Jorasses in 1904 by Valentine Ryan with Franz and Josef Lochmatter.

The Grandes Jorasses Traverse

Although the additional peaks can be reached from the Normal Route they are more elegantly attained in the process of a complete ridge traverse – one of the great classic undertakings in the Alps.

To get you into the right mood for this you should read Geoffrey Winthrop Young's lyrical account of the exploration of this dramatic ridge. There is a choice of strategies the one described being a northerly approach from the Leschaux Hut and a descent into Italy. Another way is from the Torino Hut along the Rochefort Ridge with a steep descent to the Col des Grandes Jorasses. The West Ridge then leads to Pointe Walker with a possible descent by the Hirondelles Ridge to add extra challenge. Whichever combination is chosen settled weather is essential.

Grade: D. Rock up to IV+ and IV, to a large extent also III and II. Also ice on the approach up to 55°.

Effort: Ascent to the Refuge Leschaux 650mH (3 hrs), ascent to the Bivacco Canzio 1400mH (6 hrs), ridge to the Pointe Walker 400mH with a ridge length of 1500m (8 hrs). Descent from there 1400mH (4 hrs) as far as the hut and another 1300mH (3 hrs) into the valley.

Dangers: The approach via the Mallet glacier with plenty of crevasses and an awkward rimaye. The cliffs above the bivouac hut can be icy in the early morning and on the ridge itself temperature changes can be problematic.

Highlights: Terrific high alpine ambiance on a complex route.

Access, maps: See Aiguille Verte, p.171.

Approach to the Leschaux Hut and the Canzio Bivouac: Take the Aiguille Verte approach by the Mer de Glace. Where the Couvercle path heads left, continue east on the Leschaux glacier and then over moraine and glacial striations northwards for about 100mH up to the Refuge Leschaux (2431m, staffed in summer, 15 B, usually overcrowded in good weather).

Cross the Leschaux Glacier and ascend near to the western edge of the heavily crevassed Mont Mallet Glacier, and at the top go below the jagged ridge of the Périades. Eventually move up to

The western summits of Grandes Jorasses from Dôme de Rochefort with Pts Young and Marguérite prominent. Col des Grandes Jorasses is below the slabby lower rocks of Pointe Young.

the left below the flank of the Calotte de Rochefort and over a steep ice slope (rimaye often difficult) to the Col des Grandes Jorasses and the Canzio Bivouac Hut on its eastern side (3825m, 10B). This final section of the approach is AD and serious.

Traverse – Col des Grandes Jorasses to Pointe Walker: Above the col is a triangular north-west facing rock wall. Climb rocks on the left of an obvious couloir/depression on the right of the wall (leading to the right-hand ridge). After 20m go left along a slanting ramp (30m) to a snow ledge on the North Face. Continue 25m left up cracks (often icy) and move round to the right of an overhanging block and then move directly up to the summit of **Pointe Young** (sustained IV, 2 hrs from the col, the face may be cold and icy with the difficulties accumulating as height is gained). Descend on the north flank to a ledge above a notch. Descend or abseil 30m on the right-flanking (west) rocks of a couloir/gorge (III) which is then crossed to reach and traverse the slabby buttress beyond by a hand traverse along a horizontal finger crack (IV+). Go up a crack to another couloir which is followed for 20m until rocks on the right lead up to the twin summits of **Pointe Marguérite** (2 hrs from Pointe Young). Continue along the knife-edged rock ridge down to the notch, then up to **Pointe Hélène** and after passing the ridge towers continue to the less prominent **Pointe Croz**. A snow ridge leads to **Pointe Whymper** and further snow climbing soon gains **Pointe Walker** (8 hrs from Col des Grandes Jorasses). If not descending the Hirondelles Ridge it is best to return to Pointe Whymper and go south down the Whymper Rib (III, II). Cross below the right-hand (western) glacier arm to the Rocher du Reposoir. From their foot trend left down and across the glacier to the Grandes Jorasses hut (3–4 hrs).

Dôme de Rochefort 4015m
Aiguille de Rochefort 4001m

These peaks are linked by an elegant snow ridge. Narrow and exposed, it is impressively decorated with baroque scroll work of cornices, and offers a range of fascinating views. The first ascent of the Aiguille de Rochefort was made in 1873, that of the Dôme de Rochefort eight years later, both by James Eccles with the Michel-Clement and Alphonse Payot.

Their ascents were made via the very crevassed Mont Mallet Glacier and then up the rather monotonous North Face. Today's Normal Route, along the West Ridge from the Dent du Géant, was first carried out in 1900 by Ettore Allegra with Laurent Croux, Pierre Dayné and Alexis Brocherel (in descent from the Aiguille), and in ascent with the continuation to the Dôme de Rochefort by Karl Blodig and Max Horten in 1903.

Maps, sketches, travel: See Grandes Jorasses p.181.

Hut climb: The concrete stairs up the tunnel from the téléphérique station to the Torino Hut (3371m, CAI Torino & Aosta, 170B, hotel and self-service restaurant from May – end of September Tel. 0039 0165-844034, from France Tel. 0039 0165-846484). To avoid an overnight stay one can start – at an unfavourably late hour – from the Pointe Helbronner, 3462m.

Summit Route by the Rochefort Ridge: From the hut cross to the Col du Géant (3365m, crevasses) and head north-eastwards round the rock spur of the Aiguilles Marbrées into the wide snow basin under the Col de Rochefort. Pass this col and continue in the same direction up to the base of the prominent Aiguille du Géant. First ascend on easy rocks on the left of a small snow

Difficulties: AD. Snow or ice to 50°, with some climbing to II and I.
Effort: The climb to the Torino Hut involves a mere 50mH from the téléphérique station or, on foot, a punishing 2000mH up a dilapidated path. The summit climb to Aiguille is 1050mH (4–6 hrs from the Torino Hut), to the Dôme a further 250mH (2 hrs from the Aiguille). As the ridge is level the return may take longer in deteriorating snow.
Dangers: On the Glacier du Géant there are some open crevasses. On the ridge there are many cornices, in some sections overlapping. The worn track doesn't always take the safest line circumspection is required – do not be misled by romantic postcards of figures on the crest ignoring all the rules about likely fracture lines. Also care is necessary (later in the day) on the descent to the Glacier du Géant, a south-west facing mixed slope that has been the scene of several fatal accidents.
Pleasures: To climb this ridge in the morning sun is one of life's perfect experiences. In a pristine (untracked) state it looks like a piece of scenery shortly after the creation of the world.

On the Rochefort Ridge

couloir to gain an adjacent ridge with a gendarme. From this, move across and climb on the right of the couloir, up to the broad main ridge. Move up the ridge, turning a gendarme on the right (east), to approach the Salle à Manger (breakfast place) below the South Face of the Géant (2–3 hrs from the hut).

Before reaching this, turn right and, staying on the narrow ridge (or, less satisfactory, below on the right on the rock), cross the intermediate summit P.3933 and descend steeply on the other side. Continue along the sharp snow ridge to the rocky summit block of the Aiguille de Rochefort. Traverse right to a not very prominent gully. Climb this – steeply and on somewhat unstable rock, but with good holds – to gain the summit.

Make a rapid descent to the north-east to the broad saddle south-east of Mont Mallet (3989m) and go over a snow top. After that, pass the Doigt de Rochefort on the left (north-west) and keeping on the ridge reach the rocky summit block and gain the Dôme de Rochefort.

View: To the west the Dent du Géant, passed on the ascent, dominates the scene, and behind it is Mont Blanc. To the east is the adjacent Grandes Jorasses. The Chamonix Aiguilles are to the north-west and opposite them, on the other side of the Mer de Glace, the Drus and the Aiguille Verte. In the foreground, looking north-east the pinnacled ridge of the Périades descends to the Leschaux Glacier.

Adjacent peaks: Mont Mallet (3989m) can be incorporated

into the expedition by an ascent from the saddle behind the Aiguille (III), and gives a good view down to the Mer de Glace. The Calotte de Rochefort (3974m), east of the Dôme, is climbed by those heading for the Col des Grandes Jorasses.

Other worthwhile routes: *North Face* (PD, dependent on the glacier conditions, preferably done in descent, so that one can abseil over an awkward rimaye – take a wooden stake).

The Grandes Jorasses Traverse: (D, a long, large-scale mixed route, with sections of IV; Col du Géant to Col des Jorasses/Canzio Bivouac 6–7 hrs, continuation to Pointe Walker 6–8 hrs, see p.185, descent to Col des Hirondelles 5–6 hrs – only recommended in really settled weather. The descent from the Col on the French side is by a series of abseils down a rocky rib with fixed anchors to gain the Leschuaux Glacier in 1½ hrs).

Dent du Géant 4013m

The Giant's Tooth – one of the most recognisable of all alpine pinnacles standing proudly above Courmeyeur, the steep rock obelisk defining the western end of the Rochefort Ridge. Despite the many fixed ropes on the final section the climbing is impressively exposed giving this ascent a very exciting quality.

After the failure of such notable climbers as Alexander Burgener, Alfred Mummery and others, even rockets were used in an attempt to shoot a rope over the summit as a climbing aid. In 1882, after eleven years of trying, Pointe Sella, 4009m was reached with massive use of artificial aids by Jean-Joseph, Baptiste and Daniel Maquignaz guiding Alessandro, Alfonso, Corradino and Gaudenzio Sella. The first ascent followed some weeks later when Pointe Graham, 4013m was gained by William Woodman Graham, Alphonse Payot and Auguste Cupelin, Graham leading the final section. They climbed the slabs properly by a different line without using the fixed ropes which they encountered (and used) higher up. The first unaided ascent was made in 1900 by the Austrians Heinrich Pfannl, Thomas

Grandes Jorasses, the Rochefort Ridge and Dent du Géant at sunset.

> **Difficulties:** AD. Climbing to III and with aid (strenuous and ungainly) from thick fixed ropes which is difficult if the ropes are iced up. It is worth taking tape slings for belaying on the ropes and their huge anchor pegs.
> **Effort:** Ascent to the Salle à Manger 550mH (2–3 hrs), summit block 180mH (1–2 hrs), 4–6 hrs from the Torino Hut.
> **Dangers:** Objectively a very safe route, but beware of storms and deteriorating snow conditions on the descent to the Glacier du Géant.
> **Pleasures:** The pleasures would be untrammelled if the junk of the fixed ropes were dismantled and one could just enjoy the excellent rock.

Maischberger and Franz Zimmer who climbed the (usually iced) North Ridge. In 1935, the short but steep South Face was climbed (with many pitons) by Herbert Burggasser and Rudolf Leitz. There are many that think it would now be correct for the ropes to be removed so the Dent du Géant can assume its true stature as one of the hardest alpine 4000m peaks.

Maps, travel, hut climb: See Aiguille de Rochefort p188.

Summit climb by the South-West Face: From the Torino Hut follow the Aiguille de Rochefort route to the Salle á Manger. Descend a little and traverse mixed ground to the left to the south-west edge. On a detached slab move left to the edge and up it a few metres to a piton. Then traverse 10m left to a shallow gully (peg) and climb it for 30m to a terrace. Climb the 'Plaque Burgener' the beautiful gold-brown slabs which are sadly disfigured by thick hemp ropes. These lead to a good stance on the left (west) edge. Now traverse right and climb two chimneys (peg, ropes). Continue up walls and polished steps to Pointe Sella. Descend a chimney on the north-west (exposed) and from the notch climb a crack to the top of Pointe Graham.

View: On all sides this is extraordinarily impressive, like looking from a balloon gondola. The Rochefort Ridge is close below. Across the Glacier du Géant and Vallée Blanche are the rock spurs of Mont Blanc du Tacul and beyond them the overpowering bulk of Mont Blanc.

Other worthwhile routes: *North Ridge/North-West Face* (D, IV and III, 280mH, 3 hrs from start of climb).
South Face (TD, V, A1, at least VI if done free, 160mH, 3 hrs).
Guidebook: *Mont Blanc Massif*, Vol 2 (Alpine Club, 1991).

Mont Blanc Massif

The highest mountain in the Alps is – like the second highest, Monte Rosa – a range in itself. The ridges radiating from the summit carry proud mountain forms which only through their proximity to the monarch are made satellites. Have no illusions about their immense scale and height, a factor reinforced by the lack of easy escape routes should the weather threaten.

Mont Blanc du Tacul 4248m

A broad snow trapezium, Mont Blanc du Tacul forms the lowest step of a gigantic staircase to the summit of the Alps. One can admire it, yet, because of the milling crowds and swarming throng also loath it. The terrace of Aiguille du Midi is full to bursting with people who having packed the cable cars to come up and then hang around for hours, without going out, waiting

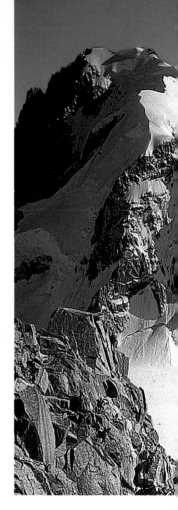

Mont Blanc du Tacul's North Face seen from the Brevent, with Mont Maudit and Mont Blanc on the right. Glacier changes have forced the Normal route to the steeper left slopes in recent years.

for the journey down. Heretical thoughts come to one here and still more on the way over to the glacier under the buzz of the gondolas of the téléphérique to Pte. Helbronner that has been hit by jet fighters. This cableway is a grotesque intrusion into the heart of the wild Mont Blanc Massif and should be removed.

The official first ascent took place on 8 August, 1855 when Rev. Charles Hudson broke away from a party returning from a Mont Blanc attempt to reach the top. During previous years there had been several forays hereabouts so others may have preceded Hudson in what is a modest diversion above the passage towards Mont Blanc.

Difficulties: PD. A glacier ascent with snow or ice to 40° though, of late, steeper ground further left has been taken to turn wider crevasses.
Effort: Using the almost irresistible téléphérique to the Aiguille du Midi, the approach consists of merely a 300mH descent to the Col du Midi and then a 730mH ascent (3 hrs).
Dangers: The lower part of the glacier is threatened by infrequent but unpredicable sérac avalanches. The face is also prone to avalanche after new snow. Rope up at all times on the glacier, even if many people don't. Time and again this catches audacious climbers making ascents at the end of the season. In bad visibility navigating can be difficult on the Col du Midi.
Pleasures: Impressive glacier scenery.

Amongst the fine climbs on the eastern flank is the pinnacled Diable Ridge linking the Grand Capucin to the summit (see next section). The Gervasutti Couloir (55°) was first climbed in 1929 by the Italians P. Filippi, Piero Ghiglione and Francesco Ravelli, and more directly in 1934 by Giusto Gervasutti and Renato Chabod. In 1936 Gabriele Boccalatte and Nina Pietrasanta managed (in one day!) the first ascent of the longest buttress. In the struggle for the harder twin buttress Gervasutti died in an abseiling accident. When his compatriots Piero Fornelli and Giovanni Mauro completed the route in 1951, they found his ice-axe and named the buttress after him. The lower, ice-encrusted (70°), rock triangle of the North Face was climbed in 1963 by André Contamine and Pierre Mazeaud. The development of ice technique in the early 1970s led to the ascent of the almost vertical (400m) 'Supercouloir' over three days in 1973 by Patrick Gabarrou and Jean-Marc Boivin.

Maps and travel: See Aig. Verte (p.170) and Mont Blanc (p.204).

Hut climb: This is a descent because the téléphérique distorts the situation. The Cosmiques Hut which used to stand on the Col du Midi and was burned down, is now rebuilt with 120 B. Bivouacing in the Midi station (3800m) is always refused.

Summit climb by the North-West Face: From the station, tramp through the tunnel and move out on to the slippery and exposed East Ridge. Descend this until it becomes flatter and then head south down and across to the level Col du Midi (3532m).

Go up the slopes to the west of the steep rock and ice triangle of the North Face, over usually snow-clogged rimayes (later in the season they are often open) and, keeping right, climb steeply up to a snow shoulder (Epaule du Mt. Blanc du Tacul, c.4060m). Now move left (east) up the broad ridge to the summit.

View: To the north is the much ravaged Aiguille du Midi, teeming with people and reminiscent of a bee-hive. To the south-west are the steep glacier flanks of Mont Maudit, the next step in the gigantic staircase to Mont Blanc. To the east across the Glacier du Géant, the Dent du Géant and Grandes Jorasses catch the eye. And to the south-east beyond the pinnacles of the Diable Ridge is the Tour Ronde.

Adjacent peaks: The East Summit (4247m) is reached with a short descent. Other than the newly ratified UIAA (difficult to attain) summits of the Diable Ridge there is also the Pilier du Diable (described opposite). The sheer/vertiginous Tour Rouge (about 4100m) is only possible in conjunction with an ascent of the Gervasutti Pillar.

Other worthwhile routes: *Central (Boccalatte) Pillar* (D+, in good conditions on the easiest line V, IV and III, but in snow and ice it is far harder, 800mH, 5–8 hrs from foot of face).

Gervasutti Pillar (ED, VI and V with pitches of A1. A fine climb on superb rock with escape possibilities higher up, 800mH, 8–12 hrs from foot of face).

Guidebook: *Mont Blanc Massif,* Vol 1 (Alpine Club, 1990).

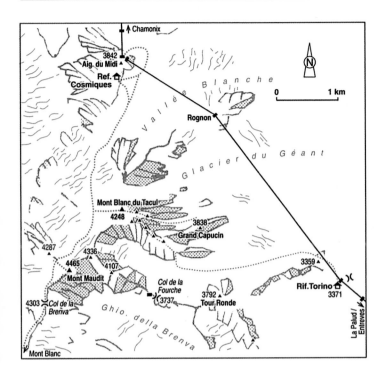

Pilier du Diable 4067m

This pinnacle at the top of one of the lesser spurs of Mont Blanc du Tacul's North-East Face presents a real problem for the UIAA (and was therefore left off the 1994 list). Yet it fulfils all the conditions with its exactly measured 40m col depth, its demanding ascent route and of course its dramatic ambiance. The difficulty is that it clearly edges beyond the classical standards associated with 4000m peak-collecting which had hitherto not exceeded the *Difficile* grade. Even if you try to reach it by abseiling from the summit of Mont Blanc du Tacul it will still be a complicated undertaking.

But this summit cannot logically be disregarded and its ascent will thus present a real challenge to mountaineers. The adjoining

Couloir du Diable was climbed in 1930 but it was not until 13 August 1963 that the Pilier itself was climbed by the Italian team of Enrico Cavalieri, Pier-Giorgio Ravaioni and Eugenio and Gian-Luigi Vaccari by a 250m rock pillar (TD–) high on ENE Face. If this hard rock climb does not appeal the summit can be reached by approaching up the couloir and its right hand branch with mixed climbing to reach the brèche and from there gain the summit by a short rock and snow climb.

Summit route by the Couloir du Diable: (see Aig. du Diable (opposite). From the Torino the Cosmiques huts gain the snow basin below and left of the main rock spurs of Mt. Blanc du Tacul's North-East Face (2 hrs). Cross the rimaye at the avalanche cone and hasten up the narrows of the Cordier Couloir or steep rocks on the left for 70m. Continue up the couloir and after passing the Pilier du Diable on the right (c.3817m) trend right and get into right-hand branch of the couloir and take the best line (mixed ground or ice) to the bréche at P.4027. From there climb a rock and snow ridge to the top of the Pilier du Diable.

Difficulties: *by the Couloir du Diable* to the notch, a short ascent to the summit, and finally up the final section of the Boccalatte Pillar to the summit of Mont Blanc du Tacul. D+ with ice to 55°, average 50° (the lower part only tolerable if there is enough ice there), and rock to IV+ and IV. *Descent from Mt. Blanc du Tacul:* 250mH. Abseiling/down-climbing sections that on the reascent give lengthy passages of IV+ and IV. *Original Route:* TD with long passages of V+ and V with A1.

Effort: Approach 2 hrs, summit route 750mH and then a further 250mH ascent to summit of Mont Blanc du Tacul. Alternatively a 730mH ascent by the Normal Route, a descent of 250mH to P.4027 and 40mH to the top.

Dangers: The Couloir du Diable is a gun barrel which, though not threatened by sérac falls like the Gervasutti Couloir, has enough potential ammunition to fire extensively at climbers. Setting out at night and having the stamina for a fast ascent cannot guarantee perfect safety in the lower section. Higher up the climb is relatively safe in good conditions which are desireable. The rock route of the first ascentionists is also endangered by stone fall at the start, after that it is objectively very safe. Retreat on the couloir could be problematic, less so from the rock route.

Highlights: Being on the move in a wild corner of the Alps.

After returning to the bréche ascend over a rise and small gendarmes (III and IV) to the P.4154 below the last steep section of the Boccalatte Pillar. Go round to the right of the gendarmes and climb the last one directly (30m, IV and IV+) and to the eastern summit of Mont Blanc du Tacul.

Pilier du Diable, Original Route: After crossing the rimaye, in good conditions approach up the couloir. Alternatively take rocks on the right (as for Pilier des Trois Pointes), with a steep step (V), as far as the ledges below the yellow tower of the Pilier des Trois Pointes. Then trend diagonally left, with less difficulty, on rubble, below the Pilier Sans Nom, to the base of the Pilier du Diable in a kind of basin, close to the couloir (6 hrs).

Start the climb at the foot of a red tower with a conspicuous boulder. On the right (east side) go up a crack and slabs (III and IV) until stopped by a vertical red slabby wall. Cross over to the right and descend (V) to a broad crack which brings you to the left to a terrace (V+). Left up slabs, cracks and two dihedrals (V, A1), then right (IV+, V) to a crack system. Follow these (V, A1) to the edge of the pillar and to the summit. (13 hrs from the glacier, and a further 5 hours to the Tacul summit).

Aiguilles du Diable:
Corne du Diable 4064m
Pointe Chaubert 4074m
Pointe Médiane 4097m
Pointe Carmen 4109m
L'Isolée (Pointe Blanchard) 4114m

The impressive towers of brilliant granite rising from the South-East Ridge of Mont Blanc du Tacul are now given summit status by the UIAA. The towers are in three groups: Diable/Chaubert; Mediane/Carmen; L'Isolee. Pointe Carmen, the most prominent of the pinnacles was climbed in August 1923 by Jacques de Lépiney, Henri Bregeault and Paul Chevalier. L' Isolee, the highest, succumbed on 8 July 1925 to Armand Charlet and

Mont Maudit and Mont Blanc du Tacul in a view across the upper basin of the Glacier du Géant.

Mont Blanc du Tacul

Mont Maudit

Aiguilles du Diable

Pilier du Diable

Point de la Androsace

Pilier Sans Nom

Frontier Ridge

Chandelle

Trident du Tacul

Grand Capucin

Petit Capucin

Couloir du Diable

Pilier des trois Pointes

Pointe Adolphe Rey

from Torino Hut

from Aig. du Midi

GLACIER DU GÉANT

Anthoine Ravenel. Two months later Pointe Chaubert and Corne du Diable fell to Jean Chaubert, Charlet and Ravenel. In July 1926 Chaubert, Charlet, Emile Robert Blanchet and Jean Devouassoux climbed Pointe Mediane. The traverse of all the peaks was made on 4 August 1928 by Armand Charlet and Georges Cachat with the Americans Miriam O'Brien and Robert Underhill. The climb was done in classic style with pitons used only for abseil anchors and a jammed axe giving aid on hard pitch of L'Isolee – a fabulous adventure thoroughly chronicled in Miriam Underhill's engaging book, *Give Me the Hills*.

Hut approach: see Aiguille de Rochefort, p.188.

Summit route from the Torino Hut: Follow the ski lift down

into the Vallée Blanche and head west to a point behind the prominent Grand Capucin and the Clocher du Tacul rising to its west. Begin the climb in the second couloir northwest of this (scree later in the year) and further up ascend diagonally left and after crossing several subsidiary gullies gain the Col du Diable (3951m, 2–2½ hrs). This point can also be reached in good conditions starting in the fall line of Pointe Chaubert and then keeping to the right across slabs to the big couloir (see pages 2 and 3).

Go along the snow ridge to the foot of the Corne du Diable. Go round it to the left (S) to the snow col – Brèche Chaubert (4047m, ½hr). From there climb steeply right on the NW ridge with good holds (III+) to the *Corne du Diable* (4064m) and

Grade: D+. Climbing to V, mostly IV+ and IV. The difficulties are increased by altitude. These are the most technically difficult 4000ers compounded by the sustained nature of the rock climbing which is, at times, surprisingly athletic and bold. At least 30m of double rope is needed for abseiling.

Effort: To the Cirque Maudit (3550m) from the Rif. Torino 150mH descent and 300mH ascent (1½ hrs) or from the Aiguille du Midi 600mH descent and 300mH ascent (2 hrs). From Cirque Maudit 400mH to the Col du Diable (2–2½ hrs), from there about 400mH climb/scramble with about 150mH of abseil. In good conditions 8–10 hrs from the Cirque Maudit to the summit of Mont Blanc du Tacul. Descent from there 730mH to the Cosmiques Hut on the Col du Midi (1–2 hrs).

Dangers: In mid summer a danger of stone fall below the Col du Diable from previous roped parties. The ridge is very exposed to the wind and should definitely be avoided in unsettled weather.

Highlights: One of the finest ridge crossings in the Alps, with breathtakingly airy sections of climbing on the best rock.

The five Aiguilles du Diable all of which exceed 4000 metres: from the right – Corne du Diable, Pointe Chaubert, Pointe Médiane, Pointe Carmen and L'Isolée.

return by abseil (bolt below the summit) to the brèche (½hr).

Climb a smooth slab (IV+) and the edge of the ridge to **Pointe Chaubert** (4074m, ½hr). Make three abseils on the north-west side to a notch and go right around little towers to the lowest point (Brèche Médiane, 4017m, ½hr).

To ascend Pointe Médiane at first go to the right, then left to a prominent dihedral. Climb this for 15m (IV) and either continue (IV+ and V) or traverse right (IV) until 1m before the edge of the ridge and climb a crack 15m (IV) to ledge/platform. Go around the ridge to the right for 6m on the ledge, then up slabs for 10m (IV) to regain the edge of the ridge and descend 2m on the southern flank to rejoin the prominent dihedral. Ascend diagonally left over two small terraces and a crack leading to the left opening of two ridge windows. Go through this and climb on the SW side to the summit of **Pointe Médiane** (4097m, 1hr). Return to the same window and there make a free abseil 30m to the north-west to Brèche Carmen (4057m).

From the north side of the Brèche Carmen climb often icy cracks to the flat notch behind summit spikes and go up the knife-edged south-east edge (V) by *à cheval* and laybacking (exposed and poorly protected) to the sharp western pinnacle of **Pointe Carmen** (4109m. 1hr). Return to the notch between the summit spikes and make two abseils to the Brèche du Diable (4054m) from where it is possible to miss out L'Isolee and take the main ridge to Mont Blanc du Tacul. To complete the rock climb go left up an easy ridge section to Brèche de l'Isolée (4078m, 1hr from Pointe Carmen).

Descend 15m south-east, then go up cracks to a platform. Either go up directly on the cracks on the left (original route, V) or by the Contamine variation crossing to the left lower down below an overhanging projection and climbing up on the south side, to the summit of *L'Isolée* (4114m, 1hr). Abseil from a platform on the eastern edge back to Brèche de l'Isolée.

To finish keep a little to the right on crumbly rock steps on the north to outflank towers on the main ridge, then ascend a little to the left of the ridge to the East Summit (4247m, 1hr).

Mont Maudit 4465m

The accursed mountain: halfway to the highest dome of Mont Blanc, yet far away from all easily accessible places, this peak can quickly become a killer in a sudden change of weather. On a good day however it provides a wonderful experience on one of the highest and sharpest ice pinnacles of the Alps.

Ignored for nearly 100 years by passing Mont Blanc caravans, the first ascent was not 'recorded' until 1878. The party was William Edward Davidson, Henry Seymour Hoare and the guides Johann Jaun and Johann von Berge. The superb Frontier Ridge was climbed in 1887 by Moritz von Kuffner with Alexander Burgener, Joseph Furrer and a porter in a three-day struggle.

Mont Maudit is usually climbed in the course of a traverse of Mont Blanc. Anyone who begins one of the more difficult climbs, should bear in mind that if the visibility deteriorates the descent to the Col du Midi is long and very hard to find.

Maps, approach: See Aig. Verte and Mt. Blanc pp. 170, 204.

Summit route by the North Face: Take the Mont Blanc du Tacul route as far as the Epaule du Mont Blanc du Tacul and from there make a slightly descending traverse south to the snow saddle of Col Maudit (4035m). Traverse right (west) on a glacier terrace, under some séracs, working steadily across the steepening face. Cross the (often large) rimaye and continue right, across

Approaching Mont Maudit from Col de la Brenva.

a very steep slope to the modest saddle of the Col du Mont Maudit (P.4345) often equipped with an abseil stake.

Now follow the North-West Ridge with easy climbing (I) or traverse in a wide arc across and up the snow of the West Face to the bold rock tooth of the summit block.

Approach from Mont Blanc: On the traverse of Mont Blanc one descends north-eastwards from Mont Blanc over the broad slope, passing right of two rock outcrops, to a flatter slope (keep

Difficulties: PD. A long high glacier climb, with snow to 50°, which should not be underestimated. In late season, as the rimayes widen, ascents from the north can be problematic.

Effort: From Aig. du Midi 300mH descent and 1000mH ascent (6–8 hrs).

Dangers: Starting this climb from the Midi can cause problems if one has not properly acclimatised. The late hour of starting (if using the first téléphérique) will inevitably mean a descent on soft snow with crampons balling-up (Mont Blanc traverse teams also take note). At such times there may also be increased avalanche danger on both the North Face of Mont Maudit and the North-West Face of Mont Blanc du Tacul, particularly after new snow. The principal dangers of the climb lie in the weather. The summit area is very exposed to storms. The route-finding is more difficult as the compass does not work reliably on this mountain because of minerals present in the rock – advance map and photograph study is a wise precaution. In thoroughly bad weather, waiting for an improvement in a snow hole is the best life-saver (if well clothed and with provisions and fuel).

Pleasures: A splendid vantage point to view the highest peak of the Alps.

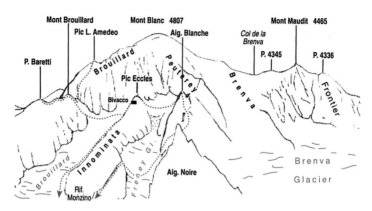

your distance from the Brenva Face cornices on the right). Follow a spur descending to the left over the steep Mur de la Côte and go down to Col de la Brenva (4303m, cornices on the right). Go north on the broad ridge (cornices) over P.4361 and P.4369 to the saddle P.4342. Then go north-west up the steep but easy slope to the summit (2–3 hrs from Mont Blanc; for the rest of the way to Col du Midi allow a further 3–4 hrs). It is wise to carry a wooden stake for Col du Mont Maudit rimaye unless one elects to descend the N.E. Ridge to Col Maudit.

View: To the west it is dominated by Mont Blanc. To the east, behind Mont Blanc du Tacul, there extends a wide selection of high peaks, with the Grandes Jorasses especially conspicuous. To the south are the exciting views down across the Brenva Face.

Adjacent peaks: At the end of the Frontier Ridge the North-East Summit (4336m) tops a stylish snow ridge and below the Pointe de l'Androsace (4107m) may now be considered a summit.

Other worthwhile routes: *South-East, Kuffner* or *Frontier Ridge* (D, climbing to IV and III, mixed, large-scale classic route at great height, along an extensive, narrow ridge, in part corniced, snow on long stretches at 45°, sometimes steeper; from the Col de la Fourche 800mH over 1.6km length of ridge, 4–8 hrs).

South-East Face (D+, a large-scale, mixed climb in places IV and often harsh ice passages; 700mH, 7–10 hrs from the rimaye).

North-East Ridge from Col Maudit (PD) An elegant snow ridge with mixed sections. A useful alternative ascent/descent route.

Guidebook: *Mont Blanc Massif*, Vol. 1 (Alpine Club, 1990).

Pointe de l'Androsace   4107m

The rock tower that marks the halfway point and crux of the splendid Frontier Ridge (aka Kuffnergrat) between the Brenva and Géant Glaciers. This famous route was first climbed in 1887 by Alexander Burgener with Josef Furrer, an unknown porter, and their client, the Austrian brewer Moritz von Kuffner. They bypassed the gendarme on the left and it was eventually climbed in 1933 by the Swiss V. Bressoud, René Dittert, Francis Marullaz, and W. Marquart. With sections of grade IV rock it is harder and more time-consuming than the traverse of the western base, but in poor snow conditions or with traffic jams, going over the top is a tempting alternative. A short abseil and some down-climbing soon gains the col about 30m below the summit.

Mont Blanc   4807m

The glittering dome high above Chamonix and Courmeyeur in the deep blue sky, the monarch, the highest peak in the Alps.

Over two centuries ago, alpinism was founded by its first ascent. The reward of 20 gold thalers offered by the Geneva scientist Horace Bénédict de Saussure motivated the crystal hunter Jacques Balmat and the doctor Michel-Gabriel Paccard to make the ascent on 8 August 1786 by a route up the Rochers Rouges and the north-east slope. A year later de Saussure himself made the ascent, enthusing about the sky's depth of blue and readings on his barometer, which sank so 'magnificently low'.

The superlatives are certainly justified. The mountain offers an host of beautiful climbs of all grades of difficulty. But not all who start out so enthusiastically come away unharmed. Time and again sudden storms bring tragedy. Climbers die of hypothermia, loss of direction in mist and driving snow, delirium, frostbite and crevasse falls – the annual death toll comes to almost three figures. Today the rescue helicopters of the Gendarmerie des Hautes Montagnes, weather permitting, collect accident victims thus saving many who earlier would have died of exposure.

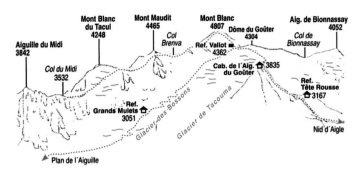

Aiguille du Midi
3842

Col du Midi
3532

Mont Blanc
du Tacul
4248

Mont Maudit
4465

Col
Brenva

Mont Blanc
4807 Dôme du Goûter
4304

Ref. Vallot
4362

Cab. de l'Aig. 3835
du Goûter

Aig. de Bionnassay
4052

Col de
Bionnassay

Ref.
Tête Rousse
3167

Ref.
Grands Mulets
3051

Glacier des Bossons

Glacier de Tacouma

Nid d'Aigle

Plan de l'Aiguille

Further highpoints of the mountain's history should be mentioned. In 1808 Marie Paradis a peasant girl from Chamonix was the first woman on the summit. About 1840 the ascent from Grands Mulets over Grand Plateau and Bosses Ridge was first carried out by Marie Couttet and company. In 1861 Leslie Stephen and Francis Fox Tuckett with Melchior Anderegg, J.J. Bennen and Peter Perren climbed today's Normal Route over the Aiguille du Goûter and Bosses Ridge. Just four years later the mighty Brenva

The upper slopes of Mont Blanc seen from the Dôme du Gouter. The Vallot Hut is obvious on the spur above the Col du Dôme, with the Bosses Ridge rising to its right.

Spur was climbed by Melchior and Jakob Anderegg with George Matthews, Adolphus Warburton Moore and Frank and Horace Walker (father and son). In 1872 Thomas Stuart Kennedy with Jean-Antoine Carrel and Johann Fischer made a route up the serious South-West Face. The Italian Normal Route was found in 1890 by Achille Ratti (later Pope Pius XI) with his guides L.and J.Bonin, J.Gadin and A.Proment.

The first ascent of the Peuterey Ridge was carried out in 1893 by Paul Güssfeldt guided by Emile Rey, Christian Klucker and César Ollier. In 1901 the Brouillard Ridge with north-west approach fell to Guiseppe and Giovanni Battiste Gugliermina with Joseph Brocherel and (ten years later) more directly from Col Emile Rey by Joseph Knubel with Geoffrey Winthrop Young,

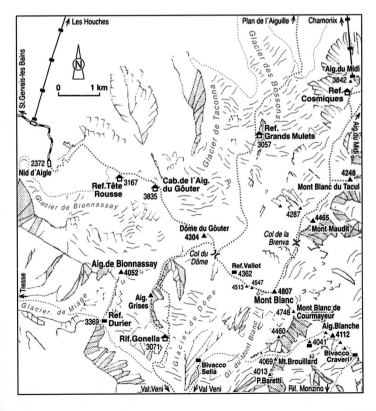

The Mont Blanc massif seen in dawn light from Dent du Géant
Mont Blanc du Tacul. The Frontier Ridge runs across the middle o

From the left: Aiguille Blanche, Mont Blanc, Mont Maudit and the photo defining the upper edge of the Glacier du Géant basin.

Humphrey Owen Jones and Karl Blodig. The Innominata Ridge was conquered in 1919 by S.L. Courtauld, Edmund G. Oliver, Adolphé and Henri Rey and Adolf Aufdenblatten.

Attention then focussed on the difficult faces: the Brenva Face was explored between 1927 and 1934; the Frêney Face with climbs in 1928, 1940, 1961 and 1963; the Brouillard with climbs

---

Difficulties: On the Aiguille du Goûter Route (PD), rock to II, otherwise only snow plodding, to 40° on the Bosses Ridge. The Grands Mulets Route (F) is twice as long, but involves only normal glacier work with many crevasses and a constantly changing line. The route from the Gonella Hut (PD) also utilizes a long, disrupted glacier (or a non-glacier variation over the Aiguilles Grises) is PD with mixed climbing to II. In all these cases these easy grades disguise the overall seriousness of a long ascent on a very high mountain that is very exposed to rapid weather changes.

Effort: From the rack railway to the Tête Rousse Hut 800mH (2–3 hrs), from there to the Goûter Hut 700mH (2–3 hrs), and to the summit a further 1050mH (4–5 hrs). From the téléphérique station Plan de l'Aiguille to the Grands Mulets Hut 800mH (3 hrs), from there 1700mH (6–7 hrs) to the summit. From Lac Combal in the Val Veni 1050mH (4 hrs) to the Gonella Hut, from there 1736mH (7–8 hrs) to the summit.

Dangers: The Goûter Hut climb is menaced by stone-fall (especially if one crosses the big couloir above the Tête Rousse Hut in order to ascend the technically easier rock rib south of that). Above the hut the route is more exposed to the wind, as compensation there are few crevasses. The Grands Mulets route is occasionally exciting on account of crevasses, especially if one of the helpfully placed ladders is missing. The route-finding presents no difficulties in good weather but quickly becomes desperate in a snow storm. Some of the slopes above the hut are prone to localised slab or powder snow avalanches. The Italian route has a likewise disrupted glacier. It is well to note that the often swift weather changes on Mont Blanc can transform the peaceful, sunny Normal Routes full of people into a hostile maelstrom within a short time. The Vallot Hut is merely a survival box for emergencies – a miserable, neglected thing. Nevertheless, it is as well to make a careful note of its position as it could be a life-saver in poor weather. Apart from the objective dangers, it is also essential, to be sure that one's fitness and acclimatization are sufficient for the task and, if in serious doubt, to turn back at the right time.

Pleasures: If all goes to plan, then the hours on the roof of the Alps are an unforgettable experience. As a precaution against disappointment in good weather, prepare yourself for a frightful crowd, with awkward passing manoeuvres on the narrow Bosses Ridge, and with many inconsiderate people. If you plan this as an expectation, the reality may just be bearable.

---

in 1959, 1965 and 1971; and the Grand Pilier d'Angle has been criss-crossed with powerful and challenging climbs since 1959. These days the customary Normal Route is that over the Aiguille du Goûter. Only a few climbers ascend from the far lower Grands Mulets Hut. The same is true of the route from the Italian side. From the Col du Dôme onwards, all three routes finish up the Bosses Ridge to the highest point. The other popular approach is that from the Aiguille du Midi over, or past Mont Blanc du Tacul and Mont Maudit, though many climbers prefer to use that for descent having climbed the Goûter Route.

Maps: IGN carte touristique 1:25,000, 1 *Chamonix-Mont Blanc* and IGN 3531 ET *St Gervais.*

Travel: Rail or car to Chamonix (1030m, 40km from Martigny, 86km from Geneva, 59km from Aosta; tourist resort and alpinists' Mecca (also see Aiguille Verte) from there 8km to Les Houches.

Hut climb: From Les Houches by téléphérique up to Bellevue (1790m, station on the tramway from St Gervais les Bains). Take the tramway to the terminus Nid d'Aigle (2386m). Go south on the path for 200m, then head left (east) in zig-zags under a rocky step up into a scree hollow. At a small hut, go right (south-east) over debris to the ridge which leads up in the direction of the Aiguille du Goûter. On a small plateau on the right is the Tête Rousse Hut (3167m, 60 B, managed: June – September, Tel. 450-544093; if one is going to the Aiguille du Goûter, there is no need to divert to the Tête Rousse Hut). Cross the small Tête Rousse Glacier to the rock rib that runs left (north) of the Grand Couloir. In recent years the rockfall on both the rib and couloir has increased. Choice of route therefore calls for judgement, speed and good luck. Many climbers cross the Grand Couloir to its south rib, but even there descending climbers can trigger rock-falls. Alternatively the northern rib can be taken straight up to the north summit of the Aiguille du Goûter. Follow the ridge to the Goûter Hut on the west side close under the summit (3817m, CAF Paris & Chamonix, 100 B, managed: end of June – end of Sept., often overcrowded in mid summer, winter room with 16 B always open, Tel. 0039 450-544093, advance booking advisable).

Summit climb from Aiguille du Goûter: From the Goûter Hut head south, then south-east along the broad snow ridge to

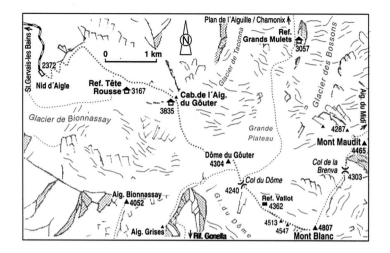

the Dôme du Goûter. Cross the summit (4303m) or turn it on the south, make a slight descent to the Col du Dôme (4240m). Continue in the same direction, up the steepening slope. Pass the Vallot Hut, standing on a rock on the left (4362m, 8 B; squalid). Climb the narrowing and steepening ridge (often on a broad track) to two snowy ridge humps (Grande Bosse 4513m and Petite Bosse 4547m) and after that go along a sharp snow ridge passing the rocks of La Tournette (4677m) on the right, and then head east to the last top (4740m) and 300m further, the summit.

View: All the surrounding summits are dwarfed by Mont Blanc's height. To the south are Gran Paradiso and the Haut Dauphiné. There is a distant view to the Valais peaks in the east. In all directions are dominating views, as Edward Whymper described when commenting on the disappointment of purely panoramic views. '[The view] is notoriously unsatisfactory... There is nothing to look up to; all is below; there is no one point for the eye to rest upon.' Whymper was right. If one only climbs Mont Blanc for the view then there will be a sense of anti-climax.

Summit climb via Grands Mulets: From Chamonix take the Midi téléphérique to the halfway station Plan de l'Aiguille. From there follow the marked path to the south to the Glacier des Pélerins. The bare tongue of this is crossed at about 2400m.

Continue on a good path to the derelict téléphérique station 'Gare des Glaciers' (2414m). Ascend on the left side of the Glacier des Bossons, under a big couloir of the Aiguille du Midi (stone-fall danger) to gain the glacier. Traverse this to the south-west to the badly disrupted area of 'La Jonction' (usually ladders over the most awkward crevasses). Now work southwards, going up over the crevassed snow slopes, first keeping right (west) of the rock island and then moving onto it where a path with an iron handrail leads up to the Grands Mulets Hut (3051m, private, 68 B, managed in spring and summer, Tel. 450-531698).

From the hut, cross the glacier heading obliquely south-west in the direction of some rocks at the foot of the long north ridge of the Dôme du Goûter. Near the séracs of the Dôme, go left over a steep slope (the Petites Montées) to a flatter ramp-like section (Petit Plateau, 3650m, 2 hrs). Keeping well away from the séracs of the Dôme, climb this flat section. After that, go up a further steep slope. Higher up, after an especially big crevasse, bear right to the extensive snow-field of the Grand Plateau (3980m).

Looking down the northern slopes of Mont Blanc to Mont Maudit, Mont Blanc du Tacul and the Aiguille du Midi.

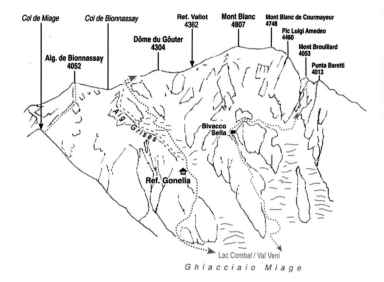

Col de Miage
Col de Bionnassay
Ref. Vallot 4362
Mont Blanc 4807
Mont Blanc de Courmayeur 4748
Dôme du Goûter 4304
Pic Luigi Amedeo 4460
Aig. de Bionnassay 4052
Mont Brouillard 4053
Punta Baretti 4013
Aig. Grises
Bivacco Sella
Ref. Gonella
Lac Combal / Val Veni
Ghiacciaio Miage

Traverse this west-south-westwards and climb the seemingly endless slope to the Col du Dôme (6–7 hrs from the Grands Mulets Hut). Continue as for Goûter route (see above).

The Italian Route via the Gonella Hut: Start from the Val Veni from Cantine de la Visaille (1653m, bus from Courmayeur – see map on p.223). Take the path along the moraines on the northern bank of the Miage Glacier. Alternatively, from Lac Combal (1940m), further up the valley, take a path over the big moraine on the south side to reach the Miage Glacier. Ascend the middle of the glacier. Pass below the Dôme Glacier (2493m) on the right and go on to P.2530 at the foot of the southern spur of the Aiguilles Grise. Take a path on the right, 150m beyond P.2530, first up a scree couloir, then working steeply up east to cross a shoulder on the ridge to reach the Dôme Glacier side. Continue up and across, bending right, across couloirs and snow slopes to a rock spur leading to the Gonella Hut (3071m, CAI, 40 B, managed: mid-July – end of August, Tel. 0039 0165-885101).

From the Gonella Hut climb near the west edge of the glacier, then move towards the centre (crevasses). Higher up take the left (west) arm of the glacier, cross the bergschrund and go left to the

Col des Aiguilles Grises (3809m, 3 hrs). This point can also be reached by taking the Aiguilles Grises ridge from the hut (PD), climbing over the first two towers, turning the third on the west side with a slight descent and after that on the broad snow ridge over the summit of the Calotte des Aiguilles Grises, 3826m (4 hrs). Now continue north along the ridge. Turn a rock rise on the left and continue on the snow ridge to the shoulder (4003m) on the frontier ridge just above the Col de Bionnassay.

Follow the (often corniced) frontier ridge north-east to a further shoulder (4153m, iron posts) and then on to the Dôme du Goûter (4303m) to join the Goûter route (see page 211).

Adjacent peaks: Mt. Blanc de Courmayeur, Dôme du Goûter, Pic Luigi Amedeo and Grand Pilier d'Angle (all new UIAA summits) and Pic Eccles are discussed later. Grande Bosse (4513m) and Petite Bosse (4547m) are on the Goûter route. The Grande Chandelle (c.4600m, 20m col depth) forms the top of the Central Frêney Pillar. Aiguille de la Belle Étoiles 4349m is high on the Pear Buttress route below Mt. Blanc du Courmayeur.

Other worthwhile routes: *South-West Face* (PD, mixed and snow to 50°, 1400mH, 6–8 hrs from the Quintino Sella Hut).

Brouillard Ridge (AD+, a classic ridge, in part on loose rock, to III+, 2200mH, 10–18 hrs from the Monzino Hut).

Innominata Ridge (D+, a classic ridge, mixed, 1450mH, 12–17 hrs from the Monzino Hut, 7–10 hrs from the Eccles Hut).

Traverse of Aiguille Blanche and Peuterey Ridge (D+, rock to IV–, over a long distance III and II, mixed, with snow or ice to 55°, 2500mH, 10–20 hrs from Monzino Hut).

Brenva Spur (AD to D, according to conditions, mainly snow or ice to 50°, sometimes hard at the exit, fine line, objectively safe, 1300mH to summit, 7–10 hrs from the Fourche Hut).

Sentinelle Rouge Route (D+, snow or ice to 55° and rock to III, ideal line up the Brenva Face to the main summit, but with danger of falling ice, 1400mH, 9–13 hrs from the Fourche Hut).

Route Major (TD, ice to 57°, rock to V and IV, mixed, great danger of falling ice, particularly in the Grand Couloir, 1300mH, about 11–16 hrs from the Fourche Hut). *Note:* The previous three routes are now more difficult to access because of a major rockfall above Col Moore. Also the old Trident Hut is no longer available (collapsed).

Right-Hand Frêney Pillar (Gervasutti Pillar) (TD, rock to VI, and A1, mixed, 800mH, 8–12 hrs from the Col Peuterey).
Central Frêney Pillar (ED+, rock to VI and A3, mixed – at the end of the world and, given bad luck, delivered up to all the hells of sudden changes of weather, 15–25 hrs from Col Peuterey).
Guidebook: *Mont Blanc Range*, Vol 1 (Alpine Club, 1990).

Dôme du Goûter 4304m

This is an important thoroughfare peak (58m above the Col du Dôme), crossed by the Goûter and the Italian routes on the way to Mont Blanc. It was first climbed by Jean-Marie Couttet and François Cuidet in 1784 during the early probes up the Goûter Ridge in search of an alternative Mont Blanc route to the Grands Mulets Glacier approach. The glacier route was subsequently used for the first and early ascents of Mont Blanc but Couttet's way was eventually adopted as the most logical route up the mountain.

Climbing Mont Blanc's Bosses Ridge with Aiguille de Bionnassay in the background, its South Ridge on the left.

Mt. Blanc de Courmayeur 4748m

It is true that the southern fore-summit of Mont Blanc is only separated by a flat col (with a mere 18m col depth) from the highest point. But being at the apex of both the Peuterey and the Brouillard ridges it forms one of the most prominent topographical summits of the Mont Blanc massif when viewed from Italy. In calm weather it can be reached from the main summit without difficulty in 20 minutes.

Aiguille de Bionnassay 4052m

Coyly hidden from the prying eyes of Chamonix this stylish western satellite of Mont Blanc offers folds of an elegant icy northern flank towards the Aiguille du Goûter – an austere North Wall decorated (to its right) by the easier-angled, furbelowed North-West Face. The first ascent of the peak was made in 1865 up the latter's intricate hanging glacier folds by Edward Buxton, Florence Craufurd Grove, Reginald Somerled MacDonald, Jean-Pierre Cachat and Michel-Clement Payot.

Seen from the Dôme du Goûter the peak's allure continues with the East Ridge curving sensuously down to the Col Bionnassay, and the corseting rock and snow rib of South Ridge seen in profile on the left. Not surprisingly the South Ridge is now considered the key to the easiest ascent route (first climbed in 1888 by the diplomat Georg Gruber, Kaspar Maurer and Andreas Jaun) it is the way by which most modern suitors approach the summit.

Difficulties: PD+. A mixed ridge climb with passages of II. The summit slope is steep snow 45°, there is also troublesome ice.

Effort: To the Durier Bivouac Hut from Tresse is 2250mH (8 hrs), from the south-east from Lac Combal in the Val Veni 1700mH (5–7 hrs). Summit climb by the South Ridge 700mH (3–5 hrs). Continuation toward Mont Blanc by the East Ridge (AD, 150mH, 1hr to the Col de Bionnassay).

Dangers: A beautiful rough approach. On the ridges, beware of cornices.

Pleasures: Protected from crowds by the sheer effort of getting there. One should appreciate such rarity and leave things behind in good condition.

Maps: IGN 3531 ET, 1:25,000, *St Gervais*.

Travel: By rail to St Gervais-les-Bains, from there by bus through the Val Montjoie in the direction of Les Contamines 6km to Tresse (1050m). For the Italian side, see Mont Blanc.

Approach to the Durier Hut: From Tresse, head east through the village, then left (north) to the Torrent de Miage. Follow a path on the south-west bank (2hrs) to the Miage chalets (1559m). Cross to the other side and follow an indistinct path up the valley. Climb the rock steps to the right of a waterfall. Continue on a steep grass ridge and rock slopes to the northern moraine of the Glacier de Miage. Ascend the moraine path laboriously to P.2566, and continue to a flat part of the glacier on the right. After turning the rocky foot of the South-West Face of the Aiguille de Tricot. Cross the glacier ascending to the east to the central rock rib descending from the Col de Miage. (*Note:* On the right of the upper end of the upper moraine is the new Plan Glacier Hut, 2740m, no warden). Cross the (often awkward) rimaye as soon as possible (far left), then climb the crumbling rib (or the left-hand couloir) to the new Durier Hut on the col (3349m, CAF St Gervais, 20B, wardened).

Approach by the Miage Glacier: Take the Gonella Hut route to P.2530 (see p.214). Continue along the left side of the glacier. At the Bionnassay Glacier junction, go north-west starting on the left and up over a step to a steep snow-field. Follow a rock rib, or the less steep glacier on the right to gain the Col du Miage.

Summit climb by the South Ridge: From the Col de Miage take the snow ridge to a shoulder. Continue to a second snow shoulder with blocks and on to a notch beyond it in front of a rock step. Turn this by the steep gully on the right and so regain the ridge above. If this is verglassed go up further right across the South-East Face, first keeping low along a snow ledge, passing below ribs/couloirs until an ascent up a steep, right-slanting snow band and a funnel through a rock band regains the ridge (AD). This leads to a final steep snow slope and the summit (4 hrs).

East Ridge: From the Italian Mont Blanc Normal Route (see p.213) descend to the Col de Bionnassay from P.4003 and follow the narrow snow/ice ridge (often corniced) to the summit (1 hr). This can also be descended by those heading to Mont Blanc.

Aiguille de Bionnassay seen from Dôme du Miage. Col de Miage catches the sun on the right, the South Ridge leading from there to the summit. Dôme du Goûter is high above, wreathed in clouds.

View: Blocked on the west by the bulk of Mont Blanc, the attention is drawn by Trélatete and Miage groups to the south.
Other worthwhile routes: *West-North-West* or *Tricot Ridge* (AD, rock-climbing to II, 2250mH, 3.8km, 10 hrs from Col de Tricot). *North-West Face* (AD, popular classic, a snow and ice climb, mostly 40°, but in places 55°, after new snow there is avalanche danger, 1050mH, 5–9 hrs from the Tête Rousse Hut).
Guidebook: *Mont Blanc Range*, Vol. 1 (Alpine Club, 1990).

Mont Brouillard 4069m
Punta Baretti 4013m

On the south-west side of Mont Blanc are the gigantic glacier basins of the Miage and Brouillard Glaciers, which can only be linked by the difficult Col Emile Rey at the foot of the mighty Brouillard Ridge. These two ridge tops are lost in this 'Himalaya of the Alps', at the end of the world and only visited by people who are addicted to 4000m peak collecting or those who have a weakness for the last lonely corners of the continent.

Naturally these are also the sort of mountains whose independence has been exhaustively debated, as the col depth of the lower Punta Baretti is distinctly greater than that of the higher Mont Brouillard. The first ascent of that was disputed because after climbing Punta Baretti in 1880 Martino Baretti and Jean Joseph Maquignaz gave inexact details about the traverse to Mont Brouillard and may well have gained only an intermediate point. Karl Blodig, Oscar Eckenstein and Alexis Brocherel found no cairn in 1906 and their's is now the accredited first ascent.

Maps, travel, sketches: See Grandes Jorasses (p.180) and Mont Maudit (p.204).

Hut approach: As for the Gonella Hut (see Mont Blanc p.214) along the Miage Glacier to its junction with the Mont Blanc Glacier. Turn the ice-fall on the left (west) close to the edge, battling with crevasses, and over the usually very complicated rimaye to the first grassy rock gully of the ridge. Climb it over broken rocks following the tracks as far as one third height. Then go obliquely right over broken slopes to a rock wall which is climbed using a gully to gain the ridge. Climb this with easy scrambling, first of all to the remains of an old hut, then to the

---

Difficulties: AD. Rock difficulties to II, mostly I and scrambling, mixed, snow or ice to 50° and disrupted glaciers.
Effort: From the west by the Sella Bivouac Hut 1400mH (5 hrs), summit climb 800mH (5 hrs).
Dangers: Many problems – crevasses, avalanche danger, stone-fall, falling ice and all the additional factors which go with remoteness.
Pleasures: Extreme remoteness.

The Brouillard Ridge from the west. The 1901 Gugliermina route takes
the left of the big buttress with the sunlit Piloni Rosso in its centre and
right of this is Col Emile Rey, Mont Brouillard and Punta Baretti.

newer Quintino Sella Bivouac Hut (3371m, 15 B).

Summit climb by the West Couloir: Traverse the snow slopes
eastwards. Cross three rounded ribs and three snow gullies and
descend over the disrupted Mont Blanc Glacier to the foot of the
snow gully which descends from the Col Emile Rey. According
to conditions, ascend this near the middle or on the right (south)
bordering rocks up to the Col Emile Rey (4012m). Now go south
on the ridge on easy mixed ground to the summit of Mont
Brouillard (15–30 minutes from the col).

To reach Punta Baretti from Mont Brouillard use the connecting
ridge, turning obstacles as necessary (1 hour).

View: Mont Blanc's Brouillard Ridge rises to the north blotting
out all views in that direction. To the west is the Trélatete group,
to the east the Peuterey Ridge and to the south the Gran Paradiso
range. Below are huge glaciers riven with hungry crevasses.

Other routes: *South-West Ridge* (PD, pitches of II, seemingly endlessly long and boring, 2100mH from the Miage Glacier).
From the south-east (AD, snow or ice to 50º, long glacier ascent using Eccles Bivouac Hut and with snow traverses and rock ribs to the Col Emile Rey, 1500mH, 2–3 hrs from the Eccles Bivouac).
Guidebook: *Mont Blanc Range*, Vol 1 (Alpine Club, 1990).

Pic Luigi Amedeo 4469m

Originally called Picco Luigi Amedeo and also referred to in French as Pointe Louis Amédée this is now the accepted hybrid title that honours the mountaineering Duke of the Abruzzi. It is the unassertive peak (defined only by a 35m notch) at the lower end of the complex Brouillard Ridge and therefore very remote. The first ascent was probably made on 19 July 1901 in the course of an expedition by Guiseppe and Giovanni Battiste Gugliermina with the porter Joseph Brocherel. They had climbed (two bivouacs) the rocky north flank and continued up the upper Brouillard Ridge with a further bivouac on the summit of Mont Blanc before descending to Chamonix. This might also be considered the first ascent of the Brouillard Ridge and though less direct than the 1911 route it has more rock climbing.

The route which is usual today taking the ridge above Col Emile Rey, was made on 9 August 1911 by Geoffrey Winthrop Young, Humphrey Owen Jones, Karl Blodig and Joseph Knubel in one day, starting from the Quintino Sella Hut. This ascent was notable for Blodig as by topping Pic Luigi he won the race for the 4000ers (as it was then understood), beating his two rivals Dr Pühn and Hans Pfann (though why Pic Luigi Amedeo did not appear in later versions of Blodig's book is something of a mystery). The quartet were so speedy that they reached Mt. Blanc's summit by noon and, intent on avoiding a bivouac, hastened down the horrendously crevassed Dôme Glacier. They reached Courmayeur by 10.30 p.m. to confound observers who had predicted one or even two bivouacs.

The least difficult way of reaching Pic Luigi by a descent from Mont Blanc will involve hazardous abseils to gain Col Emile Rey or a re-ascent over Mont Blanc.

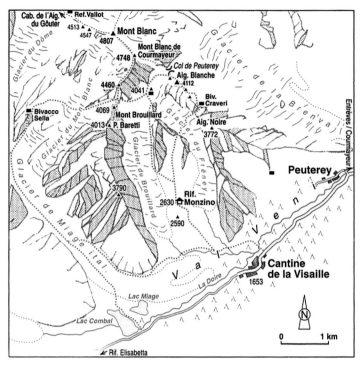

Another alternative approach would be on the north-west facing buttress overlooking the Mont Blanc Glacier. The nature of the Gugliermina Route is unknown but on 29 July 1983 Gian Carlo Grassi and Jean Noel Roche did a fine 650m rock route here called *Piloni Rosso* (TD–, one pitch of V but mainly VI+ and VI, plus mixed climbing to III) starting from the Sella Hut. Though much harder, this might well be a less fraught approach to Pic Luigi Amedeo than the steep part of the Brouillard Ridge.

Approach: see Mt. Brouillard (p.223) and Aig. Blanche (p.227).

Summit route: First climb to the Col Emile Rey (see Mt. Brouillard, 1½ hours, or from the Eccles Hut gain the snow plateau below the Brouillard Pillars and thence by a couloir, 1½ hrs). From the Col descend about 20m to the east then go up the left-hand side of a steepening slabby gully. Climb a steep slab of crumbling rock (IV). After three awkward rope lengths (danger of stone and ice-fall) continue on easier terrain working

Mont Blanc's Brouillard Ridge (skyline) from the south. Col Emile Rey and Pic Luigi Amedeo are on the left, Mont Blanc de Courmayeur high on the centre right and Pic Eccles is centre-right, below the face.

diagonally left (west) to a notch by a gendarme. Now head north at first over snow and scree, then up friable rock to the summit of Pic Luigi Amedeo (2½–5 hours from Col Emile Rey).

Descend on the east side for about 20m to a small notch. Cross a few metres below this and go two rope lengths on stepped terrain to the next sudden rise in the ridge (steep pitch). After a snow ridge go right over another steep rise. Ascend the now less steep snow ridge to P4650m (junction with the Innominata Ridge). Above go west below the last rock step of Mt. Blanc de Courmayeur ascending diagonally left to the connecting ridge and Mont Blanc's summit (4–6 hours from Pic Luigi Amedeo).

> **Grade:** AD+. IV and III in sections but mainly sustained mixed climbing.
> **Effort:** 1000mH from the Eccles Bivouac Hut to the Mont Blanc summit (8–12 hrs), plus the extra expedition to reach the hut (PD+, 2191mH, 8 hrs).
> **Dangers:** Dramatic/wild glaciers on the approach. Above Col Emile Rey the south-facing buttress has the attendant stone fall danger in the gullies and very friable rock. The great length at high altitude gives the undertaking all the elements of adventure – only justifiable in really safe weather which would be a cold, clear (but not sunny) day.
> **Highlights:** A trip in an extremely remote mountain area.

Pic Eccles 4041m

It is true that a small snow-covered peak standing below the huge south flank of Mont Blanc offers few challenges of its own in the form of rock walls, ice faces or ridges, but it does have historical links as a staging point for attempts on the South Face of Mont Blanc, a role that its nearby bivouac hut retains to this day. The first ascent was made on 31 August 1874 by J.A. Garth Marshall with Johann Fischer and Ulrich Almer during their ill-fated Innominata Ridge attempt when Marshall and Fischer died in a crevasse accident during the descent. In 1877 James Eccles with Michel-Clement and Alphonse Payot used the bivouac site and the peak as a base for their successful ascent of the South Face of Mont Blanc by a route across the upper Frêney basin and the upper section of the Peuterey Ridge. The Innominata Ridge was eventually climbed (after many attempts) in 1919 by the Courtauld/Oliver/Rey/Aufdenblatten team (see p.210), and between 1959 and the 1971 the hut served as a base for attempts and ascents of the various Brouillard Pillars.

Although the summit has a notch of about 35m deep the peak was not included in the UIAA list – perhaps to avoid further demand on the usually overcrowded bivouac hut.

Summit Route: See Aiguille Blanche (p.227) for route to the Col Eccles and along the narrow north ridge up to the summit. About one hour from the Eccles Bivouac.

Grand Pilier d'Angle 4243m

This large corner pillar forms a shoulder that marks the start of the upper section of the Peuterey Ridge. Due to the demanding routes on its impressive East and North Faces it has been included in the UIAA list despite the very modest col depth of 15m. It will probably be visited in combination with a trip to Aiguille Blanche with a finish up the Peuterey Ridge or at the end of one of the very hard routes on the Brenva flank. For description see Aiguille Blanche p.228.

Aig. Blanche with Pt. Seymour King (left), Pt. Güssfeldt (centre) and
Pt. Jones (right). Pic Eccles is seen above the Col du Peuterey (right).

Aiguille Blanche de Peuterey:
Pointe Güssfeldt 4112m
Pointe Seymour King 4107m

One of the most fascinating and menacing mountains in the Alps,
with the elegant rock pillars on its south-western flank and equally
well-sculpted ice ramparts on the north-east. Between them, the
mighty Peuterey Ridge rises to the summit from Brèche Nord des
Dames Anglaises. The downside is that this peak inveigles one
into a position of extreme hazard where the sudden onset of bad
weather can project the climber into a desperate fight for survival.

The peak is generally climbed in the course of a traverse to
Mont Blanc, when the need for speed means that only the straightforward Pointe Seymour King is crossed with the higher Pointe
Güssfeldt being turned and Pointe Jones being missed out too.
Anyone who embarks on this long ascent must be very well prepared in terms of both fitness and experience for this is the most
difficult independent 4000er in the Alps. The approaches are long
and complicated, and threatened by both ice and stone-fall and
with plenty of scope for going astray. The mountain itself is big
and complicated and when one finally reaches the knife-edged
summit ridge, the quickest way to safety involves either a further

Difficulties: D+. Rock-climbing sustained at III and II with passages of IV, mixed, seldom easy, snow or ice to 50°. The principal difficulty lies, nevertheless, not in individual pitches, but rather in the length and the sustained and changing demands. For that reason, the ascent can only be recommended to fully fit, experienced climbers who should only set out in favourable conditions and when the weather is settled. Most will hope to complete the climb, crossing Grand Pilier d'Angle *en route*, to Mont Blanc.
Effort: Hut climb 1000mH (3 hrs), bivouac approach 1100mH (4–7 hrs), summit climb 700mH (5–6 hrs), descent to Col Peuterey 150mH (2 hrs), descent by the Rochers Gruber to the Monzino Hut 1650mH with 150mH of ascent (5–8 hrs). Col du Peuterey to Mont Blanc 850mH (5–10 hrs).
Dangers: A full range – crevasses on the very disrupted glaciers are a particularly serious problem when retreating; stone-fall in the couloir below the Dames Anglaises, especially in 'good' conditions; loose rock on the South-East Face; hypothermia on the summit ridge in storm conditions; avalanches on the Rochers Gruber in bad weather, etc.
The principal problem remains the danger of being overtaken by bad weather with the consequent forced retreat. This will usually be down the Rochers Gruber, which is difficult, complicated and dangerous (with difficult ascent to the Col de l'Innominata) and must not be under-estimated. An alternative is to cross the Upper Frêney Basin to take refuge in the Eccles Bivouac Hut. Abundant food and fuel can become life-saving. Two parties climbing together can give additional security by speeding the abseiling at the critical stages.
Pleasures: An aesthetically stunning expedition for well-trained experts.

very long ascent, or a choice of complicated and hazardous descents.

The South Summit was first climbed in 1885 by Henry Seymour King with Emile Rey, Ambros Supersaxo and Aloys Anthamatten. They approached up the short North-West Ridge via the Col de Frêney and Col de Peuterey. The higher Central Summit was gained in 1893 during the first ascent of the Peuterey Ridge with an approach up the Brenva flank. This was made by Paul Güssfeldt guided by Emile Rey, Christian Klucker and César Ollier. Today's usual ridge route, via the Frêney Glacier/Dames Anglaises approach, was first climbed in 1928 by Ludwig Obersteiner and Karl Schreiner. The North Face was done in 1933 by Renato Chabod and Aimé Grivel and Punta Gugliermina's South Face fell to Giusto Gervasutti and Gabriele Boccalatte in 1938.

Maps: IGN 1:25,000 Sheet 3531 ET *St Gervais*.
Travel: To Courmayeur (1230m) via the Val d'Aosta or from the north through the Mont Blanc tunnel.

The Peuterey Ridge – one of the finest alpine climbs. Aiguille Noire and the Dames Anglaises pinnacles are on the left. Aiguille Blanche, Col du Peuterey and the steep step to Grand Pilier d'Angle lead to the final ice ridge rising to Mont Blanc du Courmayeur and Mont Blanc.

Hut climb: Take a bus or drive along the Val Veni to Cantine de la Visaille (1653m). Cross the main stream to the Chalets de Frêney. From there, take the marked track over a huge scree fan and then, keeping left (west) of the Frêney Glacier stream, climb the rugged face with many bends. Finally take the path with fixed wires etc. up three tiers of slabs to the saddle by the Aiguille du Châtelet and the Monzino Hut (2561m, Guides de Courmayeur, 60 B, managed: mid-June – end of September, Tel. 0165-809553).

Bivouac approach: From the hut go north under the walls of the Aiguille Croux, and ascend over debris and snow into the cirque in front of the Punta Innominata. Go right (east) over rocks and up a gully to the Col de l'Innominata (3205m, 2–3 hrs). On the other side, abseil down a steep gully and then descend to the Frêney Glacier. Take an adventurous route through the crevasse labyrinth to reach and climb the snow couloir descending from the Brèche Nord des Dames Anglaises. If the rimaye is impassable, or there is acute danger of stone-fall, the Schneider Couloir, running parallel to the left wall of the couloir, is less dangerous. Higher up take the left (north) branch, to the notch (3470m, obliquely left above is the Craveri or Dames Anglaises Bivouac Hut, 3490m).

Summit climb by the Peuterey Ridge: Above the notch, a steep rise bars the way ahead. Go left (west) and climb up and down on the wall of the rise, climb a short chimney and then, on shelves and ledges, cross some 40m (III and II) to a slabby, gully-like couloir. Climb the couloir (III) to the notch on an adjacent ridge, right of a thin pinnacle. On the right go up a sort of gully (III) for 10m to easy ground above the first steep rise. Go up the ridge for a short way, then traverse right (Brenva side) over debris and snow to rubble ribs separated from one another by snow gullies. The third rib is the best, climb this directly, high above the criss-crossed Brenva Glacier, with occasional crumbling rock, until it ends at a notch on the main ridge (about 100m to the side and above Punta Gugliermina). Ascend the ridge, then descend on the right to a prominent notch before a tower. Turn this airily on the left (IV) then regain the ridge and finally, on a broad snow ridge, gain the south-east top (4107m, Pointe Seymour King).

On the other side, go down a short brittle gully to the narrow snow ridge. Traverse across on its knife-edge (exposed) to the central summit (4112m, Pointe Güssfeldt) and continue to the North-West Summit (4104m, Pointe Jones). These summits are often turned – the Central on the Brenva Flake, the North-West on the Frêney side – which can involve climbing on very hard ice.
View: An intense panorama of Mont Blanc's greatest faces.

On the summit ridge of Aiguille Blanche with Pic Eccles on the left, Pointe Güssfeldt on the right and the upper Frêney Basin between.

Descent: Head north down to a rocky shoulder. Go steeply down from a fixed abseil point on the North-West Face and, most conveniently, abseil 40m from the lowest rocks to clear the rimaye and thence descend to the Col de Peuterey (3934m).

Continuation to Mont Blanc: For the next stage there are two possibilities (both taking 2–4 hrs), on the left (west) of the ridge edge leading to the top of the Grand Pilier d'Angle: either traverse left a short distance until below where the ridge angle eases, cross the rimaye (often awkward) and work back right to the ridge; alternatively, make a 150m traverse left before heading directly up a ramp (mixed climbing, stone-fall danger) to gain the ridge behind the Grand Pilier by a gendarme. After this climb the corniced ridge and finally up the steepening snow or ice face to the cornices of Mont Blanc de Courmayeur (long and very taxing in bad weather).

Descent by Col Eccles: In good conditions, a feasible descent is to cross over the Frêney Glacier and climb up to the Col Eccles and the bivouac box there, usually over-crowded in good weather. From there, descend to the Monzino Hut, down the crevassed Brouillard Glacier, possibly helped by tracks. This is a good way providing the col can be reached before the weather breaks, for the Frêney basin quickly becomes avalanche prone with new snow.

Descent by the Rochers Gruber: The steep rognon beside the highest ice-fall of the Frêney Glacier is reached by descending south-south-westwards from the col to the beginning of a snow ridge (not easy to find in mist). Descend this until it changes into a steep snow and rock rib. Go down steep snow on the left (east) of as far as a steep drop. Here move back right to the rocks. Now abseil, keeping right using several small traverses to gain the lower Frêney Glacier. Descend (many crevasses) until under the Col de l'Innominata which is reached by a steep gully (difficult). From the col an easier descent leads down to the Monzino Hut. If a Rochers Gruber descent is thought too dangerous, digging a snow hole (best done on the Col de Peuterey to reduce avalanche risk and for ease of indentification) will buy time to consider the remaining options.

Other worthwhile routes: *North Face* (TD, a pure ice face averaging 52° with some 55°, 800mH, 5–7 hrs for the face).
Punta Gugliermina South Face (TD+, a sustained rock climb at V+ and V, with sections of VI, 600mH, 11–16 hrs from the hut).

Guidebook: Mont Blanc Range, Vol 1 (Alpine Club, 1990).

Further Reading (G) pocket guidebooks, *books in print

John Brailsford *Écrins Massif*★ (G) Alpine Club, London 1987.

Ronald Clark *The Early Alpine Guides* Phoenix House, London 1950; *The Victorian Mountaineers* Batsford, London 1953. *Excellent historical commentaries.*

R.G. Collomb *Graians East*★ (G) West Col, Reading 1969.

Helmut Dumler and Willi. P. Burkhardt *The High Mountains of the Alps*★ Diadem, London/The Mountaineers, Seattle 1993. *Acclaimed international compendium.*

Charles Gos **Alpine Tragedy** Allen and Unwin, 1948. *Analysis of early accidents.*

Lindsay Griffin *Bernina and Bregaglia*★ (G) 1995; *Mont Blanc Massif*★ (G – two vols), 1990, 1991; *Valais Alps West*★ (G) Alpine Club, London, 1998.

Christian Klucker *Adventures of an Alpine Guide* John Murray, London 1932. *First ascent accounts on Liskamm and Aiguille Blanche.*

Will McLewin *In Monte Viso's Horizon*★ Earnest Press, Holyhead, 1992, Menasha Ridge Press, Birmingham, Alabama, 1993. *Informed, illustrated and anecdotal.*

Martin Moran *Alps 4000*★ David and Charles, Newton Abbot, 1994. *A modern commentary on the 4000m peaks and tops climbed in one summer campaign.*

Martin Moran and Iain Whyte *The Alpine 4000m Peaks (and adjoining peaks)*★ Hillwalker CD Rom Series, Glasgow 2003.

A.W. Moore *The Alps in 1864* (2 Volumes) Blackwell, Oxford 1939.. *First ascents on Obergabelhorn, Gross Fiescherhorn and Mont Blanc (Brenva).*

A.F. Mummery *My Climbs in the Alps and Caucasus* Fisher Unwin, London 1895. *First ascents: Matterhorn (Zmutt/Furggen) and Täschhorn (Teuffelsgrat).*

Gaston Rébuffat *The Mont Blanc Massif*★ Baton Wicks, London/The Mountaineers, Seattle 1996. *Guidebook style introduction to the classic climbs.*

Guido Rey *The Matterhorn* Blackwell, London 1946. *General history.*

Dieter Seibert *Eastern Alps*★ (G), Diadem / Menasha Ridge Press 1992.

Leslie Stephen *The Playground of Europe* Longmans Green, London. *First ascents on Zinalrothorn, Schreckhorn and Mont Blanc (Gouter Route).*

Les Swinden and Peter Fleming *Bernese Oberland*★ (G); *Valais Alps East*★ (G) Alpine Club, London 2003 and 1999.

John Tyndall *Hours of Exercise in the Alps* Longmans, London 1871. *The Weisshorn first ascent and major attempts on the Matterhorn.*

Miriam Underhill *Give Me the Hills* Methuen, London 1956. *Climbs on Dent Blanche, Lauterarrhorn, Finsteraarhorn and the first traverse of the Diable Ridge.*

Edward Whymper *Scrambles Amongst the Alps*★ John Murray, London 1871. *First ascents: Barre des Écrins, Aiguille Verte, Grandes Jorasses, Matterhorn (attempts/ascent/tragedy).*

Geoffrey Winthrop Young *On High Hills* Methuen, London/Dutton, New York, 1928. *Brouillard, Grandes Jorasses, Weisshorn, Breithorn and Täschhorn adventures.*

Also note instructional books mentioned on page 11.

Alpine 4000m peaks and tops in order of height

Peaks customarily taken as independent are marked in bold type (including UIAA 1994 additions marked * and my 1997 suggestions for further additions marked **). Names in medium type are minor tops. The depth of the col between the peak and the next highest peak (showing the independence of the summit) is on the right.

Mont Blanc 4807m	**4600m**
Mont Blanc de Courmayeur* 4748m	**18m**
Dufourspitze 4634m	**2165m**
Dufourspitze East Ridge tower c.4630m	15m
Monte Rosa, Grenzgipfel 4618m	15m
Nordend 4609m	**94m**
Dufourspitze, western foresummit c.4600m	7m
Mont Blanc, Frêney Gr. Chandelle c.4600m	20m
Zumsteinspitze 4563m	**111m**
Signalkuppe 4556m	**102m**
Mont Blanc, Petite Bosse 4547m	2m
Dom 4545m	**1018m**
Signalkuppe, East Ridge gendarme 4545m	15m
Nordend, South Ridge top 4542m	5m
Liskamm East 4527m	**376m**
Mont Blanc, Grande Bosse 4513m	5m
Weisshorn 4505m	**1055m**
Dufourspitze, high West Ridge top 4499m	20m
Täschhorn 4490m	**209m**
Dom, western foresummit 4479m	20m
Liskamm West* 4479m	**62m**
Matterhorn 4478m	**1164m**
Matterhorn, West Summit 4476m	c.15m
Mont Blanc, Pic Luigi Amedeo* 4469m	**35m**
Dom, North-East Ridge summit 4468m	c.15m
Mont Maudit 4465m	**162m**
Zumsteinspitze, South-West Ridge top 4463m	c.15m
Liskamm West, eastern foresummit c.4450m	58m
Parrotspitze 4436m	**136m**
Liskamm, saddle summit 4430m	15m
Täschhorn, North Ridge summit 4404m	10m
Dufourspitze, lower West Ridge summit c.4385m	15m
Mont Maudit, lower south shoulder 4369m	4m
Weisshorn, higher North Ridge top 4362m	25m
Dent Blanche 4356m	**897m**
Mont Maudit, North-West Summit (shoulder) 4345m	10m
Ludwigshöhe 4341m	**58m**
Mont Maudit, North-East summit 4336m	23m
Liskamm East, Cima Scoperta 4335m	10m

Weisshorn, North Ridge Gr. Gendarme★★ 4331m	**35m**
Nadelhorn 4327m	**206m**
Schwarzhorn (Corno Nero) 4321m	**50m**
Grand Combin de Grafeniere 4314m	**1517m**
Mont Blanc, Dôme du Goûter★ 4304m	**58m**
Dufourspitze, lower West Ridge summit c.4280m	30m
Lenzspitze 4294m	**90m**
Nadelhorn, north western foresummit c.4290m	c.10m
Mont Maudit, Pointe Mieulet 4287m	c.10m
Finsteraarhorn 4273m	**2108m**
Nadelhorn South Ridge higher twin tower c.4280m	c.15m
Liskamm, Schneedomspitze (Il Naso)★★ 4277m	**40m**
Nadelhorn, South Ridge, lower twin tower c.4270m	c.10m
Aiguille du Croissant 4250m	15m
Mont Blanc du Tacul 4247m	**213m**
Mont Blanc du Tacul, East Summit 4247m	20m
Mont Blanc, Grand Pilier d'Angle★ 4243m	**15m**
Stecknadelhorn 4241m	**25m**
Matterhorn, Pic Tyndall 4241m	15m
Lenzspitze, North Ridge Gendarme c.4240m	c.10m
Nadelhorn, South Ridge 4235m	c.15m
Castor 4228m	**165m**
Zinalrothorn 4221m	**471m**
Hohberghorn 4219m	**77m**
Piramide Vincent 4215m	**128m**
Zinalrothorn Kanzel c.4210m	c.15m
Grandes Jorasses 4208m	**843m**
Alphubel 4206m	**355m**
Castor, North Summit 4205m	12m
Weisshorn, small North Ridge gendarme c.4205m	15m
Weisshorn, lower North Ridge summit 4203m	20m
Liskamm, South-West Ridge top 4201m	20m
Lenzspitze, South Ridge Gendarme c.4200m	c.15m
Rimpfischhorn 4199m	**410m**
Aletschhorn 4195m	**1017m**
Strahlhorn 4190m	**401m**
Weisshorn, small North Ridge top c.4190m	c.20m
Alphubel, North Summit 4188m	15m
Castor, south-eastern foresummit 4185m	15m
Grand Combin de Valsorey★ 4184m	**52m**
Grandes Jorasses, Pt. Whymper★ 4184m	**40m**
Rimpfischhorn, southern foresummit 4180m	c.10m
Weisshorn, lower small North Ridge top c.4190m	c.20m
Weisshorn, East Ridge tower 4178m	10m
Täschhorn, South-East Ridge top 4175m	10m
Rimpfischorn 5th North Ridge Tooth c.4175m	c.15m
Castor, Felikhorn 4174m	10m
Dent d'Hérens 4171m	**692m**

Balmenhorn 4167m	12m
Finsteraarhorn, South-East foresummit 4167m	15m
Breithorn (west) 4164m	**433m**
Rimpfischhorn, 4th North Ridge Tooth 4160m	c.10m
Breithorn Central★ 4159m	**83m**
Jungfrau 4158m	**684m**
Dôme du Goûter, West Ridge summit 4155m	15m
Bishorn 4153m	**120m**
Rimpfischhorn, South Shoulder summit c.4150m	c.20m
Zinalrothorn, North Ridge "Bosse" c.4150m	15m
Dent d'Herens, Foresummit 4148m	c.20m
Combin de Tsessette★ 4141m	**55m**
Rimpfischhorn 3rd North Ridge Tooth 4140m	c.10m
Breithorn Twin (West)★ 4139m	117m
Bishorn, Pointe Burnaby 4135m	25m
Rimpfischhorn, 2nd North Ridge Tooth 4130m	c.10m
Aiguille Verte 4122m	**579m**
Combin de Tsessette, West Summit 4121m	31m
Zinalrothorn, Gabel c.4120m	15m
Dufourspitze South-West Ridge Tower 4120m	15m
Rimpfishorn 1st North Ridge Tooth 4120m	c.10m
Mont Blanc du Tacul, L'Isolée (P. Blanchard)★ 4114m	**36m**
Aiguille Blanche, P. Güssfeldt 4112m	**178m**
Grandes Jorasses, Pointe Croz★ 4110m	**20m**
Mont Blanc du Tacul, Pointe Carmen★ 4109m	**54m**
Weisshorn, lowest North Ridge top 4108m	19m
Rimpfischhorn, Grand Gendarme★★ 4108m	**40m**
Mont Maudit, Pointe de l'Androsace★★ 4107m	**20m**
Aig. Blanche, Pointe Seymour King★★ 4107m	**30m**
Mönch 4107m	**415m**
Breithorn Twin (East)★ 4106m	**40m**
Aiguille Blanche, Pointe Jones 4104m	15m
Grande Rocheuse 4102m	**70m**
Barre des Écrins 4101m	**2043m**
Zinalrothorn, North Ridge "Sphinx" c.4100m	10m
Mont Blanc du Tacul, East Pillar Tour Rouge c.4100m	20m
Dent Blanche, Grand Gendarme 4098m	10m
Mont Blanc du Tacul, Pointe Médiane★ 4097m	**25m**
Castor, Felikjoch top 4093m	20m
Pollux 4092m	**247m**
Lenzspitze E.N.E. Ridge Gendarme 4091m	c.10m
Wengener Jungfrau 4089m	25m
Finsteraarhorn, North-West Ridge top 4088m	10m
Mont Maudit North-West Face P.4087m	c.10m
Barre des Écrins, Pic Lory 4086m	10m
Aletschhorn, North East Ridge top 4086m	8m
Schreckhorn 4078m	**788m**
Dent d'Herens, East Ridge 'Epaule' 4075m	20m

Breithorn, Schwarzfluh/Roccia Nera★ 4075m	**20m**
Mont Blanc du Tacul, Pointe Chaubert★ 4074m	**57m**
Aletschhorn, W.N.W. Ridge top 4071m	5m
Mont Blanc du Tacul, Pilier du Diable★★ 4067m	**40m**
Grandes Jorasses, Pointe Marguérite★ 4066m	**30m**
Mont Blanc du Tacul, Corne du Diable★ 4064m	**17m**
Obergabelhorn 4063m	**405m**
Schreckhorn, eastern foresummit 4060m	10m
Gran Paradiso, summit towers 4061m	**1879m**
Gran Paradiso, Madonna summit 4058m	7m
Mont Brouillard 4053m	**39m**
Aiguille de Bionnassay 4052m	**160m**
Weisshorn, East Ridge, Lochmatterturm c.4050m	c.5m
Piz Bernina 4049m	**2234m**
Gross-Fiescherhorn 4049m	**391m**
Punta Giordani 4046m	**5m**
Grandes Jorasses, Pointe Hélene★ 4045m	**20m**
Gross-Grünhorn 4044m	**305m**
Lauteraarhorn 4042m	**128m**
Mont Blanc, Pic Eccles★★ 4041m	**35m**
Aiguille du Jardin 4035m	**37m**
Dürrenhorn 4035m	**119m**
Allalinhorn 4027m	**265m**
Mont Blanc du Tacul, East Face, P.4027	20m
Gran Paradiso, East Summit, Il Roc 4026m	20m
Aiguille du Jardin, Pointe Eveline 4026m	10m
Dufourspitze, lowest West Ridge tower 4026m	20m
Hinter-Fiescherhorn 4025m	**102m**
Weissmies 4023m	**1185m**
Aiguille Verte, Pointe Croux 4023m	10m
Piz Bernina, Spalla 4020m	8m
Zinalrothorn, North Ridge shoulder 4017m	5m
Dôme de Rochefort 4015m	**190m**
Lauteraarhorn North-West Ridge Tower★★ 4015m	**30m**
Grande Rocheuse, Pt. 4015 by Col. A. Charlet	10m
Gran Paradiso, Central Summit 4015m	15m
(Barre des Écrins) Dôme de Neige★ 4015m	**40m**
Dent du Géant 4013m	**139m**
Punta Baretti 4013m	**56m**
Lauteraarhorn, lower N.W. Ridge Tower★★ 4011m	**25m**
Lagginhorn 4010m	**511m**
Rimpfischhorn, West Summit 4009m	15m
Dent du Geant, Pointe Sella 4009m	c.10m
Mont Brouillard, South-West Ridge Summit c.4005	c.10m
Aiguille de Rochefort 4001m	**106m**
Les Droites 4000m	**204m**

*And now, if inclined, the reader can choose which of these elevations
are significant enough for a visit to be worthwhile!*

The climbs in categories of difficulty

Each section has climbs in book order plus their height-gains from the main hut, sometimes with a stop (h) at an intermediary hut. Some climbs* have grades that belie their remoteness and extra seriousness if the weather deteriorates. Others have very long approaches to their base huts.

D+

Aiguille Blanche to Mont Blanc (via Grand Pilier d'Angle)	2217m (h)*	226
Aiguilles du Diable traverse and over Mt. Blanc du Tacul	1100m	197
Pilier du Diable (by Diable Couloir) and Mt. Blanc du Tacul	1000m	195
Lauteraarhorn Towers: Scheckhorn to Lauteraarhorn	1760m	57

D

Grandes Jorasses: West Ridge	1777m (h)	185
Aiguille du Jardin	1400m	175
Pointe de l'Androsace (Frontier Ridge to Mont Maudit)	1700m	205
Weisshorn: Grande Gendarme (Younggrat to Weisshorn)	1750m	110

AD+

Aletschhorn by the Hasler Rib from Konkordiaplatz	1400m	32
Schreckhorn	1558m	49
Lauteraarhorn (either route)	1550m	54
Täschhorn (either route) and traverse to Dom	1650m (h)	87
Grand Combin (North-West Face)	1450m	166
Grandes Jorasses : Pte. Marguérite (from Pte. Whymper)	c.1600m	183
Weisshorn Gr. Gendarme (from Bishorn and over Weisshorn)	1600m	110
Pic Luigi Amedeo (via the Brouillard Ridge to Mont Blanc)	2900m	222

AD

Piz Bernina: North Ridge Biancograt (from Tschierva)	1500m	16
Dürrenhorn / Hohberghorn /Stecknadelhorn/ Nadelhorn	1500m	72
Lenzspitze: ENE Ridge (and on to Nadelhorn)	1000m	80
Rimpfischhorn North Ridge (with Great Gendarme)	1600m	97
Weisshorn: East Ridge	1600m	109
Obergabelhorn	850m	117
Breithorn Traverse	350m (h)	149
Matterhorn: Italian Ridge	1663m (h)	158
Dent Blanche	850m	121
Dent d'Herens: WNW Face (from the Schönbiel Hut)	1500m	162
Aiguille Verte (Whymper Couloir and Moine Ridge)	1450m	172
Grande Rocheuse	1430m	175
Les Droites	300m	177
Rochefort Ridge	1300m	187
Dent du Géant	730m	191
Aig. de Bionnassay and on to join the Gouter Route	1500m	218
Mont Brouillard / Punta Baretti	800m	220

AD–

Aletschhorn: South-West Face from Oberaletsch Hut	1700m	31
Zinalrothorn	1050m	111
Liskamm	920m	140
Matterhorn: Hörnli Ridge	1200m	157
Grand Combin: West Ridge	1300m	167
Grandes Jorasses: Pointe Walker (and Pte. Whymper – optional)	1400m	181

PD+

Barre des Écrins	1000m	24
Jungfrau	850m	33
Gross-Fiescherhorn	750m	39
Gross-Grünhorn	1400m	45
Dom: Festigrat	1620m	84
Rimpfischhorn	1600m	97
Nordend	1820m*	123
Liskamm Traverse (Lisjoch to Feikjoch) (from Gnifetti Hut)	950m	142
Roccia Nera and **Breithorn Twin (East)** (from Ayas Hut)	700m	147
Breithorn Twin (West) from west, then to **Breithorn Central**	350m	149
Dent d'Hérens: South-West Face (from Aosta Hut)	1400m	161
Grand Combin: South Face	1300m (h)	167
Mont Blanc: Gonella Route	1736m*	214
Pic Eccles (from the Monzino Hut)	1450m (h)	225

PD

Piz Bernina: Spallagrat	1550m (h)	16
Aletschhorn: North-East Ridge	1200m*	29
Mönch	500m	37
Hinter-Fiescherhorn	750m	43
Finsteraarhorn	1300m	58
Lagginhorn	1280m/960m	63
Weissmies: North-West Face (from Hohsaas Hut)	1050m	67
Weissmies: South Face (from Almageller Hut)	1150m	71
Nadelhorn: North-East Ridge	1000m	77
Lenzspitze: South Ridge	1350m*	81
Dom: North Face	1650m*	82
Alphubel	1330m	90
Allalinhorn: Hohlaubgrat	1050m	94
Strahlhorn	1250m	101
Dufourspitze	1880m*	126
Signalkuppe plus its satellites in various combinations	1000m (h)	132
Piramide Vincent / Punta Giordani	600m	138
Liskamm West (from Quintino Sella Hut)	900m	142
Castor (from Quinto Sella Hut)	650m	144
Pollux (from Klein Matterhorn)	600m	146
Breithorn: Roccia Nera (from Klein Matterhorn)	350m	147
Mont Blanc du Tacul	730m	192
Mont Maudit (from Col du Midi)	1000m*	202
Mont Maudit (from Grands Mulets)	1400m*	204/212
Mont Blanc: Goûter Route	1050m*	205–212

PD– /F

Gran Paradiso	1350m	18
Dôme de Neige	900m	27
Allalinhorn: West Ridge	580m	93
Bishorn	900m	104
Liskamm: Il Naso/Schneedomspitze	960m	139
Breithorn	350m	150
Breithorn Central (from west)	350m	149
Mont Blanc: Grands Mulets Route	1776m*	212

The Very Pronounced Peaks

For those who seek a simpler interpretation of alpine peak significance, there are twenty-three peaks (in **bold** type) that are '**Very Pronounced**' with more that a 150m col depth. The total is thirty-two if the nine **Pronounced** 4000m peaks (medium type) are added, these with a col depth of at least 100m. For those who wish to add similarly high assertive peaks to this list, the seven that exceed 13,000ft but fall below 4000m (in ***bold italics***) might be considered.

BERNINA GROUP

Piz Bernina 4049m	**2234m**
Piz Zupo 3996m	*805m*

BERNESE ALPS

Finsteraarhorn 4273m	**2108m**
Aletschhorn 4195m	**1017m**
Jungfrau 4158m	**684m**
Mönch 4107m	**415m**
Schreckhorn 4078m	**788m**
Gr. Fiescherhorn 4049m	**391m**
Gr.-Grünhorn 4044m	**305m**
Lauteraarhorn 4042m	128m
H.-Fiescherhorn 4025m	102m
Eiger 3970m	*356m*
Gletscherhorn 3983	*214m*

PENNINE ALPS (VALAIS)

Dufourspitze 4634m	**2165m**
Dom 4545m	**1018m**
Liskamm East 4527m	**376m**
Weisshorn 4505m	**1055m**
Täschhorn 4490m	**209m**
Matterhorn 4478m	**1164m**
Nadelhorn 4327m	**206m**
Grand Combin 4314m	**1517m**
Dent Blanche 4356m	**897m**
Castor 4228m	**165m**
Zinalrothorn 4221m	**471m**
Alphubel 4206m	**355m**
Rimpfischhorn 4199m	**410m**
Strahlhorn 4190m	**401m**
Dent d'Hérens 4171m	**692m**

Breithorn 4164m	**433m**
Pollux 4092m	**247m**
Obergabelhorn 4063m	**405m**
Allalinhorn 4027m	**265m**
Weissmies 4023m	**1185m**
Lagginhorn 4010m	**511m**
Zumsteinspitze 4563m	111m
Signalkuppe 4556m	102m
Parrotspitze 4436m	136m
Piramide Vincent 4215m	128m
Bishorn 4153m	120m
Dürrenhorn 4035m	119m
Fletschhorn 3993m	*299m*
Schalihorn 3974m	*215m*

MONT BLANC MASSIF

Mont Blanc 4807m	**4600m**
Mont Maudit 4465m	**162m**
Mt. Bl. du Tacul 4247m	**213m**
Grandes Jorasses 4208m	**843m**
Aiguille Verte 4122m	**579m**
Aiguille Blanche 4112m	**178m**
Aig. de Bionnassay 4052m	**160m**
Dôme de Rochefort 4015m	**190m**
Les Droites 4000m	**204m**
Dent du Géant 4013m	139m
Aig.de Rochefort 4001m	106m

PARADISO AND ÉCRINS GROUPS

Gran Paradiso 4061m	**1879m**
Grivola 3969m	*c.700m*
Barre des Écrins 4101m	**2043m**
La Meije 3963m	*596m*